Catskill Mountain Guide

Third Edition

AMC's Comprehensive Guide to Hiking Trails in the Catskills

Written by Peter W. Kick

Appalachian Mountain Club Books
Boston, Massachusetts

The Appalachian Mountain Club (AMC) is a nonprofit organization, and sales of AMC Books fund our mission of protecting the Northeast outdoors. If you appreciate our efforts and would like to become a member or make a donation to AMC, visit outdoors.org, call 800-372-1758, or contact us at Appalachian Mountain Club, 5 Joy Street, Boston, MA 02108.

outdoors.org/publications/books

Distributed by The Globe Pequot Press, Guilford, Connecticut.

Front cover photograph © John F. Reece
Back cover photograph, © Michael R. Martin, author of *AMC's Best Backpacking in the Mid-Atlantic*
Maps by Larry Garland, © Appalachian Mountain Club
Cover design by Matthew Simmons, myselfIncluded.com
Interior design by Jennie Sparrow

Library of Congress Cataloging-in-Publication Data
Kick, Peter, 1951–
 Catskill Mountain guide : AMC's comprehensive guide to hiking trails in the Catskills / Written by Peter W. Kick. — Third edition.
  pages cm
 Includes bibliographical references and index.
 Summary: "This guide from the Appalachian Mountain Club offers hikers turn-by-turn descriptions of more than 300 miles of trails in New York's Catskill Mountains. These trails suit every ability level—from an easy walk to Kaaterskill Falls to strenuous climbs on the Devil's path. Includes topographical maps"— Provided by publisher.
 ISBN 978-1-934028-94-0 (pbk. : alk. paper) 1. Hiking—New York (State)—Catskill Mountains—Guidebooks. 2. Trails—New York (State)—Catskill Mountains—Guidebooks. 3. Catskill Mountains (N.Y.)—Guidebooks. I. Title.
 GV199.42.N652C374 2014
 917.47'38—dc23
                    2013038751

The paper used in this publication meets the minimum requirements of the American National Standard for Information Sciences-Permanence of Paper for Printed Library Materials, ANSI Z39.48-1984. ∞

Outdoor recreation activities by their very nature are potentially hazardous. This book is not a substitute for good personal judgment and training in outdoor skills. Due to changes in conditions, use of the information in this book is at the sole risk of the user. The author and the Appalachian Mountain Club assume no liability for accidents happening to, or injuries sustained by, readers who engage in the activities described in this book.

Interior pages contain 30% post-consumer recycled fiber.
Cover contains 10% post-consumer recycled fiber.
Printed in the United States of America,
using vegetable-based inks.

MIX
Paper from responsible sources
FSC
www.fsc.org FSC® C005010

10 9 8 7 6 5 4 3 2 1   14 15 16 17 18

DEDICATION

For Ryan

Editions of the Catskill Mountain Guide

First Edition	2002
Second Edition	2009
Third Edition	2014

KEY TO LOCATOR MAPS

The numbers within the boxes on the locator maps presented at the beginning of each section indicate which AMC maps show trails discussed in that section. The page numbers listed at the beginning of each section indicate the start of trail descriptions covering a given area.

Map 1: Catskill Forest Preserve–East
Map 2: Catskill Forest Preserve–West

CONTENTS

FOREWORD

With the object of keeping pace with the constant changes in mountain trails, the Appalachian Mountain Club publishes a revised edition of this guide at intervals of about five years.

Hiking and climbing in the Catskill Mountains should provide a combination of outdoor pleasure and exercise. Plan your trip schedule with safety in mind. Determine the overall distance, the altitude to be reached, and the steepness of the footway. If you are returning to the starting point the same day, allow ample time, as you will most likely be less energetic in the afternoon than you were in the morning. Read the caution notes where they appear in this book. They are put there for your guidance and protection.

Catskill Park Statistics

The Catskills encompass 1,102 square miles, or 705,500 acres. Of these, 287,500 acres are state forest preserve (public lands) and 381,000 are private lands. There are also 40,500 acres of New York City-owned watershed lands within the park, many of them open to hikers. Four counties make up the public lands in the park: Delaware County, with 42,000 acres; Sullivan County, with 18,800 acres; Greene County, with 79,200 acres; and Ulster County, with 154,200 acres. There are five wilderness areas representing 51 percent of the forest preserve, with 143,000 acres, and fourteen wild forest areas (not all of these have hiking trails), with 130,000 acres, representing 47 percent of forest preserve lands. The remaining lands are made up of administrative and intensive use areas, as well as primitive bicycle corridors (156 acres) and conservation easements. There are seven state campgrounds with a total of 738 campsites, 303 miles of hiking trails, 80 miles of snowmobile trails, two horse trails with a total length of 34 miles, 60 miles of public fishing rights, and 187 primitive campsites. Based on trail registrations, it is estimated that 34,000 people use the wilderness areas annually, and 66,000 use the wild forest areas. Nearly a half million use intensive use areas (primarily campgrounds), with 5,000 using the administrative areas, totaling more than half million visitors annually.

The forest preserve lands of New York State are protected in perpetuity by the Forever Wild clause, created by the NYS Legislature in 1894 and preserved in the state constitution:

"The lands of the state, now owned or hereafter acquired, constituting the forest preserve as now fixed by law, shall be forever kept as wild forest lands. They shall not be leased, sold or exchanged, or be taken by any corporation, public or private, nor shall the timber thereon be sold, removed or destroyed . . ."

Article 14, Section 1 of
the New York State Constitution

ACKNOWLEDGMENTS

I would like to recognize the following individuals for their assistance, enthusiasm, and encouragement: June Sanson, for hiking companionship and moral support; Dr. John C. Dwyer, historian; Jim Morton, lifelong Platte Clove resident; Tom Alworth, New York State deputy commissioner of Natural Resources; Glenda Gustafson, former public relations consultant; Inverna Lockpez, former art director, Catskill Center for Conservation and Development; Justine Hommel, historian, former president of the Mountain Top Historical Society; Alf Evers, author, historian; Howard Dash, former Catskill Trails chair, New York–New Jersey Trail Conference; Jeremy D. Apgar, cartographer, New York–New Jersey Trail Conference; Jeffrey Rider, supervising forester, Division of Lands and Forests Region 3; Jim Beil, Division of Lands and Forests for the New York State Department of Environmental Conservation; George Profous, DEC Region 3 urban forester; Barbara Lucas-Wilson, DEC Region 4 forester; and New York State forest rangers Pete Evans, Dennis Martin, Patricia Rudge, Steve Preston, Stephen Scherry, Frederick Dearstyne, and Jeff Rider, supervising forester. Special thanks go to the editorial staff at the Appalachian Mountain Club, including Books Project Editor Victoria Sandbrook Flynn, Publisher Peter Tyson, Vice President of Communications Kevin Breunig, Production Manager Athena Lakri, and the creator of the maps for this series, Larry Garland.

HOW TO USE THIS BOOK

This is a practical trail guide, in which each trail within a given wild forest or wilderness area is described individually. The trails you will need to reference, accordingly, are determined by your own particular route. Certain trails in the Catskills are very long—including the Escarpment Trail, the Devil's Path, and other trunk trails—and for these trails descriptions are continuous and only side trails used for obtaining water or for egress need to be referenced. The trails are organized by region, then by area. In the case that a trail spans two different wild forest or wilderness areas, you will need to reference two separate chapters.

TRAIL DESCRIPTIONS

Each trail in this book is described individually and usually in the ascending direction. In some cases where a hike uses a combination of trails, several descriptions may need to be consulted. A typical trail description first provides an overview of the trail, including its origin and destination and, if notable, its general character (gradient, roughness, etc.), and perhaps the view to be seen from the summit. Driving directions to the trailhead are then given, where appropriate. This is followed by concise directions for following the trail. The description notes important features such as trail junctions, stream crossings, viewpoints, summits, and any significant difficulties.

For example, if you wanted to climb Overlook Mtn. from the Meads trailhead and continue to your spotted car (a shuttle car placed ahead of time) at the Devil's Path trailhead at Prediger Road, you would first consult Overlook Mtn. Trail, following it to the top of the mountain. Descending Overlook the way you came up, you would then turn to the Overlook Trail description, following the trail to the north. On the way, you might like to visit Echo Lake, in which case you would read the Echo Lake Trail description, later returning to Overlook Trail, following it to the Devil's

Path. Since the Devil's Path is described from the trailhead on Prediger Road, which lies to the west, you would follow it in the opposite direction of the text and interpret accordingly. For this particular hike, you will have consulted four separate trail descriptions.

SUGGESTED HIKES

The end of each section of this guide lists suggested hikes, selected to provide a number of options for easy, moderate, and strenuous hikes within a region. Criteria can vary from trail to trail, but in general, an easy hike may have little to no elevation gain, covers a relatively short distance, and can be completed in several hours or less. A moderate hike can take as long as half a day and cover a longer distance with more elevation gain. A strenuous hike will require a full day of six to eight hours, with significant mileage or elevation gain. The abbreviations "rt," "ow," and "lp" denote "round-trip," "one-way," and "loop," respectively. The numbers indicate distance, elevation gain, and time required. When choosing a trail, hikers should consider mileage, elevation gain, time required, available daylight, and difficulty of the terrain as well as the experience, physical fitness, ambition, and size of the group.

DISTANCES, TIMES, AND ELEVATION GAINS

The distances, times, and elevation gains that appear in the tables at the end of trail descriptions are cumulative from the starting point at the beginning of each table. Elevation gains are given for the reverse direction only when they are significant and are not cumulative—they apply only to the interval between the current entry and the next one. The following example shows users how to read tables that are at the end of trail descriptions.

Colgate Lake Trail (map 1: B9)

Distances from CR 78 parking area (2,100 ft. **[elevation]**) to
• view of beaver meadow (2,200 ft. **[elevation]**): 2.5 mi. **[distance]**, 250 ft. **[elevation gain]**. (rev. 150 ft. **[reverse elevation gain]**), 1 hr. 25 min. **[time]**

Elevation gains are generally estimated and rounded to the nearest 50 ft.; some elevation gains can be determined almost to the foot, but others, such as where several minor ups and downs are traversed, are only roughly accurate. Elevations are estimated as closely as possible when not given precisely by our source maps. The United States Geological Survey maps are used as the basis for such information.

There is no reliable method for predicting how much time a particular hiker or group of hikers will actually take to complete a particular hike on a particular day. However, to give experienced hikers a rough basis for planning, estimated times have been calculated for this book by allowing 30 minutes for each mile of distance or 1,000 ft. of climbing. During winter, with heavy packs or in deep snow, hikes may take two or three times the summer estimate.

MAP AND COMPASS

If you do not know how to read and orient yourself with a map, which is easier than using a Global Positioning System (GPS) unit, you should learn to do so before hiking anywhere. Spend time walking with someone who does know how to read a map, or study the skills in a book and practice them in the field. The same holds true for using a compass. You may not need either on the easiest of this guide's trails, but walking the easier routes with map and compass will allow you to become comfortable with their use so you can extend your hikes beyond the trails described or to more difficult hikes. In a very few cases, trails may not be self-guiding for short distances (although they will invariably be marked), and your compass and map will help you to stay oriented. In the event that you do walk off a trail, which can happen when you're not paying close attention or when the trail traverses rock and the treadway disappears, backtrack to the previous trail mark and begin again.

Distances shown on state-trail signs in a great many instances will not match distances given in the text, and these differences are not always reconcilable. Errors in sign placement, errors in calculation, disagreements in calculation, different means of calculation, and other human effects all play a role in any computations. Hikers in the Catskills will very quickly discover that state-trail signs do not always add up and that no two publications will always reflect identical distances to identical destinations.

Considering this, hikers must take it upon themselves to judge book information against field observation with a degree of skepticism, and in doing so, make reasonable calculations and decisions. By becoming familiar with the map's scale—something that will become second nature after a few hikes—determining a reliable working sense for distance will become routine. Distance is a reference, not an absolute, and should be used accordingly. Rarely will conflicting distances between state-trail signs and the text equal more than a few tenths of a mile.

USING THE TRAIL REGISTERS

Use the registers that have been placed at important trail access points and junctions. Everyone using these trail systems is urged to sign the registers and give the information requested. This will enable the Department of Environmental Conservation (DEC) to ascertain the number of people using a particular area and will assist field personnel in locating a party more quickly in the event of an emergency. Looking at the register will also give you some idea of how many parties are ahead of you on the trail.

DEC RULES AND REGULATIONS
FOR HIKERS AND CAMPERS USING STATE LANDS

The following are illegal and enforced by DEC:

- Camping is prohibited within 150 ft. of any road, trail, spring, stream, pond, or other body of water except at areas designated by a "camp here" disk.

- Groups of ten or more persons or stays of more than three days in one place require a permit from the New York State Forest Ranger responsible for the area.

- Lean-tos are available in many areas on a first come, first served basis. Lean-tos cannot be used exclusively and must be shared with other campers.

- Use pit privies provided near popular camping areas and trailheads. If none are available, dispose of human waste by digging a hole

6 to 8 inches deep at least 150 ft. from water or campsites. Cover with leaves and soil.

- Do not use soap to wash yourself, clothing, or dishes within 150 ft. of water.

- Drinking and cooking water should be boiled for five minutes, treated with purifying tablets, or filtered through a filtration device to prevent *Giardia* infection.

- Fires should be built in existing fire pits or fireplaces if provided. Use only dead and down wood for fires. Cutting standing trees is prohibited. Extinguish all fires with water and stir ashes until they are cold to the touch. Do not build fires in areas marked by a "No Fires" disk. Camp stoves are safer, more efficient, and cleaner.

- Carry out what you carry in. Practice "Leave No Trace" camping and hiking.

- Keep your pet under control. Restrain it on a leash when others approach. Collect and bury droppings away from water, trails, and campsites. Keep your pet away from drinking water sources.

- Observe and enjoy wildlife and plants but leave them undisturbed.

- Removing plants, rocks, fossils, or artifacts from state land without a permit is illegal.

- The storage of personal property on state land is prohibited.

- Carry an approved personal flotation device for each person aboard all watercraft.

- Except in an emergency, or between December 15 and April 30, camping is prohibited above an elevation of 4,000 ft. in the Adirondacks.

- Except in an emergency, or between December 21 and March 21, camping is prohibited above an elevation of 3,500 ft. in the Catskills.

- At all times, only emergency fires are permitted above 4,000 ft. in the Adirondacks and 3,500 ft. in the Catskills.

DESIGNATED CAMPSITES

Throughout the Catskills (both within the forest preserve in proximity to the trails as well as on many remote roadsides) are designated free primitive campsites, identified by state markers: the symbol of a teepee against a yellow background. These sites are in flux—often they are closed or relocated because of overuse. On this book's map, these same sites are identified in the key by the use of a red teepee symbol superimposed with the letter P. Because it is legal to camp 150 ft. from a road or water source in the Catskill Wild Forest and Wilderness areas, the designated campsites that are closest to the road (and drive-up sites) are of most interest to hikers who may be arriving late at night to a trailhead and wish to stage or organize themselves before setting out. They are also of interest to the general public, members of whom are often found car camping or long-term camping (permit required) in the more attractive sites. Note that the yellow designated camping disks with a red line on them indicate that camping is prohibited.

PARKING

Designated, marked parking areas exist at the majority of the trailheads in the Catskills and are identified on the map. These may be used for extended day outings as well as long-term, overnight hiking and camping. In cases where designated parking is not identified, non-designated, informal pull-off parking often exists. Unless these are marked "No Parking" at the site, they are legal for day use and overnight parking. Most municipalities in the Catskill Park allow roadside parking as long as a vehicle does not block the road. Be sure to check with any township where you intend to use such sites for overnight parking, especially during the winter months. To aid in your trip planning, parking icons appear on the map; more details on specific sites are given in trail descriptions.

STATE AND LAND-USE CLASSIFICATION

There are five basic land-use categories in place for the Catskill Park and Forest Preserve. These have been created because the preserve's wide variety of terrain, soil types, and forests have different capacities to support and recover from recreational use. Most of these classifications follow the same guidelines used for the Adirondack Forest Preserve. These management areas have been created and are being continuously developed based on physical land characteristics, biological considerations, established facilities, and both social and psychological factors. The DEC describes these management units as follows:

Wilderness: The area (1) generally appears to have been affected primarily by the forces of nature, with the imprint of humans' work substantially unnoticeable; (2) offers opportunities for solitude or a primitive and unconfined type of recreation; (3) has at least 10,000 acres of land (and/or water) or is of sufficient size and character as to make practicable its preservation and use in an unimpaired condition; and (4) may also contain ecological, geological, or other features of scientific, educational, scenic, or historic value.

Wild Forest: A wild forest area is a section of forest preserve where the resource can sustain a somewhat higher degree of human use than a wilderness area. It may contain within its bounds smaller areas of land or water that are essentially wilderness in character, where the fragility of the resource or other factors require wilderness management. A wild forest area is further defined as an area that lacks the sense of remoteness of wilderness areas and that permits a wider variety of outdoor recreation.

Intensive Use: An intensive use area is a location where the state provides facilities for highly concentrated forms of outdoor recreation. These facilities include ones designed to accommodate significant numbers of visitors, such as campgrounds, ski centers, and visitor centers. These areas provide for congregations and/or accommodation of visitors to the park and sometimes function as a base for day use of wild forest and wilderness areas.

Administrative: Administrative areas are locations within the Catskill Park under the jurisdiction of the Department of Environmental Conservation. They were acquired and are managed for non-forest preserve purposes.

Primitive Bicycle Corridor: A primitive bicycle corridor is a linear area of forest preserve land, adjacent to or going through a wilderness area, where bicycles are permitted, but which is otherwise managed under wilderness guidelines.

STATE LAND MASTER PLAN

In addition to creating new wilderness areas for the protection of the resources, the 2008 Catskill Park State Land Master Plan provided for designated corridors for bicycle use. These linear corridors are 100 ft. wide and were created to allow all-terrain cyclists (mountain bikers) to pass through wilderness areas, which are otherwise off limits to mechanical vehicles. Although the public will be permitted to use bicycles on these corridors, they otherwise will be managed according to wilderness guidelines. The corridors follow old roads that have had a history of bicycle use. Now, where it was prohibited in the past, hikers may encounter mountain bikers coming down the trail. It is the cyclists' ethical responsibility—as espoused by the International Mountain Biking Association, as well as by common sense and courtesy—to yield to pedestrians. Still, take the initiative in avoiding conflicts by stepping to the side of the trail when you see a cyclist coming. Most of the primitive corridor hiking terrain in the Catskills is suitable only to technically advanced mountain bikers, as it is quite rough and difficult in many cases, full of rocks over steep grades on narrow trails with many obstacles. Stay alert and signal your intentions. The corridors are as follows:

- Indian Head Wilderness: Mink Hollow Road through the Indian Head Wilderness, 3.2 mi.

- Indian Head Wilderness: Overlook Turnpike from the Overlook Mtn. Wild Forest boundary (Meads) to Platte Clove and Prediger Road, 4.5 mi.

- Hunter-West Kill Wilderness: Diamond Notch Road through the Hunter-West Kill Wilderness, 3.2 mi.

- Windham-Blackhead Range Wilderness: Colgate Lake-Dutcher Notch Trail to Stork's Nest Road, 2.4 mi.

Hikers should also be aware that in wild forests, bicycle use is allowed on roads open to the public, state truck trails, old woods roads, foot trails, snowmobile trails, and horse trails, unless such use is deemed unsuitable by the DEC. Roads and trails in wild forest areas are therefore open unless signed as closed.

A 2013 draft amendment to the State Land Master Plan proposed was under review at the time of this guide's publication. Should the amendment be approved, land acquired in the town of Shandaken adjoining the Belleayre Mountain Ski Center Intensive Use Area, the Big Indian Wilderness, and the Shandaken Wild Forest will be classified in individual portions: one 114-acre parcel will be added to the Intensive Use Area, one 542-acre parcel will join the Shandaken Wild Forest, and the final 510 acres will be added to the Big Indian Wilderness. More information on the State Land Master Plan can be found at dec.ny.gov/lands/43013.html.

LEAVE NO TRACE

AMC is a national educational partner of Leave No Trace, a nonprofit organization dedicated to promoting and inspiring responsible outdoor recreation through education, research, and partnerships. The Leave No Trace Program seeks to develop wild land ethics—ways in which people think and act in the outdoors to minimize their impact on the areas they visit and to protect our natural resources for future enjoyment. Leave No Trace unites four federal land management agencies—the United States Forest Service (USFS), the National Park Service (NPS), the Bureau of Land Management (BLM), and the United States Fish and Wildlife Service (USFWS)—with manufacturers, outdoor retailers, user groups, educators, organizations such as AMC, and individuals. The Leave No Trace ethic is guided by these seven principles:

- Plan ahead and prepare
- Travel and camp on durable surfaces
- Dispose of waste properly
- Leave what you find
- Minimize campfire impact
- Respect wildlife
- Be considerate of other visitors

leave no trace
CENTER FOR OUTDOOR ETHICS

AMC is a national provider of the Leave No Trace Master Educator course. AMC offers this five-day course, designed especially for outdoor professionals and land managers, as well as the shorter two-day Leave No Trace Trainer course at locations throughout the Northeast.

For Leave No Trace information and materials, contact the Leave No Trace Center for Outdoor Ethics, P.O. Box 997, Boulder, CO 80306, 800-332-4100 or 302-442-8222, or lnt.org. For a schedule of AMC Leave No Trace courses, see outdoors.org/education/lnt.

User impact has become a serious issue everywhere, but especially here in the Catskills, a relatively small and fragile mountain range within a four-hour drive of 40 million people. One of the most direct results of the high impact caused by both day and overnight hikers in the Catskills has been the prohibition of campfires above 3,500 ft. Campfires continue to be one of the biggest impact issues in the Catskill Forest Preserve, even at lower, "legal" elevations, but this is just one example. The DEC is grappling with a variety of impact issues, including both deliberate abuse (littering, vandalism) and "unconscious abuses" such as impact on wildlife populations, plant communities, soil conditions, and water quality. The Catskill Park State Land Master Plan is designed to limit such environmental impact, but the rest is up to us, the hikers and campers, the Catskills' largest user group.

TRAILLESS PEAKS

It is not consistent with the conservation ethic and practice of the Appalachian Mountain Club to identify suggested routes or trailheads to trailless peaks. There are several reasons for this restraint. First, the proliferation of recommended routes to these summits has caused the development of herd paths in several areas. Because hikers tend to climb a trailless peak by the most direct and logical means (i.e., the path of least resistance), no consideration is given to the potential design, carrying capacity, or terminal impact such trails can have on the environment.

Professionally designed, DEC-designated trails take into account the most inoffensive routing of a trail as well as its proximity to sensitive or important ecozones; after a trail's construction, a maintenance program is developed for its upkeep. Herd trails are not designed, designated, or maintained, and ultimately they produce undesirable patterns of erosion, vegetative destruction, alterations in wildlife habitat and populations, and deterioration of water resources. Trailless peaks are trailless for a reason, and discussing approaches to trailless peaks defeats the purpose of having them trailless to begin with.

User patterns reflect the popularity of climbing the trailless peaks, and many hikers join organized groups in order to do so, keeping tally cards and signing in at summit canisters (small metal boxes attached to trees). The establishment and maintenance of canisters on trailless peaks is a practice that has been called into question and debated in the public forums of the unit-management planning process. It should be noted that some public input to the Catskill Unit Management Plans has called for the removal of canisters on Catskill summits. The Catskill Park State Land Master Plan does not call for the construction of trails on any of the trailless peaks, nor for the removal of the canisters. It is felt that the existing trails in the forest preserve are adequate at this time.

SAFE TRAVEL IN THE FOREST PRESERVE

Cell Phones

Cell phones will work from most mountain summits and many upper-elevation areas in the Catskills but seldom from valleys and hollows, and generally will not work from main roads in the interior Catskill Forest Preserve. They will work from slopes only if there is no significant geology between the phone and the tower. It can be difficult or impossible to reach 911 even from secondary roads that are surrounded by ridges. It is possible that a caller will be able to connect with and listen to a 911 operator, even when that operator can't hear the caller, because 911 transmitters are more powerful than cell phones. While the opposite is rarely the case, if you think your call may be being monitored by someone, it is helpful to supply your exact location, ideally using GPS coordinates if you are carrying a GPS unit and can establish them. If, during an emergency, you reach a voice recording, take the precaution of leaving a message with your situation and coordinates.

If you or a member of your party are injured or incapacitated but someone is still able to walk to a higher elevation or open area (sometimes even moving a short distance will help), your chances for getting through could improve. If you are confident in leaving an injured party (with a companion), make sure to mark their location with a GPS unit if you have one. Also try calling local forest rangers' numbers or the number of the nearest state campsite. Under certain conditions it may be possible to reach information (845-555-1212 or 411) or any local land line that can relay a message for you. Hikers are advised never to rely on a cell phone for emergencies. The only fail-safe wireless communications from any remote area are provided by satellite telephones, and even these, like your GPS, are subject to satellite positions and weather.

Global Positioning Systems

Several GPS coordinates are given in the text, primarily for difficult-to-spot trail junctions, or for the sake of orientation afield, but it is not necessary to carry a GPS in order to use this book, or even to travel safely and accurately in the Catskills. However, with the Catskill Forest Preserve map included with this book, which was created by hikers carrying GPS units recording coordinates every five seconds, it is now possible to navigate the Catskills off-trail very accurately with your handheld GPS unit by lifting coordinates from the AMC map. If you're not certain about a trail junction, or if signs have been destroyed, decayed, or otherwise removed, you can extract coordinates from the map and double check your location using a GPS. Be aware that a thick tree canopy or heavy cloud cover will substantially alter (if not prevent) an accurate GPS fix.

Almost everyone can afford a GPS unit these days, and they are very useful tools. Proficiency comes with practice, and there is a good deal to learn about the GPS and its many features. Carry a compass to back up your unit. Carrying a set of spare batteries is always a good idea.

Bring a Compass

Even if you plan to stay on marked trails in the Catskills, it is still advisable to carry a compass. Not only will a compass help you to verify directions or help you find your way back to a trail you have wandered from, it will also aid in your identification of landmarks, which adds to the fun of hiking. The best compass for the identification of peaks is an orienteering compass, the kind with a flip-up sight that enables you to take bearings with about a 2-degree error or less. In using the book's bearings you will be able to identify points that are identified in the text. All bearings are given as magnetic. If you plan to navigate over land with your compass, be sure to correct for declination (13 degrees W).

Binoculars

A pair of binoculars will add significantly to the enjoyment of your trips to the mountains and to many other places as well. There are many things a good pair of binoculars will allow you to do—from identifying the elusive hermit thrush on Slide Mtn. to finding important landmarks. The ability to locate many of the landscape features identified in the text, especially those that are not clearly visible with the naked eye, will give you a much better sense for regional geography than you will experience without magnification. For hiking, you can see all you want with 8 x 21mm to 10 x 25mm magnification, still staying within the very light 6- to 10-ounce range.

Trekking Poles

Hikers have been catching on to the advantages of trekking poles. They help you to travel faster, easier, safer, and with less fatigue. In icy conditions, they increase your stability. Descending, they'll help save your knees. During ascents, they'll give you a little extra push and will contribute to upper-body tone, making a hike more of a "total-body" form of exercise. For traversing slopes, adjustable poles can be adapted to the angle of the slope. Poles are a great advantage during slippery stream crossings. And they can be used as tent and tarp poles.

Adjust your poles according to the slope and your comfort level. For climbing, use a shorter length. For descents, a longer adjustment will give you increased options for support points. For walking across a slope, make your downhill pole longer. For hiking on the level, adjust your poles so that your forearm is parallel (or a bit higher) to the ground when you're holding the grip. Once you get used to traveling with poles, you will want them on every hike, particularly in winter. A day pack with ski slits or compression straps will come in handy during times when you want your hands free. Bear in mind that trekking poles can at times contribute to environmental impact in sensitive areas.

INTRODUCTION

Welcome to the Catskills—the Land in the Sky. It is to these rocky hills and mountains between the Hudson and Delaware rivers that the trails described in this guide will take you. Today the Catskill Forest Preserve contains nearly 300,000 acres in four counties: Greene, Ulster, Delaware, and Sullivan. Within the Catskills there are 35 peaks higher than 3,500 ft., 98 peaks higher than 3,000 ft., and more than 300 miles of state-marked hiking trails—including a 94-mile section of the Long Path, which begins at the George Washington Bridge and ends in the Northern Helderbergs. Slide Mtn. (4,190 ft.) is the Catskills' highest peak. First occupied by native people more than 5,000 years ago, the Catskills of today look much the same as they did then, with a few important changes. The many early settlers who arrived in the area marked the landscape with evidence of their industry—a history that is written in the hills.

The Catskill region occupies 1,500 square miles. Next to the Adirondacks, these are New York's highest and most rugged mountains and have the highest elevations. Four distinct regions define the Catskill plateau: the escarpment (northeast), the southern, the central, and the western. There are several smaller topographic regions as well, many of which run east–west or perpendicular to the southward movement of ice during the Pleistocene epoch (1.6 million to 10,000 years ago).

The profusion of streams that formed when the vast thickness of ice melted and retreated resulted in the erosion that produced the rugged character we see in the Catskills today. The plateau is drained to the north by the Schoharie Creek, a tributary of the Hudson via the Mohawk. To the east, the Rondout, Esopus, and Kaaterskill creeks join the Hudson.

To the south and west, the Delaware and Neversink rivers are the major watersheds. Hiking is made fun and adventurous by the trees, slope, elevation, and the resulting sense of wilderness they offer—all things determined by geology. The Catskills were lifted up and out of a shallow sea during the Devonian period, approximately 400 million years ago. The uplift of the Devonian sediments took place in several stages, and in the much later Miocene epoch, 24 million years ago, while subsequent stages were influenced by Pleistocene glaciations. Today the higher peaks are located where the uplift was greatest and where their conglomerate sandstones were able to resist erosion by the advance of the continental ice sheets and later by glacial meltwaters.

During this uplift, streams began to carve out the shapes of today's Catskills. A minimum of folding or faulting occurred, however, and the rocks were not changed by igneous or metamorphic activity. Later glaciations put their final erosive mark of character on the Catskills. Deep ravines, called cloves (from the Dutch word *kloove*, meaning "a cleft or gash in the landscape"), frightened early settlers. The cloves later inspired the artists of America's first school of painting (the Hudson River School of Landscape Painting), a number of the country's early writers (William Cullen Bryant, Washington Irving, and James Fenimore Cooper), and others whose efforts shaped the literary and artistic climate of the New World.

High, flat plains offered attractive areas for early settlements. Remote, forested peaks provided native people with winter hunting encampments, and later, provided hideaways and forts for the various revolutionaries and counterrevolutionaries of the eighteenth century. As more settlers reached the area, mountain houses and railroads appeared. Bluestone quarries and the tanbark industry (which milled bark for tannins used to make leather) followed. The hiker owes a considerable debt to these historical developments (forgetting, for the time being, their ruinous impact on the environment), because they resulted in the construction of footpaths, stagecoach and tote roads, railway beds, and later the hiking trails that have provided access to the Catskills' most remote and scenic destinations. Because these old and remote interior wilderness roads now form many of the upper-elevation trailheads, especially in the eastern escarpment area of the Catskills, it is possible to start hiking at relatively high elevations. This allows Catskill hikers to reach isolated summits and remote wilderness areas fairly quickly.

The most interesting aspect of the underlying geology of the Catskills may be the vegetation that flourishes there. The region represents the southernmost occurrence of boreal coniferous forests on glaciated uplands in North America. In contrast with this summit forest of spruce and paper birch is the valley-forest type. Known as the Carolinian zone forest, it consists of oak, hickory, occasional black birch, tulip tree, and, until recently, chestnut. According to Catskills forest historian and botanist Dr. Michael Kudish, "The proximity of the Carolinian and Canadian zones, especially in the Eastern Catskills, together with the effects of humans over two centuries, produces a rich, diverse flora and creates a vegetation so complex that it nearly defies explanation."

While they are unique historically and geologically, the Catskills have yet another distinguishing characteristic: their youth. Surrounding ranges that are visible from the Catskills are considerably older. To the east lie the 450 million-year-old Taconics, formed during a continental collision that displaced older sediments in a period called the Taconic orogeny. South of the Catskills are the Shawangunks, and although they are close to the Taconics in age, their evolution is more related to that of the Catskills. Extensive sands and quartz-rich gravels were deposited in a shallow sea during the Silurian period, about 450 million years ago. Much later, the resulting sandstones and conglomerates were uplifted and differentially eroded.

Views of the distant mountain ranges of southeastern New York are outstanding from many of the Catskills' higher peaks. From the resistant limestone of the Helderberg Escarpment, to the dissected plateau of the Catskills, and into the crystalline Hudson Highlands lying beside the younger folded rocks of the Appalachians, you can see the parts of the puzzle that make up the region's geological history.

HIKING IN THE CATSKILL REGION

The wide variety of trails in these mountains offers the hiker an excellent range of opportunities. For residents of southern New York State, the special appeal of most of these trails is their proximity to New York City. The majority of the trailheads lie within two hours of the city.

There are two ways to enjoy the Catskills. Social hikers will find many hiking groups that offer regularly scheduled hikes and trips. The New York-North Jersey and Mohawk Hudson chapters of the Appalachian Mountain Club (AMC) conduct dozens of outings in the Catskills, year round. Other organizations such as the Catskill 3500 Club, the Sierra Club, and chapters of the Adirondack Mountain Club all offer outing schedules for a variety of hikers. The New York-New Jersey Trail Conference can put you in touch with many of these groups. Each organization also fills an additional role by providing hikers the opportunity to give something back to the land. By offering trail maintenance and conservation programs, working to prevent overuse, and promoting wise use, these organizations help protect our wild lands. To become involved in these projects, consult AMC on its website or at the New York office of the AMC New York-North Jersey chapter (see Appendix C for contact information).

Those who seek quiet can also find that in the forest preserve. Some of these routes are never heavily used. Others are, but early spring and late fall trips mix solitude with expanded vistas in ways sure to please any wilderness seeker. The forests of the Catskills have been preserved as the Hudson Valley's water source and as part of the New York State Forest Preserve. Protection under the state constitution ensures these lands will remain "forever wild." Lands within the Blue Line (as it appears on maps) surrounding the Catskill Park contain all of the trails in this guide.

Almost all of the lands traversed by today's trails were once settled and used by farmers, miners, loggers, and visitors to the great mountain hotels. Their presence is reflected in the lore that surrounds the trails. While this guide serves as an invitation to the Catskill Mountains, it cannot even begin to probe the vast history that enlivens each route. If you want to learn more, consult the bibliography at the end of this book.

BEFORE YOU START

This guide provides an enormous range of trails, offering everything from easy strolls to strenuous climbs. The information about distance and time, and the trail descriptions, will help you gauge the difficulty of each trail and your level of preparedness. As you read this guide, you will occasionally see an exclamation point (⚠) in the margin, indicating a potentially dangerous area on the trail. Read the material about your area of interest before you go! All of the trails in this guide are clearly marked, state-maintained trails, although this can change. Trail maintenance groups and outdoor organizations such as the Appalachian Mountain Club, the Adirondack Mountain Club, and the New York-New Jersey Trail Conference have worked hard to design, build, and maintain sections of trail in the Catskill forest preserve. Without such efforts, the trails would not be in the condition that we now enjoy. The lands surrounding the Catskills offer many more natural areas than are described in this book, and references to other excellent books are given in the bibliography. To discover other hikes or to become better prepared for outdoor adventures, you could join one of the hiking groups listed at the end of the introduction.

Preparedness is essential to your enjoyment, and you should be well equipped before you start. This includes knowing how to use a map and compass to complement the information in this guide. If you are new to hiking, it is definitely a good idea to join a hiking group and learn from those with experience. The more background you have on hiking in the woods, the greater your safety and enjoyment. Do not count on the following summary to prepare you for every situation you are likely to encounter. This introduction is not a comprehensive primer for beginning hikers. Treat it instead as a checklist and a set of reminders.

THE WEATHER

When possible, wait for a sunny day. The pleasures of hiking are much greater and the problems more predictable. But even on sunny days you should be prepared for changes and extremes. The temperatures on the mountaintops of the Catskills can be 12 or more degrees colder than in the nearby Hudson Valley. Storms can appear on short warning.

The temperature in the summer is often too hot for strenuous hikes. There are many who prefer hiking the Catskills in fall and spring, but these are the most changeable times. Extremes from heat waves to snowstorms can occur. But the rewards of fewer people and expanded distant vistas in the leafless season make it worthwhile.

PREPARATIONS

Even when a forecast calls for ideal weather, your watchwords should be "plan for the unexpected." Possible changes in temperature mean you should take extra clothing, especially rain gear. Experiment with layers of light, waterproof gear. In the mountains you will want a layer of wool or fleece, even if in summer it is only a sweater or light jacket in your day pack.

Many of the trails are as smooth as a sidewalk; some are as rubble-filled as a rock pile. For most of these hikes, a sturdy pair of broken-in, over-the-ankle boots is essential. Boots made of lightweight Gore-Tex or a similar material, in addition to being water-resistant, provide good traction and support, and they are usually sufficient. More support is required when hiking on the higher mountain trails in early spring or winter, or when carrying a heavy backpack. An old piece of hiking advice still holds true, especially for the tenderfoot: wear two pairs of socks, an inner lightweight pair and a heavy outer pair that is at least partially wool.

Even for a day hike, carry a sturdy day pack, large enough to hold your lunch and a few necessities. These include a whistle, a waterproof case with dry matches, a knife, lip balm, and a space blanket. Bring a map and compass (and know how to use them), a flashlight or headlamp in case you are delayed beyond dusk, and a watch. You also need a small first-aid kit containing a few bandages, antibiotic cream, and moleskin for the unexpected blister. Take along a small squeeze bottle of insect repellent; you will encounter blackflies in early spring and mosquitoes through the summer. Fill a plastic bag with toilet paper and throw in a few towelettes to use before lunch on those dry mountaintops. You will need another bag to carry out used toilet paper.

You may enjoy carrying a small, lightweight altimeter. On relatively steady days it is a good clue to progress on a mountain; on unstable days a barometric altimeter can alert you to sudden changes in the weather—although a sudden drop in pressure is not always a sign of impending bad weather.

WATER

Of course, you should always carry water when you hike. The Catskills are dry much of the year, and few reliable springs exist. It is becoming increasingly dangerous to trust open water sources because of the spread of *Giardia* parasites. Remember to take enough water—2 liters per person per day seems enough in summer, and most AMC hike leaders will require that you bring at least that much. Dehydration on temperate days is a possibility; it can happen even on a sunny, leafless day in the colder seasons. If you refill from a spring, treat your water before you drink it, as discussed in the *Giardia* section later in this chapter.

PERSONAL SAFETY

Remember, hiking should be fun. If you are uncomfortable with the weather or are tired, turn back and complete your hike another day. Do not put yourself or your companions at risk.

Walking alone is not always a good idea, although many hikers will have no choice, and just as many prefer to do so. If you do hike alone, make sure someone knows your intended route and when you expect to return. Always sign in at the DEC trailhead registers where they are available. The unexpected may occur—weather can change, trail markings can become obscured, you can fall, and you can get lost. However, you will minimize the danger if you anticipate the unexpected.

LYME DISEASE

Lyme disease is caused by a tick-borne spirochete that may produce a rash, flulike symptoms, and joint pain. If untreated, it may cause chronic arthritis and nervous system disorders. Though difficult to diagnose, it is treatable if diagnosed early. The deer ticks that transmit Lyme disease are found in the Catskills, and their range is expanding rapidly north and west. Users of this guide should take preventive measures, although there is no foolproof way to protect yourself from these minute ticks. Check yourself frequently; tuck pants into socks and boots; put insect repellent containing DEET on your pants, shoes, and socks (note that DEET does weaken elastics and is a suspected carcinogen); and wear tightly woven, light-colored clothing (making it easier to see the ticks). Most important, shower and change clothes at the end of your hike; this is the best time to make a complete body check. Remove your hiking clothes to prevent any ticks present on the clothing from biting you. If you suspect you have contracted Lyme disease, call your physician right away—early detection is important.

GIARDIA LAMBLIA

Giardia, that renowned genus of single-celled intestinal parasites, is here to stay and should be feared. The cysts are transmitted in the feces of animals and humans and are present in most water sources. They can survive for months in near-freezing water. Because they are small (16,500 can fit on the head of a pin), they are difficult to avoid without a quality filter of 0.2 microns or less. Other waterborne pathogens also require attention, such as the hepatitis virus, *Leptospira* (from cattle urine), and *Cryptosporidium*, which are smaller than *Giardia* cysts. These may not be effectively removed by a 0.2 micron ceramic microfilter. A quality filter will remove bacteria, cysts, protozoa, algae, spores, and sediment, and will reduce bad taste and odors.

Boiling is the safest precaution against *Giardia*, *E. coli*, and other protozoa. *Giardia* parasites die at 176 degrees Fahrenheit, and the other microorganisms die after 10 minutes at 212 degrees Fahrenheit. Halazone, bleach, and iodine will also work, but these disinfectants require a 30-minute wait. If you must drink from streams or lakes in the forest preserve, use four drops of bleach, five halazone tablets, or ten drops of 2 percent iodine per quart of water for safety. The colder the water, the longer the disinfecting process takes. Try to carry enough water for the trip. Piped springs and other subterranean sources at high elevation also require treatment. The official position of DEC forest rangers is that all water from natural sources should be filtered or treated.

WATER FILTERS VS. WATER PURIFIERS

It is important to recognize the difference between water filters and water purifiers. Water filters use microfiltration to rid water of protozoa and bacteria to a level that is considered safe by the health standards and environmental conditions in the US and Canada. Water purifiers also use microfiltration, with the addition of chemical agents that kill bacteria and protozoa, but also viruses. Purifiers are recommended more for international travel where the risk of viral contamination is greater. Viruses are rarely found in wilderness water sources in the US.

Another means of purification (without chemicals) is ultraviolet (UV) light. UV purifiers kill all microorganisms quickly by destroying their DNA and their ability to reproduce. Most portable units can purify a quart of water in under a minute. These systems require batteries and they do not work with murky water—in which case a purifier must first be used.

WINTER ACTIVITIES

Snowshoeing and cross-country skiing have steadily become more popular. Increasing numbers of hikers have discovered the beauty of the woods in winter, and advances in clothing and equipment have made it possible for experienced winter travelers to enjoy greater comfort and safety.

The greatest danger is that it begins to look too easy and too safe, while snow, ice, and weather conditions are constantly changing, and a relatively trivial error of judgment may have grave, even fatal, consequences. Because conditions can vary greatly from day to day and from trail to trail, much more experience is required to foresee and avoid dangerous situations in winter than in summer. Days are very short, particularly in early winter when darkness falls shortly after 4 p.m. Trails are frequently difficult or impossible to follow, and navigation skills are hard to learn in adverse weather conditions (as anyone who has tried to read a map in a blizzard can attest). Breaking trail on snowshoes through new snow can be strenuous and exhausting work. The most dangerous aspect of winter in the Catskills, however, is the extreme variability of the weather. It is not unusual for a cold, penetrating, wind-driven rain to be followed within a few hours by a cold front that brings subfreezing temperatures and strong winds.

Winter on most Catskills trails may require only snowshoes or skis and some warm clothing. Even so, summer hiking boots are usually inadequate, flashlight batteries can fail quickly (a headlamp with battery pack works better), canister fuel may be too cold to properly burn, and water in canteens freezes unless carried in an insulated container or wrapped in a sock or sweater held close to the body. The winter hiker needs good physical conditioning from regular exercise, and must dress carefully in order to avoid overheating and excessive perspiration, which soaks clothing and soon leads to chilling. Cotton clothes are not useful; only wool and synthetics retain insulating value when wet. Because dehydration can be a serious problem in the dry winter air, fluid intake must increase.

No book can begin to impart all the knowledge necessary to cope safely with such potentially brutal conditions, but helpful information can be found in *AMC Guide to Winter Hiking & Camping* by Yemaya Maurer and Lucas St. Clair (2009, AMC Books). Hikers interested in extending their activities into the winter season are strongly advised to seek out organized parties with leaders who have extensive winter experience. AMC and several of its chapters sponsor numerous workshops on winter hiking and camping, in addition to introductory winter hikes. Information on such activities can be obtained from AMC at 5 Joy St., Boston, MA 02108 (617-523-0655; outdoors.org).

HYPOTHERMIA

Hypothermia is the loss of ability to preserve body heat because of injury, exhaustion, lack of sufficient food, or inadequate or wet clothing. The result is a dangerous lowering of the body's core temperature. Our bodies lose heat all the time, but we don't suffer hypothermia because the loss of heat is buffered by insulation. Most often this comes in the form of clothing made of fabrics that help retain body heat. Many fabrics are good insulators when dry, but when some get wet the insulating ability drops so drastically that they become very efficient at cooling the body just when you need warmth. In hiking circles, the phrase "Cotton kills" is as accurate as it is serious. Most cases of hypothermia occur in temperatures above freezing (between 32 and 50 degrees Fahrenheit) on windy, rainy days. Some fabrics, such as wool, polypropylene, and polyester, lead to hypothermia in cooler conditions.

Symptoms of hypothermia include uncontrolled shivering, impaired speech and movement, lowered body temperature, and drowsiness. The ultimate result is death, unless the victim (who may not understand the situation because of impaired mental function) is warmed up. In mild cases, the victim should be given dry clothing and placed in a sleeping bag if available (perhaps with someone else in it to provide body heat), then provided quick-energy food and something warm (not hot) to drink. In severe cases, only prompt hospitalization offers reasonable hope for recovery. It is not unusual for a victim to resist treatment and even combat rescuers.

Uncontrollable shivering should be regarded as a sure sign of hypothermia. This shivering will eventually cease on its own, but that is merely the sign that the body is sinking toward death.

For those interested in more information, a thorough treatment of the subject is contained in *Hypothermia, Frostbite, and Other Cold Injuries:*

Prevention, Recognition, Rescue, and Treatment by Gordon G. Giesbrecht, PhD, and James A. Wilkerson, MD (2006, Mountaineers Books).

HEATSTROKE

The opposite of hypothermia, heatstroke, occurs when the body is unable to control its internal temperature and overheats. Usually brought on by excessive exposure to the sun and accompanying dehydration, its symptoms include cramping, headache, and mental confusion. In New York the hot, humid days of summer pose the greatest risk of heatstroke, because the high humidity reduces the amount of sweat that can evaporate from the skin. This consequently limits the body's ability to cool itself through evaporative heat loss and can lead to a dangerous rise in core body temperature. Treatment entails rapid, aggressive cooling of the body through whatever means are available—cooling the head and torso is the most important—and drinking lots of fluids. Stay hydrated and wear sun protection on your head if you expect to travel a hot section of trail that lacks shade.

PART ONE
NORTHEAST CATSKILLS

The Northeast Catskills are made up of the Windham-Blackhead Range Wilderness, Indian Head Wilderness, Hunter-West Kill Wilderness, North Mountain Wild Forest, Kaaterskill Wild Forest, Phoenicia-Mount Tobias Wild Forest, and Bluestone Wild Forest. Travelers on the New York State Thruway will pass close to this region and marvel at the abrupt rise of the land from 500 ft. to 2,500 ft. and then up to the recessed peaks of nearly 4,000 ft. These sudden, upper elevations are often established within a mile or two of the valley floor. This great, seemingly impenetrable wall of sandstone is the Escarpment, the edge of the great inland plateau that eroded into a peneplain 17,000 years ago, leaving a high, hilly region dissected by rugged cloves (clefts), ragged defiles, and the streams, hollows, and hemlock forests that mystified and delighted a newly independent America's literary and artistic imagination—and in many important ways, forged its new national identity. It was here in the Northeast Catskills that a unique American concept of wilderness was born (seen as both picturesque and sublime), as well as the interest in its preservation that naturally followed.

The region is interesting to hikers in part because of the very same things that drew early visitors to the mountain houses, but more practically because of this sudden altitude gain. After only a short distance, hikers can reach the relatively remote areas that walkers of the past delighted in, areas devoid of the less ambitious public. These altitude gains give way to the high plateau itself, where backpackers can enjoy long ambles over undulating terrain for days on end, reveling in far-reaching vistas amid the same lonely haunts that bewitched the fictional Rip Van Winkle and astonished Natty Bumppo (aka Leatherstocking and Hawkeye), the legendary woodsman and guide imagined by James Fenimore Cooper. The stories of the Catskill trails are the stories of early American civilization itself, and perhaps nowhere else in the range does this hold more true than in the northeastern mountains, the first of the Catskills to be visited by post-revolutionary leisure-class society, and the region that had the largest impact on the concept of wilderness in the American mind.

After the disappearance of the Paleolithic hunters who followed large animal herds with the retreating Ice Age, the hunter-gatherers arrived, settling to the north and east of the Catskills, leaving evidence in the earth of their 7,000-year occupation. These people—the Lenni-Lenape of the Delaware Nation—were forced into the west after the initial contact period with European settlers. Following a series of broken treaties and land grabs, colonial expansion claimed the best of the Lenni-Lenape riparian and agricultural lands.

After the British surrendered to the colonists in 1781, valley settlers took a more confident attitude toward commercial investment, and many farmers and businesspeople began to prosper. With the rise of economical river transportation, westward expansion began, roads penetrated the Escarpment, and the bluestone-quarrying and tanning industries took hold in the Catskills. These early industries cut the first roads into the hills, and it is on many of these roads that hikers will travel today. Often these roads pass the very quarries that caused them to be made. At one time this area was a matrix of paths and skid trails, the vast majority now reclaimed by nature.

As the region was denuded of its hemlocks and the quarries came to a sudden stop with the introduction of Portland cement, the Catskills enjoyed a welcome respite from ruin. By 1850 the tourism age was in full swing in the Northeast Catskills. The hotel industry created roads as well, and established the first leisure trails for walking. America's first true hiking trails evolved from a simple love of nature. By 1840 there were more than a hundred steamships in service between New York City and the Catskill Landing, providing round trips of less than ten hours, a fact that suddenly—and for the first time—made weekend outings to the Catskills a reality for New Yorkers.

Innumerable foot and carriage trails emanating from the hotels survive today as marked state hiking trails. Scenic destinations in the Northeast Catskills are the same places walkers visited as early as 1810. The Escarpment Trail was a marked trail for at least part of its present-day length as early as 1823. And it was the remarkable landscape scenery that drew visitors to the mountain houses. Figures such as Washington Irving, Thomas Cole, Cooper, and William Cullen Bryant drew enough attention to the Northeast Catskills that most of the visitors to the Catskill Mountain House were being turned away as early as 1824—there weren't enough accommodations. The landscape painters of the Hudson River School set up easels on the ledges of the northeast mountains, immortalizing the views in a new vision of wilderness.

But it is a romantic notion to suggest that the trails of the Northeast Catskills were formed in the footsteps of early laborers and artisans alone. An active policy of acquisition followed the creation of the Catskill Forest Preserve on May 15, 1885, when Governor David B. Hill signed into law the requisite that "all the lands now owned or which may hereafter be acquired by the State of New York . . . shall be forever kept as wild forest lands . . ."

Hikes into most of the Northeast Catskills can be conveniently staged from the public North/South Lake Campground in Haines Falls and from the Kenneth L. Wilson Public Campground east of Tremper Mtn. Camping opportunities in the forest preserve itself are plentiful. Two of the region's trails, the Devil's Path and the Escarpment Trail, provide the opportunity for multiday outings. The North/South Lake area has a handful of the best day hikes in the Catskills, all from the convenience of an established campsite. All of the trails in the region are hilly and wild. Services near trails are few, and water is scarce at upper elevations in all of the Catskills. Forest rangers are always willing to answer questions and provide advice on trip planning.

Section 1
Kaaterskill Wild Forest

The Kaaterskill Wild Forest surrounds the North/South Lake Campground, and is bounded on the north by the Windham-Blackhead Range Wilderness, and on the south by Platte Clove Road. To the west are the hamlets of Tannersville and Haines Falls, while the east side is the Catskill Park boundary in Ulster and Greene counties. This is one of the most popular hiking destinations in the Catskills and has been for nearly 200 years. Scenic vistas here are among the best and most numerous in the Catskills. This area contains the southern trailhead of today's popular Escarpment Trail, which runs north and south across the eastern Catskills and is one of the oldest continuously used recreational trails in the country (sections of this trail were blazed as early as 1810 by hunters, trappers, and surveyors). This area is the location of Kaaterskill Falls, postcolonial America's most famous landmark destination hike, and the Catskill Mountain House, America's first luxury resort hotel, which was built on the wild ledges of Pine Orchard in 1824. The falls themselves received national attention with the paintings of Thomas Cole and the publication of James Fennimore Cooper's *The Pioneers* in 1823—the same year the Catskill Mountain House began construction. With the advent of transcendentalism as espoused in the philosophies of William Ellery Channing, Ralph Waldo Emerson, and, later, Henry David Thoreau (Thoreau and Channing visited Kaaterskill Falls in the 1840s), the act of walking gained popular acceptance from its previously much lower status: typically only the poor were doomed to walk—the rich were meant to ride in carriages. The revolution in culture and the arts that followed had everything to do with what the Catskill Mountain House depended on for its success and survival—the world-class scenery that can still be enjoyed today not only in the classic paintings of the Hudson River School, but from the North Mtn. area's historical trail complex.

None of the mountain hotels remain standing today, but much of the extensive matrix of garden paths, carriage roads, and famous lookouts survives to enchant modern hikers. The visitors of old left their marks here and there, and many are still visible. As they languished over scenic outcroppings and read aloud from Cooper, Wordsworth, and Bryant, many chose to carve their names or even images into the precipice, and some of the results are astonishing for both their antiquity as well as their aesthetic refinement. Incredibly, some faded specimens at Kaaterskill Falls survive from 1810, though most of the detail has been eroded, and many of them have broken away from the precipice over time.

Hikers planning a thorough investigation of the North Mountain and North Lake Trail systems will find the public campground at North Lake ideal. Camping is legal and close at hand in the wild forest area outside the posted state recreational facility boundary, both north and south of the campground intensive-use area.

The classification of this forest area as simply a wild forest can be deceiving—its 8,550 acres have the feel and nearly the size of a true wilderness area. Its two major peaks, Kaaterskill High Peak (3,655 ft.) and Roundtop (3,440 ft.), are remote and wild. High Peak is informally marked by a private user group, yet is classified as "trailless" by the DEC. Elevations range from 900 ft. in Palenville, to the summit of Kaaterskill High Peak. The Long Path, which begins at the George Washington Bridge and ends in the northern Helderbergs, cuts through this area and is often used by thru-hikers as well as day hikers. Over the past twenty years, Huckleberry Point has increased in popularity, resulting in the trail's designation and marking with state-trail markers. It is easily one of the most scenic and appealing destinations in the Northeast Catskills.

The snowmobile trail that encircles Kaaterskill High Peak and Round-top is both long and seldom used by hikers, but it remains popular with snowmobilers and has become an oft touted though seldom traveled back-country ski route—one of the few practical and exciting routes in the east-ern Catskills.

An early trail emanating from Twilight Park in the northwestern extremes of the forest was once popular with Twilight Park residents and area hotel guests, and crossed the northerly ridgeline above Wildcat and Hillyer ravines to Poet's Ledge and Red Gravel Hill Road in the mid-nineteenth century. Abandoned for years, the trail was resurrected by the New York-New Jersey Trail Conference under permit by the DEC and formed the "missing link" of the Long Path, finally connecting to the northern Catskills in the 1980s. During the process, conference mem-bers led by Albert "Cap" Field rediscovered and flagged a route to Poet's Ledge, and this early destination once again became a marked hiking trail. It is evident from the field sketches and finished works of Sanford R. Gifford that he used this vantage to render scenes of Kaaterskill Clove. Today, Poet's Ledge makes a practical and scenic day hike from Palenville. Hikers visiting the ledge should plan to take the extra time to see Wildcat Ravine and Buttermilk Falls, just to the west.

Escarpment Trail: Section 1—
Scutt Road Trailhead to Rock Shelter Trail

This popular, scenic, and fascinating 23-mile-long trail begins outside the entrance to the North/South Lake Campground. Many hiking parties use the Escarpment Trail (ET) for extended weekend backpacking trips, going as far north as the Windham High Peak and Blackhead Range Wild For-est areas. If a shuttle is arranged at the trail's northern terminus, the ET can be hiked in a long weekend. Lean-tos and water are scarce. The sec-tion of trail between Scutt Road and North Point is very popular with day hikers, most of whom gain access to the trail from the North/South Lake Campground at the trailhead adjacent to North Lake.

Despite the fact that "Schutt Road" appears on road signage, the cor-rect spelling is "Scutt," after Peter and Jacob "Shakespeare" Scutt, the original owners of the Laurel House at the top of Kaaterskill Falls. "Shake-speare" Scutt was fond of reading aloud to his guests. (NOTE: spellings of the words "Schutt" and "Scutt" are used in the text as they appear on signage.)

Day hikers seldom travel beyond North Point if they're entering the trail from the south; they seldom travel south of Blackhead (locally known as Blackhead Mtn.) if entering the trail from the north. A long section of remote territory is in the middle, much of it less interesting than either of its extremes.

Parking for the ET is provided in the Scutt Road Corral parking area, 300 ft. south of CR 18 (North Lake Road) on Scutt Road. Forest Preserve Access Parking signs appear on the corner. A small corral located in the southwest corner of the parking lot is available to equestrians riding Sleepy Hollow Horse Trail, which originates here as well. A signboard and maps are posted, as well as camping/day us information on subjects such as ticks *Giardia*. The trail begins immediately opposite the parking area on the east side of Scutt Road, where it enters dense woods.

Mixed hardwood and hemlock shroud the heavily worn and often muddy trail. Descending gradually, the trail is bordered by tall white pine, mixed hardwoods, and small spruce trees. The trail's surface improves (it was not originally built for multiuse, and equine impact is considerable), and at 0.4 mi. it crosses two old railroad beds. The first was the Catskill and Tannersville Railway (the Huckleberry), which discontinued service in 1915. The second, more established bed (ties are still visible), belonged to the Ulster & Delaware Railroad's Kaaterskill Branch, which remained in service until 1940.

At 0.45 mi., hikers cross lively Lake Creek (South Lake's outlet) on a footbridge, and ascend easily. Past the bridge 200 ft., an obvious but unmarked side trail (be aware that this is off-route) leads left (north) away from the ET, and in a few moments arrives at the old bluestone laundry house and its barely detectable reservoir that once served the Catskill Mountain House. It is worth seeing. It appears as if there was a railroad siding and deck here, now in ruins and filled with 1940s vintage junk. Bits of coal can still be found on the trail. Because it is made of stone, this is the only structure surviving from the heyday of the great hotels. Return to the ET.

The trail continues along a gentle uphill grade, crossing a small footbridge and rising to a four-way trail junction, 0.5 mi. from the ET's trailhead at Scutt Road. The ski trail to the left (north) is marked with yellow ski trail disks but is unsigned. It gently ascends 0.5 mi. to South Lake Road. Straight ahead, red Schutt Road Trail and a yellow horse trail ascend. The blue ET continues to the right (south).

The trail turns right (west), descending through a barrier gate and over an eroded surface. A caboose, seen across Spruce Creek on a private parcel, once belonged to the Delaware and Hudson Railway. This area at the south end of Scutt Road was also the site of the historical Glen Mary (boarding) Cottage, named for Mary Scribner (as was Mary's Glen). A cottage and sawmill in this location (assumed to have belonged to the Scribners) were mentioned in the private journals of Henry David Thoreau, who visited the area in 1844. A record of the visit was never published.

Impact here has prompted the DEC to post No Camping signs. Beneath a hemlock-and-maple forest, the trail is road width and within audible range of Spruce Creek, which spills over Kaaterskill Falls 0.2 mi. to the west. Next to a narrow footbridge is the trail register. Registering here is strongly encouraged, because the country beyond becomes more remote and the trails are numerous. Be sure to describe your intended route accurately. The trail descends, reaching a T, where to the right can be seen the ramparts of a hand-laid, bluestone dam, all that remains of the Scribners' sawmill. Following left (southwest) and climbing, the trail soon flattens through white birch woods. To the right (west) avoid the herd path (an unmarked trail sustained by hikers) that persists over the older route of the ET, which originated at the base of Bastion Falls on NY 23A and was closed because of intensive use and erosion in the 1980s (see Kaaterskill Falls Trail).

Mountain laurel, which is profuse at the monument, and mountain maple and aster, along with small oak and poplar, line the trail as it descends 1.2 mi. to the Layman monument, a significant bluestone obelisk commemorating Frank Layman, a firefighter who perished in the line of duty near this spot in 1900. A cut vista looks northwest into the clove with a view of Hunter Mtn. (4,050 ft.) and the Molly Smith Lookout on NY 23A, the trailhead parking area for Kaaterskill Falls Trail. The trail ascends easily for a few hundred feet to a rock outcropping with extensive views. *Dangerous vertical drops continue from this point, many very close to the trail.*

From this vantage the first sustained views of Kaaterskill Clove begin. Kaaterskill High Peak (3,655 ft.) and Roundtop (3,440 ft.) rise above the vast expanse of the northern Kaaterskill Wild Forest. The rugged, parallel ravines dissecting that slope—from right to left (east to west) Hillyer,

Wildcat, and Santa Cruz—are made obvious by their waterfalls, landslides, and deeply gouged channels. The precariously perched, cliff-edge homes in nearby Twilight Park (private) are visible to the west of the slide. Both Onteora Mtn. (3,230 ft.) and Parker Mtn. (2,820 ft.) stand to the west. Raptors, mostly turkey vultures but sometimes a red-tailed hawk or bald eagle, can be seen along this stretch during warm weather, soaring the updrafts above Kaaterskill Clove.

Even-aged oak and dense mats of blueberry bushes populate the cliff zone. Isolated stands of large white pine dot the forest below the clove itself, the eroded valley of an ancient river and one of the most prominent landscape features of the Catskill range, spilling out thousands of feet below onto the western Hudson Valley. The trail ascends.

At 1.6 mi., the yellow connector trail to Schutt Road Trail leaves to the left (north), while the ET continues straight, following the cliff edge. The trail levels, following the edge of Kaaterskill Clove, and reaches Sunset Rock, with its *treacherous vertical drops*, at 1.7 mi. (There is another, more popular Sunset Rock on a spur off the ET beyond Artist's Rock at 5.1 mi.) The trail climbs a steep pitch to a large, open sandstone ledge covered in silt dust, projecting out over the clove above a vertical ledge at 1.9 mi. This is Inspiration Point. These ledges were popular spots for summer boarders, artists, and the literati of the nineteenth century. General Ulysses S. Grant, a frequent visitor to the Catskill Mountain House, enjoyed discharging his shotgun here in order to experience the echoes bouncing back from the north slopes of Kaaterskill.

The trail continues, turning slightly left into the northeast as the view to the east improves. Hardwood forest follows, yielding to one last view from a small rock facing east, known historically as Bellevue. This lookout stands above Harding Road and the southern branch of Sleepy Hollow Horse Trail. Kaaterskill Clove Lookout can be seen, as well as Indian Head (Point of Rocks). A few undesignated, illegal camping sites appear along the trail around Bellevue. At 2.5 mi., continue straight ahead where the ET joins a short section of Sleepy Hollow Horse Trail, which comes in from the left (west). The horse trail represents the fastest, shortest route back to Scutt Road from this point. Coneflower grows here, blooming in mid- to late summer. Just 200 ft. ahead, the ET leaves Sleepy Hollow Horse Trail (at this point a carriage road) and goes left (northwest), uphill, from the T.

At the T intersection with Sleepy Hollow Horse Trail (and the Long Path), the ET becomes a narrow, rocky trail, covered in loose rubble and bedrock slabs, steadily ascending as it follows the original treadway of Harding Road toward the Hotel Kaaterskill site. At 2.7 mi. and 2,250 ft., the trail flattens and assumes the character of the original stage road, and at 2.9 mi. it arrives at an intersection with Schutt Road Trail.

The Hotel Kaaterskill site lies straight ahead, off the main trail to the north of the intersection. Reputed at the time to be the largest wood-frame structure in the world, it sat atop South Mtn. (2,460 ft.). A vague, unmarked herd path leaves the intersection to the north and circles the site, where a few old foundations and dumps are all that remain. The hotel, which was completed in 1881, was destroyed by a kitchen fire in 1924.

The ET/Long Path continues to the right (northeast) toward Boulder Rock. A short distance beyond the junction, an unmarked trail departs to the left (north), leading downhill to the campground road. The ET is flat through this section. At 3.5 mi., signage is posted at a T where a red cutoff trail provides a shortcut north around Boulder Rock (this cutoff rejoins the ET in 0.2 mi.).

The ET bears right, descending among even-aged oak trees growing above mountain laurel, and passes a "balance rock" off to the right (south) of the trail. Passing Split Rock, a monolith that has fractured away from the bedrock, creating a deep fissure, the trail arrives very soon at a ledge and the large glacial erratic known as Boulder Rock. Old photographs depict the rock (then "Bowlder Rock") with a rustic gazebo perched on top. Good views up and down the Hudson River exist here, taking in a partial view of Overlook Mtn. (3,150 ft.) to the south. Here the carriage road originating from the Hotel Kaaterskill site ends. Continue uphill easily, at 3.8 mi. passing the red cutoff trail on the left (southwest). Continue straight ahead (north) along the ET.

A very short distance beyond the intersection a steep, unmarked herd trail drops off to the right (east). This is also an early route, once marked, which provided one of the few possible descents through the "Great Wall of Manitou" (the fanciful native name given to the Escarpment during the American Romantic era). It joins Sleepy Hollow Horse Trail west of Palenville Overlook. The ET descends now, through rocky, terracing terrain with views east, as the forest becomes open and boreal. A distinctive rock (Eagle Rock) appears on the left, inscribed with carvings from 1850. The trail descends gradually through an area of moss-laden boulders and thick hemlock, passes the trail register, and arrives at Pine Orchard (the pine is gone), the site of the Catskill Mountain House. The only thing that remains of the mountain house is the rear piazza steps, which lie concealed in a nearby thicket. Here there are exceptional views above the Hudson River Valley. Many interesting carvings dating from the early 1800s survive in the *ledge stone near the dangerous precipice to the east*. The derelict hotel eventually became a safety hazard and was burned by the DEC in 1963.

The ET crosses the clearing to the west before turning north, and marking becomes scarce. The old hotel service road (also the road to South Lake Beach) becomes prominent within 200 ft. Watch very carefully ahead as the dirt road forks to the right and turns north-northeast. (If you've reached the South Lake Beach parking area, you've gone too far.) Marking reappears at the fork, where the trail doubles back toward the Escarpment's edge, descending a short section of dirt road through a barrier gate. A trail sign is posted here, immediately south of the Otis Elevating Railway right-of-way, of which nothing remains but a wide scar in the earth (this flat area at the top of the railway was originally named Otis Summit). The steel was later pulled out and scrapped. To the left, North Lake is visible and the bath houses, beach, and picnic area are located a moment's walk off the ET to the left (west; yellow markers may be present).

The trail continues north directly across the Otis right-of-way, following the Escarpment. Watch carefully for markers. No trail signs exist on the north side of the Otis right of way, although one is needed here, and marking (a single trail disk) is inconspicuous. Hikers using the beach, picnic area, or restrooms can return to the trail from the north end of the beach parking lot by following the campsite road to the north. Within 500 ft. or so, a yellow spur provides access to the ET, which lies due east of the beach. A large trail sign is prominent on the right (east) side of the main campsite road.

(NOTE: Day hikers gaining access to the ET from North Lake Campground can most conveniently park at the public beach and day-use area, which has a day-use fee; cars left overnight in this lot are also subject to cumulative day-use fees, which vary by season. The campground is open from the first weekend in May through the fall foliage season in late October. At all other times, access to the ET is available from outside the main gate (Scutt Road parking area). The North Mtn. trailhead is prominent at the North Lake beach and picnic parking area's north side along the campground road (previously discussed). This yellow spur goes east, joining the ET (blue markers) in less than 0.1 mi.)

Follow blue markers as the ET goes north. Views to the east over the Hudson Valley are limited but improve dramatically ahead. *The terrain terraces up through broken ledges and rocky flats, leaving dangerous sheer ledges to the right (east).*

(This area contains some of the vestigial "pine orchards," a name given by nineteenth-century tourists to describe the pure pitch-pine stands that resembled fruit orchards in the romantic imagination. The original pine orchards were destroyed in order to build the Catskill Mountain House. The best surviving example of a pitch-pine orchard exists on Sunset Rock, a 40-minute walk north of the mountain house site.)

At 4.9 mi., the trail reaches Artist's Rock, a small ledge looking east over the Hudson Valley as far east as Mt. Everett and its associated ridges in the southern Taconic region. This is where Thomas Cole and his colleagues stood their easels, with throngs of young men and women in tow. These outings of Cole's and his students were the social "events" of the day. From here, Cole was fond of pointing out his home in Catskill, which can still be seen if you know where to look. He is buried in a cemetery near his home. The house is now a National Historic Site open to visitors.

Continuing north and climbing gently, the trail passes Prospect Rock and shortly beyond it the tilted, open crown of Sunrise Rock. The following ascent of Red Hill levels through hardwoods and passes by the western wall of a monolith, buttressed with vertical puddingstone (conglomerate). This was the site of Jacob's Ladder, a historical structure that at one time scaled the wall to the top of Sunset Rock. The trail continues to the junction with Sunset Rock Spur Trail at 5.7 mi., now the safest way to gain access to this scenic landmark (see Sunset Rock Spur Trail).

The ET continues through hardwoods, climbing to Newman's Ledge. This exposed, vertical ledge at 2,500 ft. is actually an overhang, largely unsupported from beneath. Old carvings on its face reflect its historical

⚠ popularity. *This high vertical precipice is extremely exposed and dangerous.* Views to the east are extensive, including the Hudson's two midregion bridges (Kingston-Rhinecliff and Rip Van Winkle); the Escarpment's eastern wild forests; bits of the cultivated lowlands of Ulster, Green, and Albany counties; and on a clear day, Albany itself. The trail heads north over a rocky surface, climbing terraces through ledgy hardwood and spruce thickets. Circling to the north of a bog at 5.8 mi. and turning west, it reaches the junction with Rock Shelter Trail, the site of Badman Cave, at 6.0 mi. This area is so floristically diverse that it "defies imagination," according to botanist Dr. Michael Kudish. It is the most southern and the only place in the Catskills that supports a subarctic plant community, similar to those of the Canadian Shield.

Escarpment Trail: Section 2—
Rock Shelter Trail to Arizona Mtn. Summit

The Escarpment Trail (ET) turns right (north), climbing up across a ledge and into spruce woods. Another small ledge follows, and then at 2,700 ft. and 6.2 mi. the trail enters an open bald with views of Kaaterskill High Peak, Roundtop, Plateau, and Sugarloaf to the south. Remaining level, the route retreats from its rocky ledges of spruce and pine and exposed rock to enter a shaded transition zone of striped maple, birch, and mountain laurel. The path turns to red-clay silt. Flat stones have been placed on the trail in an effort to keep it dry. Following a section of level ground and open hardwoods, the ET meets Mary's Glen Trail below North Point at 6.9 mi.

Climb steeply. Intensive use has necessitated rerouting and improvement of this section of trail on several occasions. Earlier routes are fenced
⚠ off and recovering. *Following a series of scrambles and ledges,* the trail reaches North Point (3,000 ft.) at 7.2 mi. This popular scenic destination is a large, open rock shelf 0.5 mi. east of (wooded, trailless) North Mtn. itself. On summer days, it can be a busy spot, full of day hikers and, like many of the more accessible scenic locations in the Catskills, European visitors (the Hudson Valley is often referred to as "America's Rhineland" for its European-style scenery, and has attracted many foreign visitors). The views are sensational, moving through the northwest to the southwest. A sliver of Overlook Mtn.'s summit appears (3,150 ft., the fire tower is barely visible

at 211 degrees, above Plattekill Mtn.). The northerly summit of Twin Mtn. (3,640 ft.) rises between Kaaterskill High Peak and Roundtop. The Shawangunk Ridge is obvious, and it is possible to see the Mohonk Mountain House, Sky Top, and the Hudson Highlands with binoculars. Sweeping views of the valley include several ranges in the tristate area around Mt. Everett in Massachusetts. Hikers familiar with that region will be able to pick out Bash Bish Falls, Washington, Alander, Brace Mtn., and Mt. Everett. (The Appalachian Trail crosses Mt. Everett's summit.)

To see the northerly views that are not at all obvious from the shelf, move 300 ft. to the northeast of the point through low brush, to open rocks that provide intimate views of the Windham-Blackhead Range Wilderness—Thomas Cole Mtn. (3,950 ft.), Black Dome (3,990 ft.), Blackhead (3,950 ft.), Arizona (3,400 ft.), Windham High Peak (3,524 ft.), Burnt Knob (3,190 ft.), and Acra Point (3,110 ft.); the latter four destinations are traversed by the ET. Albany is visible with the naked eye on a clear day, as well as the mountains beyond it, in Vermont's Green Mountain National Forest.

Very few day hikers venture beyond North Point. Ahead, the land becomes remote, and there is no significant scenery or water for several miles (see Dutcher Notch Trail for the location of a fairly reliable spring). A weathered signpost stands in the exposed rocks of North Point.

Proceeding straight ahead (west), with the North/South Lake viewshed to the left (south), the ET enters patches of woods, for the first 0.4 mi. keeping to the open southerly ledges of North Mtn., where blue-paint blazes guide hikers across bare, rocky flats. Within a short distance the trail crosses a bald of curiously eroded, pockmarked bedrock and arrives at an overlook that resembles a scaled-down, more private version of North Point, complete with the same southerly aspect (only higher) and similar views. Day hikers will find that this area is empty when the lower point is crowded. From here the trail winds its way up and around low ledges, passing through woods and across open vistas. At 7.7 mi., at the site of a final clearing, approximating the summit of North Mtn. (3,180 ft.), the trail enters the woods and turns right (northwest) gradually, through mixed hardwoods and extensive red spruce stands, ascending 240 vertical ft. from North Mtn. to Stoppel Point (3,430 ft.). This diminutive lookout, while small, offers an attractive resting point and a legal camping area (stay back off the trail 150 ft.), with interesting but limited views to the east from a small rock shelf in the spruces. An ancient, nearly obliterated trail leads from this point down the mountain to the Winter Clove hotel and trail matrix and is still used by some knowledgeable hikers.

The trail continues straight, trending northwest, remaining generally level until swinging gradually to the north and passing a cut vista toward the Windham-Blackhead Range Wilderness, and descending past a small, somber plane wreck on the right (east) side of the trail at 9.0 mi. (3,400 ft.). This is one of several aircraft that have fallen victim to not only the Escarpment's very sudden rise from near-sea level to 3,950 ft. (Blackhead), but also to the severe downdrafts that can develop as air masses sweep across the Catskill plateau and plunge into the Hudson Valley.

From the crash site, the trail descends through a forest of large birch and scattered spruce and levels along the Escarpment ridge to 3,000 ft., coming upon Milt's Point Lookout, where Stoppel Point, North Mtn., the village of Catskill, and the city of Hudson, as well as several mountain ranges, can be seen. Cairo Roundtop is the small hill in the foreground. Albany is at 45 degrees. Bash Bish Falls gorge and Mt. Everett can be seen on a clear day.

The trail soon descends and switches back over long, easy grades where the surface is worn to silt mineral soil. A flat ridge top of cherry, beech, and birch trees follows. After a final, brief descent the trail arrives at the four-way intersection of Dutcher Notch at 10.3 mi. Dutcher Notch is named for Jim Dutcher, the "guardian spirit" of Slide Mtn. and its best-known guide. The state wished to commemorate Dutcher, who lived beneath Slide Mtn., and had run out of suitable landmarks in the Southern Catskills.

For summer backpackers, the notch is important for its two nearby water sources. The closest is 0.4 mi. southeast on Dutcher Notch Trail (yellow), a ten-minute walk downhill. The source is obvious on the right side of the trail, trickling from a ledge into a stone basin. This spring is ordinarily reliable but runs very slowly in hot weather. Don't risk taking standing water from the basin; take the time to let your bottles fill. (It may take ten minutes or more to fill a liter bottle in late summer.) Groups are better off taking Colgate Lake Trail southwest 1.0 mi. to the East Kill or one of several (seasonal) creeks that cross the trail in the East Kill watershed area, although these are often completely dry, subject to surface contamination, or both. Don't make the mistake of underestimating the scarcity of water here. To meet their own water requirements, large college outing groups often cache water in dozens of gallon jugs throughout this area. The nearest reliable water source to the north is below Lockwood Gap on Black Dome Trail—too far to go if you're already suffering from dehydration.

Because there are no views from this deep and relatively remote wooded notch, it is not a day-hiking destination. However, it is often busy with relaxing hikers in transit, a sort of Times Square of the woods, where a member of the party will stay with gear as others descend, free of their packs, to the spring. The area has seen moderate but increasing use from outing clubs, backcountry skiers, and (rarely) mountain bikers coming in from Colgate Lake. This will mostly likely change, as the state has classified this area as a primitive bicycle corridor. Opportunities for camping in the notch are limited, if not poor, but improve ahead on the (under 3,500-ft.) flats of Arizona Mtn.

The ET continues straight ahead and rises very steeply to the northwest among pure spruce stands, yielding to birch. This is about as steep as it gets in the Catskills—nearly 1,000 ft. of vertical gain in slightly more than one mile. Most of the rise occurs immediately north of Dutcher Notch and eases as a lookout rock appears to the left (west) at the end of a short spur trail at 11.5 mi. (3,100 ft., marked with yellow markers but easy to miss). This is a popular spot and many hikers stop here. Sweeping views include, west to east, Hunter Mtn., Sugarloaf, Pecoy Notch, Twin, Indian Head, Roundtop, Kaaterskill High Peak, Stoppel Point, and North Mtn., with Parker and Onteora mtns. in the low foreground. The trail continues, offering only limited, seasonal views as the land rises and falls gently on the approach to Arizona's flat-ridge summit at 12.1 mi.

Escarpment Trail: Section 3—
Arizona Mtn. Summit to NY 23 in East Windham

Spruce and white birch give way to sparse vegetation across open blueberry balds with patches of goldenrod and reindeer moss. Although higher than many popular Catskill peaks, Arizona Mtn.'s relatively featureless summit (3,400 ft.) and remote position have compromised its name recognition as well as its popularity as a destination hike. However, the mountain's nearly viewless summit of flat rocks allows some easterly views of the Hudson

Valley as far north as Acra Point (3,110 ft.). A vague, unmarked herd trail ahead at 12.2 mi. leads west to a view of the East Kill Valley. The trail remains flat along the summit ridge, climbing piecemeal to a viewpoint at 12.4 mi. where graffiti survives from 1902 and includes the etching of a small rising sun (looking east). Ascending, hikers will see a rock painted with the words "Camp Steel, 1936" marking the site where some sustained impact becomes evident. From this point the Escarpment Trail (ET) ascends to the treed-in, thick, balsam-clad summit of Blackhead (3,950 ft.) and the intersection with Blackhead Mtn. Trail at 12.7 mi.

From the junction the ET turns right (northeast), descending steeply, and can be hazardous under icy conditions. As the trail turns toward the north, a rock appears to the right (east) of the trail, offering views over the Hudson Valley (Cairo Roundtop is the small hill to the right). The trail terraces its way downhill, through birch, balsam, spruce, striped maple, and a ground cover of asters. After a short, level stretch through a birch wood, the trail arrives at a well-marked, rocky intersection with Batavia Kill Trail at 13.5 mi.

The trail continues north, descending slightly into a densely wooded area with a thick fern ground cover. In the middle to late spring, starflower, trillium, spring beauty, and Canada violet appear, and in some areas the trail is profuse with Canada mayflower. Climbing, the path becomes rocky and penetrates a spruce forest with limited views south toward the Blackhead Range. The trail crosses to the east side of the ridge, passing a campsite, closed due to overuse and its proximity to the footway. Northern hardwoods appear and gain in maturity as you travel north and the trail flattens at 3,000 ft. in an area where ravens nest. Maple takes over, becoming a pure stand as the terrain descends almost imperceptibly and the slopes of Burnt Knob (3,190 ft.) become apparent to the north-northwest. Descending slightly to the easterly side of the narrow ridge as the trail approaches Acra Point, a small lookout point, is seen. Ascending easily through an area where very thick grass appears in the woods, the trail descends gently to a small, flat-topped boulder on the right (northeast) of the trail at 15.2 mi. This (including the small blueberry bald just ahead) is Acra Point. No Camping signs are posted on the summit itself. Acra Point provides a view of Albany, and on a clear day, the large mountain ranges of Vermont can be identified beyond the city. North of Acra Point a viewpoint looking southwest is reached within ten minutes, with views of Blackhead at 190 degrees, followed by Elm Ridge, Burnt Knob, and Windham High Peak. The trail gradually descends 300 vertical ft. into the saddle and the junction with Black Dome Trail (red) at 15.8 mi.

The ET climbs straight ahead into the west, sometimes steeply, making its way 350 vertical ft. up the southwest-facing side of the ridge, offering only broken views of the Blackhead Range. As the trail levels onto Burnt Knob (3,190 ft.) at 16.6 mi., a poorly marked spur trail leads left through a closed campsite to a ledge with excellent views southwest, including Acra Point, Blackhead, Black Dome, and Thomas Cole Mtn., and the long, flat ridge of Arizona Mtn. Views across the Hudson River include Mt. Everett and Bash Bish Mtn. At the westerly edge of Burnt Knob, the trail briefly curves left (southwest), dropping downhill between two shallow rock overhangs and making its way west again. Hikers will be expecting views to the north from this point (the trail draws close to the north edge of the ridge), which is heavily wooded. These views materialize ahead from a large, flat, rock vista at 2,900 ft. Albany and the mountains of the Taconic Range and Green Mountain National Forest are plainly visible. The trail continues, shifting to the west side of the ridge through thick hardwoods, passing another lookout point on the left of the Hunter-West Kill Wilderness. A better view is soon encountered along the trail from a south-facing spur, with spectacular views of the Black Dome Valley and Windham High Peak.

At 17.3 mi., the trail begins its ascent of the southeast shoulder of Windham High Peak, passing a shallow rock overhang on the right before entering a small, pure stand of beech. After a steep, short distance, a bald of blueberry bushes and stunted maple is crossed, and the trail continues level into dense hardwoods. Gaining elevation—never too strenuously—the 3,500 ft. sign is reached, and within a moment beyond it, Windham's first significant viewpoint at 18.0 mi. From a rock that appears to hang in midair over the Hudson Valley, Albany and views north are again visible, along with the farms and open land of the Schoharie and Mohawk valleys.

To the north, the southern Adirondacks are seen. Large mountain ranges loom beyond Albany and stretch far south, from Mt. Snow to Bash Bish in the Taconics. The rock itself is defaced with crude etchings. At 18.2 mi., Windham's true summit is reached (3,524 ft.), where bits of vintage graffiti appear on a stone that has broken away from the bedrock, dating from the mid- to late 1800s, carved by early hotel visitors hiking in from the local boarding houses. Scattered balsam fir leads the way across the summit area to more isolated views, none of them as grand as the first.

Descending, the trail becomes grassy and worn over mineral soil at 19.0 mi. Wake-robin (purple trillium) appears, and the trail flattens below the 2,700-ft. level where a seasonal creek marks the beginning of an extensive sugar maple forest, and grass carpets the ground. Soon the trail passes large plantations of Norway spruce, which continue to 2,100 ft. The trail penetrates these impressive conifer stands at several points ahead, making this the most attractive trail for day-hiking Windham High Peak. Pass through an old stone wall and a settlement area, crossing a mossy bald into another large plantation area. (These large forests can be identified from the summit of Blackhead.) At 20.3 mi. (2,350 ft.), the Elm Ridge lean-to is seen on the left of the ET. It too is situated in a very attractive evergreen forest and has an expansive, legal tent-camping area to the rear (south). A piped spring is located downhill (south) 0.2 mi. on adjacent Elm Ridge Trail, but it runs very sluggishly in the dog days of summer, and during drought periods, perhaps not at all. Within hailing distance of the lean-to, the trail junction is reached.

The trail leaves the lean-to to the left (south) and within 100 yd. reaches the junction with Elm Ridge Trail. The ET continues, bearing right (north). From the Elm Ridge saddle the ET follows an attractive, old dirt road to the north, which descends and switches back to the west at a point where an earlier road continues east again before settling into the northwest through hemlock woods. A signboard and trail register are located on the left side of the trail at 21.0 mi. Open fields and poplar appear as NY 23 comes into view. Cross a footbridge within sight of the road at 21.4 mi. Here the trail crosses the road to the trailhead parking area on the north side of NY 23 and at the corner of Cross Road (the Long Path continues northeast to Old Road). This is the northern terminus of the ET. From this point, the Long Path continues north.

Escarpment Trail (map 1: B9–A8)

Distances from Scutt Road trailhead (2,240 ft.) to:
- Schutt Road Trail, lower junction (2,090 ft.): 0.5 mi., 0 ft. (rev. 150 ft.), 15 min.
- Sunset Rock (2,190 ft.): 1.7 mi., 350 ft. (rev. 250 ft.), 1 hr.
- Inspiration Point (2,150 ft.): 1.9 mi., 350 ft. (rev. 50 ft.), 1 hr. 10 min.   ▶

- Schutt Road Trail, upper junction (2,420 ft.): 2.9 mi., 600 ft., 1 hr. 50 min.
- Boulder Rock (2,310 ft.): 3.7 mi., 600 ft. (rev. 100 ft.), 2 hr. 20 min.
- Catskill Mountain House site (2,210 ft.): 4.2 mi., 700 ft. (rev. 200 ft.), 2 hr. 35 min.
- spur trail to North/South Lake Campground (2,150 ft.): 4.6 mi., 700 ft. (rev. 100 ft.), 2 hr. 40 min.
- Sunset Rock Spur Trail (2,430 ft.): 5.7 mi., 1,000 ft., 3 hr. 20 min.
- Rock Shelter Trail at Badman Cave (2,640 ft.): 6.0 mi., 1,200 ft., 3 hr. 50 min.
- Mary's Glen Trail (2,750 ft.): 6.6 mi., 1,300 ft., 4 hr. 10 min.
- North Point (3,010 ft.): 7.2 mi., 1,550 ft., 4 hr. 25 min.
- Stoppel Point (3,430 ft.): 8.9 mi., 1,950 ft., 5 hr. 25 min.
- Dutcher Notch (2,510 ft.): 10.3 mi., 2,050 ft. (rev. 1,000 ft.), 6 hr. 30 min.
- Arizona Mtn. summit (3,410 ft.): 12.1 mi., 2,950 ft., 7 hr. 30 min.
- Blackhead summit (3,950 ft.): 12.7 mi., 3,600 ft. (rev. 100 ft.), 8 hr. 35 min.
- Batavia Kill Trail (2,870 ft.): 13.5 mi., 3,600 ft. (rev. 1,100 ft.), 9 hr. 5 min.
- Acra Point (3,110 ft.): 15.2 mi., 3,950 ft. (rev. 100 ft.), 10 hr. 10 min.
- Black Dome Range Trail (2,770 ft.): 15.8 mi., 3,950 ft. (rev. 350 ft.), 10 hr. 35 min.
- Burnt Knob (3,190 ft.): 16.6 mi, 4,400 ft. (rev. 450), 11 hr.
- Windham High Peak summit (3,524 ft.): 18.2 mi., 5,050 ft. (rev. 300 ft.), 12 hr. 25 min.
- Elm Ridge Trail (2,310 ft.): 20.3 mi., 5,050 ft. (rev. 1,200 ft.), 13 hr. 30 min.
- NY 23 in East Windham (1,770 ft.): 21.4 mi., 5,050 ft. (rev. 550 ft.), 14 hr. 10 min.

Sunset Rock Spur Trail

This short side trip off of the Escarpment Trail to Sunset Rock is the most popular day-hiking destination between North/South Lake Campground and North Point, and by popular consensus is considered among the most appealing short hikes in the Catskill Mountains. (And, when combined with North Point, it ranks as one of the greatest.)

From the Escarpment Trail, 0.9 mi. from North Mtn. Trail's signboard at the north end of the North Lake beach parking area, Sunset Rock Spur Trail goes right (east). Passing Lookout Rock to the left, the trail bends back to the south, the surroundings shifting from oak and mountain laurel to idyllic pitch-pine flats that approximate the appearance of the erstwhile Pine Orchard, the area where the Catskill Mountain House once stood. Sunset Rock is reached at 0.3 mi. *This expansive lookout is fissured* *with hazardous, deep cracks (caution children against running ahead of you).*

The westernmost (and deepest) fissure is the Bear's Den (once the name for the general area), one of several famous nineteenth-century landmarks. In reality the "den" is a series of labyrinthine crevices, most likely harboring only porcupines. Exercise caution, particularly in winter conditions, as the fissures may be concealed by blown snow. The views immediately overlooking North and South lakes, South Mtn. (2,460 ft.), the mountains to the south, and the Hudson River valley are spectacular. Kaaterskill High Peak (3,655 ft.) and Roundtop Mtn. (3,440 ft.) are most prominent to the southwest. The southerly views of the Shawangunk Ridge feature Sky Top Tower (the ridge juts out to the east of the southerly escarpment) and Overlook Mtn. (3,150 ft.), roughly 40 mi. distant. North Mtn. (3,180 ft.) is the long ridge to the northwest.

Sunset Rock Spur Trail (map 1: B9)

Distance from Escarpment Trail (2,430 ft.) to
• Sunset Rock (2,430 ft.): 0.3 mi., 0 ft., 10 min.

Kaaterskill Falls Trail

Kaaterskill Falls has proven to be one of the Catskills' most popular destinations—a century ago this waterfall was more popular than Niagara Falls. Hikers will find the trail to the falls scenic, easy, and interesting. Recent improvements have made steeper sections of the trail more negotiable. Many people use this trail, especially on weekends, and hikers in search of solitude will choose to look elsewhere.

This trail originates next to Bastion Falls at the hairpin turn on NY 23A, 3.5 mi. west of the intersection of NY 23A and NY 32A in Palenville. Parking is 0.2 mi. uphill beyond the trailhead. *Exercise extreme caution when walking from the parking area to the trailhead along NY 23A.*

Locate the trailhead at the destination sign (Kaaterskill Falls, 0.4 mi.) in the deepest part of the hairpin turn on NY 23A. The trail is marked with yellow markers and travels northeast along the banks of Spruce Creek. The path ascends very steeply at first, soon leveling through a virgin hemlock forest, and arrives at the base of the falls, where large boulders provide excellent viewing of the two-tiered falls, with an estimated height of 260 ft. (More recent estimates run from 230 ft. to 250 ft.) The first,

higher tier is said to be 175 ft. and the lower tier is roughly 85 ft. *Behind* ⚠
the lower tier (where hikers should not venture) is an area long known as the
Amphitheater—a spot that many people have died trying to reach, especially in
the winter months, as they've fallen or slid 85 ft. off the icy, narrow, near ver-
tical herd trails onto the rocks beneath the second tier. It is also—according to
some—the fabled resting place of Rip Van Winkle who, as legend has it,
while drinking a strange brew, bowled ninepins here with the ghostly crew
of Henry Hudson's *Half Moon* and slept for the next twenty years.

The Escarpment Trail once began at this trailhead on NY 23A and
continued from there, climbing the southeastern wall of the gorge to join
the present Escarpment Trail. This section of trail is closed because of
severe erosion. Presently there is no marked trail access to the top of the
falls, but they can be reached legally from the end of Laurel House Road
off CR 18, 0.5 mi. west of the North/South Lake Campground and Day
Use Area.

Kaaterskill Falls Trail (map 1: B9)

Distance from NY 23A (1,450 ft.) to
• Kaaterskill Falls (1,750 ft.): 0.4 mi., 300 ft., 20 min.

Rock Shelter Trail

Skirting the campground to the northwest, Rock Shelter Trail provides alternate access to the Escarpment Trail, as well as a quick route to Mary's
Glen and North Point from outside the campground gate. It is used by
those who wish to avoid paying the campground's day-use fees, or plan
to be hiking for several days or more. It is not an interesting trail in itself, and is not recommended as a day-hiking route. In this case the Scutt
Road Corral trailhead parking area should be used (the campground does
ask a minimal "walk-in" fee). If the primary objective is to visit North
Point, Mary's Glen Trail (the trailhead is inside the entrance gate, 0.8 mi.
down the campsite road) provides the fastest access, and is most easily and
quickly reached using the campsite road rather than Rock Shelter Trail.
This rocky, heavily wooded trail leaves from the north side of CR 18 immediately outside the North/South Lake Campground and Day Use Area
opposite the trail sign near Scutt Road.

Heading north at its departure, the trail quickly turns northeast and continues on a nearly level grade through the boulder-strewn forest northeast toward Mary's Glen. Rocks and roots beneath dense foliage result in a slow pace, and there are no views. At 1.2 mi., the trail arrives at the junction with Mary's Glen Trail.

The trail continues through the junction, following yellow markers, and begins to ascend. During wet periods, water cascades over ledges to the left and large slabs of bedrock in the trail become slippery, so use caution. The state recreation facility boundary lies on the right (no camping permitted). As the trail gains elevation, hemlock appears and the footway becomes a friendlier base of needles. The terrain ahead flattens, becoming amenable (and legal) to campers, and spruce thickets give way to the trail junction at Badman Cave, which can be found to the left of the junction. It is not really a cave, but a rock overhang, portions of which have collapsed next to the trail. This is the junction with the Escarpment Trail (blue), which at this point is also the Long Path.

Rock Shelter Trail (map 1: B9)

Distances from CR 18 outside North/South Lake Campground main gate (2,250 ft.) to
- Mary's Glen Trail (2,400 ft.): 1.2 mi., 200 ft. (rev. 50 ft.), 50 min.
- Escarpment Trail at Badman Cave (2,640 ft.): 1.6 mi., 450 ft., 1 hr. 10 min.
- North Point (3,010 ft.) via Mary's Glen Trail and Escarpment Trail: 2.8 mi., 800 ft., 1 hr. 40 min.

Mary's Glen Trail

A popular but very short hike to a small glen and Ashley Falls, Mary's Glen Trail is also commonly used as an alternate route or loop connection to North Point, although most hikers use the more scenic Escarpment Trail from the bathing-beach parking area. The trail begins inside the North/South Lake Campground, 0.8 mi. from the main gate along the north side of the main campsite road. Park at the designated parking area, and walk back (west) approximately 100 yd. along the road to the trailhead, just west of Ashley Creek, where signs are posted.

Following the western fringe of a small wetland and beaver meadow—filled with wildflowers by midsummer—the trail is sometimes overtaken by

Ashley Creek. Within a few hundred feet, the trail passes the register in a mixed forest of hemlock and hardwoods, at 0.25 mi. reaching a yellow spur that branches right. The spur ends a few hundred feet ahead, at the base of Ashley Falls, where a huge pile of broken stones has fallen away from the streambed above. Small but vigorous in the spring, the falls dry up as warmer weather arrives. Many casual walkers come in to view the falls but rarely venture beyond them. Return to the red trail, which bears right and climbs minimally into the glen itself, crossing above the falls to enter a birch-and-hemlock wood. The forest type shifts as the trail gains elevation, revealing the slow, partial recovery of an extensive red spruce stand (once considered the finest in the state) that was clear-cut during World War I to provide wood for aircraft. The trail remains rocky but footing becomes easier as the path approaches the junction with the yellow Rock Shelter Trail at 0.6 mi.

Bearing left (northwest), the trail continues through the junction (250 ft.), leaving Rock Shelter Trail to the left slightly farther ahead. Wet ledges and lush forest characterize the area. The trail ascends gently, soon becoming level in a poorly drained area that sometimes remains wet for extended periods. Climbing again, the trail arrives at the junction with the Escarpment Trail. North Point is to the left (north); the North/South Lake Campground is to the right.

Mary's Glen Trail (map 1: B9)

Distances from North/South Lake Campground road (2,170 ft.) to
- spur trail to Ashley Falls (2,170 ft.): 0.2 mi., 0 ft., 10 min.
- Rock Shelter Trail (2,400 ft.): 0.6 mi., 250 ft., 25 min.
- Escarpment Trail (2,750 ft.): 1.3 mi., 600 ft., 55 min.
- North Point (3,010 ft.) via Escarpment Trail: 2.2 mi., 850 ft., 1 hr. 10 min.

Schutt Road Trail

Schutt Road Trail begins off the Escarpment Trail, 0.5 mi. from Schutt Road Corral at the four-way intersection of the Escarpment Trail and the Nordic ski trail, just east of Spruce Creek. Part of the old carriage road system dating from the hotel's heyday, it provides a short, uphill walk to the Kaaterskill Hotel site, where nothing remains but a few stone foundation ramparts. This is the shortest trail route to the Kaaterskill Hotel site, the Catskill Mountain House site, and the North Lake state campground beach and picnic area. However, the latter two landmarks can be reached much faster by walking the campsite road. Using the yellow spur trail, ahead 0.2 mi. on Schutt Road Trail, it is also the shortest way to Sunset Rock and Inspiration Point.

Following red markers, Schutt Road Trail heads uphill on a dirt carriage road. In some areas, the road is reinforced with original stonework, and the soft silt soil washes out occasionally. At 0.25 mi. from the junction, a connector trail (yellow) turns to the right (south), joining the Escarpment Trail in 0.4 mi.

Following red markers, the trail continues through red oak that nearly tunnels overhead. State recreational facility boundary (SRFB) postings appear to the left (north). No camping is allowed within the SRFB. At 0.9 mi., Schutt Road Trail ends at a four-way trail junction. Here, a herd trail going straight ahead circles the Kaaterskill Mountain House site. From the knoll (South Mtn., 2,460 ft.) where the hotel stood, the view that made it famous is now heavily forested and no longer exists. At this intersection, Schutt Road Trail joins the Escarpment Trail.

Schutt Road Trail (map 1: B9)

Distances from Escarpment Trail, lower junction (2,210 ft.) to
- yellow connector trail (2,250 ft.): 0.2 mi., 50 ft., 5 min.
- Escarpment Trail, upper junction (2,420 ft.): 1.0 mi., 200 ft., 35 min.

Sleepy Hollow Horse Trail System

Sleepy Hollow Horse Trail system begins at Scutt Road Corral (the Escarpment Trail trailhead), just outside the North/South Lake Campground and Day Use Area's main gate, on CR 18. It provides the shortest route to scenic Palenville Overlook—and is the route of choice for backcountry skiers and experienced mountain bikers who are heading downhill to Palenville on either the Old Mountain Turnpike or Harding Road sections of the horse trail system (both of these trails are very rocky at lower elevations).

The trail follows the Escarpment Trail to Schutt Road Trail, reaching the latter at 0.5 mi. At 0.7 mi., the trail turns right (south) onto the yellow connector trail. At 0.9 mi., the horse trail leaves the connector trail to the left (east) and is from this point designated as a single-use trail (distance and time begin here). This initially flat and very attractive section of the Sleepy Hollow Horse Trail system is a multiuse trail used by hikers, skiers, and mountain bikers. The trail goes through an oak-and-laurel forest until, at 1.8 mi., it turns left (northeast) onto the Escarpment Trail for only a few hundred feet (also called Harding Road Trail at this point). Signage is posted at the junction of the horse trail and Escarpment Trail.

The trail continues straight through this junction (northeast), arriving at Shorey Point (1.9 mi.), a one-time scenic location that has become heavily wooded. From this Y, the Harding Road, also part of the Sleepy Hollow Horse Trail system, descends to the southwest and is not signed. Trail markers are prolific, and the roadlike trail is wide and self-guiding. Aqua Long Path blazes appear here along with red trail markers.

Continue northeast on the horse trail, toward Palenville Overlook, then descend slightly, crossing a seasonal creek. At a boulder the trail splits, coming together again a short distance ahead. A few unmarked side trails appear as the trail narrows and flattens out. A descent follows and the trail switches back steeply over loose stone, arriving at a T at 2.5 mi. Snowmobile markers appear on the horse trail at this point.

The trail turns right (southeast) toward Palenville Overlook, remaining flat and narrow as it follows along the edge of a high, wooded ledge, arriving at the overlook at 2.8 mi. At this writing, a picnic table, fireplace, and designated campsite exist at Palenville Overlook, an area used on a fairly regular basis by pack-tripping parties from a nearby horse ranch. In spite of multiuse exposure, the level of impact at this site is surprisingly low, and few hikers seem to visit this beautiful area. A short path south through a stand of pine reveals Palenville Overlook and excellent views over Kaaterskill Clove and the Hudson Valley. *Vertical drops here are high and dangerous, so use caution.*

To the right at the same elevation is another lookout, known as Point of Rocks or Indian Head—the latter name for its now fractured profile as seen from Kaaterskill Clove. Shelving rocks, pitch pine, blueberry bushes, and dwarf oak characterize the overlook. Kaaterskill High Peak (3,655 ft.) and Roundtop Mtn. (3,440 ft.) command the southern skyline above the extensive forests on their northern slopes. A large piece of the Hudson Valley, from the lower Taconic region to the Hudson Highlands, sprawls within view across the southeast.

The trail hairpins back on itself in a tight loop, following markers to the left (east), downhill through a small pine grove. Within a few hundred feet the trail curves left, heading north. Marking is adequate. A small unmarked, unmaintained trail to the right leads to another ledge and an interesting old foundation—the former site of Halfway House, which at one time took in summer boarders. Hikers have assembled stone seats facing the sweeping valley views at the site where a small boarding cottage once stood.

The trail continues to the north on an even elevation along an oak- and laurel-wooded terrace, heading north-northwest to a point north of the previous trail junction. Turn right (north). The terrain remains flat with only a minor descent as it approaches the Otis Elevating Railroad grade, where a cable railway (built in 1892) climbed the Escarpment, bringing guests to the Catskill Mountain House and connecting with the Catskill and Tannersville Railway to points west. Nothing remains of the scrapped elevating railway but its abandoned right of way. The trail goes north beyond the railroad grade and climbs, switching back hard and steeply toward the southwest, and quickly joins the Old Mountain Turnpike on the section known as the Long Level. To the left a 0.25 mi. section of the trail rises to the North Lake campground picnic area and beach. Turning right at 4.5 mi., the trail descends on the wide dirt road.

Descending to the first hairpin turn, winter views appear of Newman's Ledge to the left (west) and Rip's Rocks to the north. Continue the descent on Featherbed Hill, switching back to the south. At the next switchback at 5.5 mi., historically known as Cape Horn, is Little Pine Orchard, the site of a picnic area with a hitching post, fireplace, and picnic table as well as extensive valley views. From the towns of Hudson and Catskill, the panorama swings south across the Taconics, Mt. Everett, the Hudson Highlands, and the Shawangunks. The turnpike descends again, over the section long known as Dead Ox Hill, which drops down to the head of Sleepy Hollow and the site of an old tavern ruin (the foundations can still be seen on the left before crossing the bridge). This tavern and rest stop, according to Catskill Mountain House advertisements, was the fanciful home of Rip Van Winkle. The trail crosses the bridge spanning Stony Brook, turns right (east), passes the trail register, and descends along the brook and its deepening hollow, crossing Black Snake Bridge at 6.4 mi. A pine bluff on the north side of the trail precedes a northward curve in the turnpike, and the trail ends at the west end of Mountain Turnpike Road at 7.4 mi. At the turnpike trailhead, a sign is posted near the barrier gate.

Roadside parking is available to the east of a barn, within sight of the trailhead. Pelham Four Corners is 0.8 mi. east, at the corner of Mountain Turnpike Road and Bogart Road, where trail signs provide directions to Sleepy Hollow Horse Trail. From the four corners, follow Pennsylvania Avenue right (south) to Bogart Road, and at 0.4 mi. find the horse trail parking area. NY 23A is 2.0 mi. farther, at Palenville.

Sleepy Hollow Horse Trail (map 1: B9)

Distances from yellow connector trail joining Schutt Road Trail and Escarpment Trail (2,250 ft.) to

- Escarpment Trail (2,200 ft.): 1.8 mi., 50 ft. (rev. 100 ft.), 45 min.
- Shorey Point and Harding Road Trail (2,100 ft.): 1.9 mi., 50 ft. (rev. 100 ft.), 50 min.
- spur trail to Palenville Overlook (1,800 ft.): 2.8 mi., 100 ft. (rev. 350 ft.), 1 hr. 25 min.
- Old Mountain Turnpike and connector to North Lake Campground (1,870 ft.): 4.5 mi., 150 ft., 2 hr. 20 min.
- Little Pine Orchard Picnic Area (1,570 ft.): 5.5 mi., 150 ft. (rev. 300 ft.), 2 hr. 50 min.
- Mountain Turnpike Road trailhead (690 ft.): 7.4 mi., 150 ft. (rev. 900 ft.), 3 hr. 45 min.

Harding Road Trail

This trail follows the bed of an old carriage road. In the lower elevations, the old roadbed is still wide and well maintained, but as it rises to the Escarpment's upper elevations, nature has reclaimed the road and it assumes the character of a footpath.

The trail begins in Palenville, 0.3 mi. west of Whites Road on the north side of NY 23A (just before the Entering Catskill Park sign). Parking here is possible, but limited. Less secure parking is available in the DEC-designated parking area on Whites Road, 0.6 mi. north off NY 23A. Hikers using this lot will walk south through the woods 0.4 mi. to meet Harding Road Trail and turn west at the junction. Signs at both trailheads are consistently poor in terms of distances and nonexistent for destinations at this writing, but the trails are easily followed, self-guiding, and well established. The trailhead on Whites Road is identified with forest preserve access signs.

George W. Harding, a wealthy Philadelphia lawyer, built this road to deliver guests to his Hotel Kaaterskill, and it remains in good condition today. Railroad engineers considered the project and refused to undertake it—the task was impossible, they said. So Harding hired local men who were familiar with the creation of tanning and quarry roads, and they completed the task in 1880.

From the NY 23A trailhead (watch for aqua Long Path blazes), ascend first northeast, then consistently to the west over a rocky, washout surface. At 0.3 mi., the trail passes the yellow spur trail to the Whites Road parking area and begins to climb. At 0.9 mi., arrive at a scenic bend in the trail known as Kaaterskill Clove Lookout, with open views across the clove of Kaaterskill High Peak (3,655 ft.) and Roundtop Mtn. (3,440 ft.). A fireplace and hitching post are found here. At this point the trail is nearly directly beneath Point of Rocks (Indian Head) and Palenville Overlook and poised above Red Chasm. Curving right (north) the trail follows a deep hemlock ravine that drops sharply downhill to the left, and at 1.2 mi. the trail swings left (southwest) through the Gulf, crossing a rugged tributary of Kaaterskill Creek. The ascent is continual but moderate. Above a bowl of terrain historically known as the Amphitheater, the trail turns sharply right (northeast), with ledgy terrain increasing as the road narrows and erodes. At 1.6 mi., water—in season—crosses the trail. The trail rises evenly to Shorey Point at 2.7 mi., meeting Sleepy Hollow Horse Trail, then turns left, climbing 0.1 mi. to the Escarpment Trail. To the north, Sleepy Hollow Horse Trail heads toward Palenville Overlook and Bogart Road. Except for Harding Road itself, signs are clear. Harding Road Trail ends at this point, but the original imprint of Harding Road continues to the Hotel Kaaterskill site, following the Long Path and Escarpment Trail.

Harding Road Trail (map 1: B9)

Distances from NY 23A (690 ft.) to
- connector from Whites Road (810 ft.): 0.3 mi., 100 ft., 10 min.
- Kaaterskill Clove lookout (1,170 ft.): 0.9 mi., 500 ft., 40 min.
- Sleepy Hollow Horse Trail (2,100 ft.): 2.7 mi., 1,400 ft., 2 hr.
- Escarpment Trail (2,200 ft.): 2.8 mi., 1,500 ft., 2 hr. 5 min.

Kaaterskill Wild Forest Trail

This remote and wildly scenic, upper-elevation trail provides exciting opportunities for extended day-hiking, backpacking, and backcountry ski touring. It is also marked as a snowmobile trail for the first 3.3 mi., after which the foot trail descends into Kaaterskill Clove, passing a pair of vertical waterfalls and the historical Poet's Ledge.

The trailhead can be reached from the east via precipitous Platte Clove, using Platte Clove Mtn. Road (closed in winter), which is identified as CR 33 in West Saugerties (Ulster County), and as CR 16 "on the mountain" in the town of Hunter (Greene County), where the trailhead is located. Those electing to use this road should either be traveling in periods of dry weather or have a four-wheel-drive vehicle, as it is seasonally unmaintained and typically barricaded between April and November. The safest route to the trailhead is from NY 23A in Tannersville, turning south onto Spring Street (CR 16), 0.25 mi. east of the only traffic light in town. CR 16 becomes Platte Clove Road and heads east approximately 6.4 miles to Kaaterskill Wild Forest trailhead parking lot. Turn left (north) on the dirt access road and go a short distance into the parking lot. Locate the trail sign adjacent to the barrier gate, where the trail departs to the north.

The trail begins on deeply embedded Steenberg Road (named after an early quarryman and landowner) uphill through a mixed forest of hemlock and hardwood, with a private parcel on the right (east). Marking is thorough, with snowmobile-trail signs and blue Long Path trail disks. At a fork (0.7 mi), the trail levels and trail signs appear. To the left (west), the road branches off onto private property.

Bear right and ascend steadily but easily. The trail bed, made of soft, red shale, tends to wash out. At 1.0 mi. (2,300 ft.), at a fork, the trail turns right (east) off the more-established route and onto a foot trail (an old, abandoned road), following trail arrows, blue Long Path discs, and snowmobile-trail markers. Within five minutes or less of this intersection, at 1.2 mi., Huckleberry Point Trail goes right (southeast) to Huckleberry Point (signed, yellow markers). Kaaterskill Wild Forest Trail goes straight ahead here (northeast), ascending slightly. The terrain flattens through a hemlock forest, at 1.4 mi. crossing a footbridge over a sluggish creek where bear tracks often appear in the mud. It very soon crosses a plank gangway and another footbridge before ascending, beneath ash and maple trees. Touch-me-nots bloom profusely along here, where yellow blazes and cairns define the forest preserve boundary to the left (west).

Stately hemlock emerges as the trail gains altitude over rocky, rooty footing, relaxing and climbing again into a beech woods before leveling out at 2.25 mi. (3,000 ft). This picturesque section of the forest, where the trail is covered in bedrock and moss and lined with blueberry and an increasing density of spruce-fir, is called the Pine Plains. Water tends to pool here in spring and winter. The area is densely foliated; tangled blowdowns and rotting snags lie off the trail, and slender green-and-white saplings of striped maple along with viburnum lean into the trail here and there. Also visible are some of the old-fashioned, yellow steel snowmobile markers. The trail continues flat and boreal until descending gently to the northwest under a sugar maple canopy, arriving at an unsigned junction at 3.2 miles. The snowmobile loop trail around Kaaterskill High Peak (distance, 5.9 mi.) leaves to the left (southwest), where a short spur trail goes uphill to the loop itself. Kaaterskill Wild Forest Trail continues straight ahead but is not signed and shows only unofficial, plain blue trail disks at this time (for directions to the unmarked Kaaterskill High Peak foot trail, see Kaaterskill High Peak Snowmobile Trail).

The trail turns to the north at 3.7 mi. and begins to descend gradually through a mixed hemlock forest, arriving at the edge of a ridge where at 2,200 ft. a large, conspicuous boulder is blazed with yellow forest preserve boundary paint. This marks the edge of the private Twilight Park's lands and the extension, from Twilight Park, of the old Kaaterskill High Peak Trail (unofficial). Bear right, dropping downhill through a ledge at this point, as the trail switches back, trending north, continuing its descent. As the terrain flattens, the trail heads briefly northwest before making a sharp turn into the east. Marking is poor here, and for a short distance the trail is not self-guiding. Watch carefully. Heading east, the trail draws close to Kaaterskill Clove, the heavy foliage providing only hints of South Mtn. and the abyss to your left. Beginning from the snowmobile loop trail, this 100-plus-year-old foot trail that was for so long marked with rusting tin-can tops, remained unmarked until volunteers from the New York-New Jersey Trail Conference revived it as a section of the Long Path. It is a part of the old Red Gravel Hill Road. At 5.0 mi., the trail crosses the top of Buttermilk Falls, an unimaginative name for this spectacular falls that looks out across Kaaterskill Clove into North Mountain Wild Forest. *Be especially aware of the steep drop here—the precipice is spotted with slippery moss* *and the bare, wet stone is slick.*

Although there may have been no water on the trail (and there may also be none at all here in John Case Brook), there is almost always a barely audible stream of water flowing from the headwall under the falls themselves, even in very dry periods. Across Kaaterskill Clove, Stoppel Point (3,420 ft.) appears as the highest landmark, at 60 degrees. The deep ravine between Buttermilk Falls and Stoppel Point is the location of Kaaterskill Falls, which is not visible. North Mtn. is to the right of Stoppel Point. With binoculars you can see North Point to the immediate right as a series of open ledges, where the Escarpment Trail works its way north. Below, serpentine NY 23A can be seen winding its way through Kaaterskill Clove.

The trail continues straight into the southeast on level, duffy ground, spotted with remote colonies of Indian pipes. At 5.5 mi., hemlock-shrouded Wildcat Falls is seen 50 ft. to the north of the trail *and is a higher,* *more dangerous waterfall than Buttermilk Falls.* The two open rock ledges at the eastern extreme of South Mtn. are Indian Head Lookout (a historical profile rock) and Palenville Overlook, or High Rock. Stoppel Point and North Mtn. are still visible, along with an open expanse of Hudson Valley flatland to the northeast.

Mountain laurel and colorful bunchberry decorate the trail as it continues east into an extensive hardwood grove that cuts across the dual streambeds above Hillyer Ravine at 5.7 mi., below which (and not visible from the trail) is Viola Falls. The trail curves to the north, through an area of gravelly washouts that drain into Hillyer Ravine. The forest type changes to spruce and red pine, with increasing mountain laurel as the spur trail to Poet's Ledge is reached at 6.1 mi. (see Poet's Ledge Spur Trail for details). Kaaterskill Wild Forest Trail terraces its way downhill—steeply at times—through hardwoods, flattening amid laurel, and descending through deciduous forest. A level stretch over a narrow red sandy loam path follows, heading south, and the trail turns to the northeast to join the now-graded, road-width Red Gravel Hill Road, thereafter descending to a barrier gate. The trail turns left (north) after the gate, where a trail sign indicates the Hiking Trail, and follows a private easement 100 ft. to Malden Avenue at 8.0 mi. (There is no parking available at this point.) Those continuing on the Long Path should turn left, passing through the guardrail at the dead end of

Malden Avenue, turn right onto NY 23A, and left again into the forest preserve at 0.3 mi. where a small parking area, state wild forest signs, and aqua Long Path blazes are seen on the north (left) side of NY 23A. Food and services are available in Palenville, a few minutes' walk east of the trailhead.

Kaaterskill Wild Forest Trail (map 1: B9)

Distances from trailhead on Platte Clove Road (1,810 ft.) to
- Huckleberry Point Trail (2,400 ft.): 1.1 mi., 600 ft., 50 min.
- connector to Kaaterskill High Peak Snowmobile Trail (2,900 ft.): 3.2 mi., 1,200 ft. (rev. 100 ft.), 2 hr. 20 min.
- Buttermilk Falls (2,110 ft.): 5.0 mi., 1,200 ft. (rev. 800 ft.), 3 hr. 5 min.
- Wildcat Falls (2,150 ft.): 5.5 mi., 1,250 ft., 3 hr. 20 min.
- Poet's Ledge Spur Trail (2,350 ft.): 6.1 mi., 1,500 ft. (rev. 50 ft.), 4 hr.
- Malden Ave. (590 ft.): 8.0 mi., 1,500 ft. (rev. 1,750 ft.), 4 hr. 55 min.
- trailhead parking area for Harding Road Trail on NY 23A (690 ft.): 8.7 mi., 1,650 ft. (rev. 50 ft.), 5 hr. 10 min.

Huckleberry Point Trail

This popular trail is a fascinating day hike, leading to a sweeping view of the Hudson Valley beyond Platte Clove. From Kaaterskill Wild Forest Trail (snowmobile and foot trail), 1.0 mi. north of the Kaaterskill Wild Forest parking area on Platte Clove Road, Huckleberry Point Trail (aka Nature Friends Trail) goes east. A sign and trail arrow mark the junction. Old foundation stones and rock piles cleared for pasturelands by early settlers may be seen along the trail off in the woods. This junction marks the former residence of the Steenberg family, who worked a quarry northeast of here at the end of Steenberg Quarry Road. This trail was established by a group of German expatriates, escaping from their inflation-ridden, war-torn country in the 1920s. They established the trail and marked it with tin-can lids, which until recent state marking were maintained in white with a red center dot. They called themselves the *Vanderverder*—the "wandering birds." They preferred to hike in the nude.

The trail is level but soon descends gently to cross Mossy Brook, which is easily forded under normal conditions. On the brook's north side, a reclaimed (by nature) road goes to Dunkler's Clove and the site of an old quarry. Huckleberry Point Trail continues south-southwest, soon climbing amid mountain laurel, oak, and hemlock. At 0.8 mi. (2,500 ft.), the trail levels and it is possible to see Indian Head Mtn. (3,573 ft.) to the south-west, along with bits of the eastern Devil's Path, as well as Kaaterskill High Peak (3,655 ft.) to the northwest. Even Overlook Mtn. (3,150 ft.) can be seen. The trail soon descends, passing a small, vague quarry on the right (south) side of the trail. A pure pitch-pine stand covers a knoll to the north as the point is approached. Suddenly the trail ends at the top of a series of vertical ledges overlooking the valley, with uncommonly good views of Platte Clove and the Devil's Path mountains. There's a shallow quarry at this location also. The near precipice is covered in blueberry bushes.

Overlook Mtn. and its fire tower are seen at 218 degrees. The crag on the eastern slope of Overlook is the Minister's Face, known for its famous rattlesnake den. (Folklore holds that the oil of these particular snakes has medicinal properties. It is also the site of a much examined Late Woodland period hunting encampment.) Beyond, Sky Top and Eagle Cliff in the Shawangunks are visible. An arm of the Ashokan Reservoir is visible. Far south in a widening of the Hudson River, the Esopus Meadows lighthouse can be seen with binoculars. Plattekill Mtn. (3,110 ft.) is in the foreground, east of Indian Head. The rest of the Devil's Path range (with the exception of West Kill Mtn.) is visible, including Twin (3,650 ft.), Sugarloaf (3,810 ft.), Plateau (3,850 ft.), and Hunter (4,050 ft.) mtns.

Aside from its appeal to view-seekers, the strong thermal updrafts of warm air from the Hudson Valley lowlands make Huckleberry Point a popular spot for observing soaring raptors—most of them turkey vultures.

Huckleberry Point Trail (map 1: B9)

Distance from Kaaterskill Wild Forest Trail (2,400 ft.) to
• Huckleberry Point (2,150 ft.): 1.3 mi., 200 ft. (rev. 450 ft.), 45 min.

Poet's Ledge Spur Trail

From its junction at 6.1 mi. on Kaaterskill Wild Forest Trail northeast of Hillyer Ravine, Poet's Ledge Spur Trail drops 0.4 mi. to the west. At this time it ranks among the best-marked trails in the Catskills. The trail drops downhill to an open, flat rock with a makeshift fire ring and a much older, more thoughtfully constructed fireplace, its foundation stones gathering moss. The trail bears left (southwest), following a low vertical ledge, and turns to the west at a flat ledge. Bearing left again (southeast), the trail ends at Poet's Ledge (1,800 ft.), a west-facing platform divided by a narrow crevice that can be hazardous, especially when concealed by snow. This early hiking destination was known to many, most likely even to the subjects of Asher Brown Durand's *Kindred Spirits*—William Cullen Bryant and Thomas Cole—and it was more than likely the vantage used for composite sketches in several of Sanford R. Gifford's well-known works, including *Twilight in the Catskills* (1861), *Kauterskill Clove* (1862), and *October in the Catskills* (1880).

This view looking west into Kaaterskill Clove includes South Mtn. (2,460 ft.), with North Mtn. (3,180 ft.) above it, and Stoppel Point (3,430 ft.) to the left. Blackhead (3,950 ft.) and Black Dome Mtn. (3,990 ft.) stand over the top of West Stoppel Point (3,100 ft.). The solitary bump at 324 degrees is Parker Mtn. (2,820 ft.), and the large mountain sloping into it on the left is Onteora (3,230 ft.). Kaaterskill High Peak (3,655 ft.), Hurricane Ridge, and Hurricane Ledge are up high to your left. The various parallel drainages on the left (south) wall of Kaaterskill Clove are the Hillyer, Wildcat, Buttermilk Falls, and Santa Cruz ravines, each of them joining Kaaterskill Creek. This is a spur trail and does not continue. The only way out is back the way you came.

Poet's Ledge Spur Trail (map 1: B9)

Distance from Kaaterskill Wild Forest Trail (2,350 ft.) to
  • Poet's Ledge (2,050 ft.): 0.4 mi., 0 ft. (rev. 300 ft.), 15 min.

Kaaterskill High Peak Snowmobile Trail

Kaaterskill High Peak Snowmobile Trail loop begins at the 3.2-mi. point of Kaaterskill Wild Forest Trail. In addition to being only slightly popular with hikers and very popular with snowmobilers, this trail has gained some popularity with backcountry skiers. The latter should be well aware that the loop is easily underrated in terms of its remoteness, difficulty, and distance, as it requires a fairly strenuous 3.2-mi. uphill skinning or snowshoeing effort (which, depending on conditions, might be walkable), the 5.9-mi. loop itself, and the 3.2-mi. backtrack to the trailhead—a total of more than 12 miles. In addition, the track is often irregular, rocky, muddy, and icy after snowmobiles have compacted it, leaving little if any smooth diagonal striding terrain, notwithstanding fresh snowfall. Skiers should carry scrapers, skins, or snowshoes, and adequate provisions for exposed, upper-elevation travel. Steel-edged backcountry skis are advised.

Kaaterskill High Peak Snowmobile Trail loop begins 3.7 mi. from Kaaterskill Wild Forest Trail trailhead parking area in Platte Clove. The loop actually begins 300 yd. uphill (south) from this junction. Once on the loop, which circles both Kaaterskill High Peak (3,655 ft.) and Roundtop (3,440 ft.), at a mean elevation of 2,800 ft., a sign indicates the total loop distance of 5.9 mi. The trail goes left (southeast), and slightly uphill.

The first few hundred yards are grassy and thick with nettles before entering the shade of a northern hardwood forest. Turtleheads appear frequently, and do in fact resemble turtles' heads. (The genus name, *Chelone*, is Greek, for "tortoise.") In periods void of snow cover, hikers will see pieces of a shredded airplane that crashed here in 1989. Kaaterskill High Peak is close to the flatlands and subject to high winds and downdrafts. Like the rest of the Escarpment area, it has claimed several aircraft. From this somber spot, stinging nettle becomes as bad as it gets in the Catskills, growing typically in the moist, rich soils under sugar maples. A scree slope appears to the north amid pockets of fern and solitary stalks of meadow rue. Within 25 minutes of the crash site, and 1.4 mi. from the loop's beginning, the trail reaches a cairned, four-way intersection at 3,000 ft., where the unmarked, unmaintained trail to Kaaterskill High Peak departs to the right (north). To the south the trail is marked with unofficial blue trail disks and descends to cross private lands. This is not a well-identified intersection, and without the cairn, it could be missed. (See Kaaterskill High Peak Trail.)

Continuing straight (west), the trail descends gradually to the 2,700-ft. mark before turning northwest, where hemlock and very large ash trees appear. The trail ascends shortly, heading northeast and leveling. Hardwood shifts to intermittent hemlock as the trail moves farther east, at 4.3 mi. arriving at a three-way intersection. To the left (northwest), the trail is not immediately marked and descends to the trails of the old Cortina Valley ski area and Clum Hill Road. (In fact, snowmobile markers appear farther down this trail, which provides the fastest emergency egress onto private Cortina Valley ski area property.) A trail sign here reads ,"Around Loop and Return to This Point, 7.64 mi." (the distance is in error), just as it does at the loop's beginning. The trail bears right (northeast), heading uphill. Traveling on the level through hardwoods and muddy swales, pass the northerly (unmarked, unofficial) Kaaterskill High Peak trailhead, which leaves to the right (south) and over High Peak itself. This is a difficult spot to identify for hikers coming from the west, but it is just a three- or four-minute walk west of the next intersection, which is the starting point of the loop trail. Go left to return to the Long Path (Kaaterskill Wild Forest Trail).

Kaaterskill High Peak Snowmobile Trail (map 1: B9)

Distances from junction with connector from Kaaterskill Wild Forest Trail (3,000 ft.) to
- Kaaterskill High Peak Trail, south junction (3,000 ft.): 1.4 mi., 100 ft. (rev. 100 ft.), 45 min.
- three-way intersection (2,800 ft.): 4.3 mi., 250 ft. (rev. 350 ft.), 2 hr. 15 min.
- junction with connector from Kaaterskill Wild Forest Trail (3,000 ft.): 5.9 mi., 450 ft., 3 hr. 10 min.

Kaaterskill High Peak Trail, northern trailhead

This trail is not officially recognized or maintained by the Department of Environmental Conservation. However, over a period of many years, beginning in the mountain house era, it has been blazed and marked by individuals from several hiking groups, and is climbed regularly by enthusiasts and locals "in the know," among them the errant members of the Bruderhof community in Platte Clove, who are among the Eastern Catskills' most knowledgeable and dedicated hikers. Nineteenth-century hikers would climb Kaaterskill from the Mountain House at North Lake and return in time for supper that evening. They most likely used the old trail through Vera Cruz Ravine (the more difficult Harding Road, while the same distance, is double the elevation gain) and returned to Pine Orchard via Kaaterskill Falls, a fairly strenuous outing of 10 miles with a modest cumulative gain of 2,500 ft. At 3,655 ft., it is one of the "trailless" tally peaks designated by the Catskill 3500 Club. This peak is difficult to approach owing to the private property along its southern bounds. It is best approached by hiking the Long Path (Kaaterskill Wild Forest Trail) from Platte Clove Road, where it can be scaled from either the north or south from Kaaterskill High Peak Snowmobile Trail, adding considerable time and distance to the climb.

The trail itself is steep, rugged, and spectacularly beautiful, a fog forest realm of cripplebrush spruce-fir in a bold and ledgy setting, with its showcase view from Hurricane Ledge overlooking Platte Clove and the southern viewshed of the Mid-Hudson region from the interior Eastern Catskills and southeast. Upon reaching the snowmobile trail from the Long Path, turn right onto the snowmobile trail. Watch carefully on your left for the trailhead, which may not be clearly marked. Use the GPS coordinates 42° 10.057' N, 74° 04.888' W. Because the southern access is more heavily used by hikers coming in across private lands to the south, the northern trailhead is harder to find. Look for blue markers and a minimally impacted trail, which may not at first be self-guiding. Climb steeply for an hour or so to the summit through boulders and blowdowns. On the closed-in summit (3,655 ft.) you may discover the debris of an aircraft scattered through the woods—this peak has claimed several. Continue south, as the trail leads you across the summit flats and down to Hurricane Ledge, a series of grassy outcroppings with a southerly exposure. Descend, sometimes steeply, over loose rock as the trail switches back to the snowmobile trail through mixed hardwood forests. Once at the southerly, cairned trail junction (42° 09.473' N, 74° 04.942' W) of Kaaterskill High Peak Trail and the snowmobile trail, turn left (east), and follow back to your point of origin.

Experienced hikers will have little problem bushwhacking back to Kaaterskill Wild Forest Trail across the flat terrain at the southeasternmost swing of the snowmobile trail, especially if they have had the foresight to mark a waypoint at the approximate 3,000-ft. point (where the trail touches the 3,000-ft. contour on the map) on their way up Kaaterskill Wild Forest Trail. Study the map before you attempt this hike, and plan a strategy that matches your ability. An early start is key. Kaaterskill Wild Forest may not be a wilderness area, but it is just as remote, and typically attracts fewer people than the neighboring wilderness areas.

Kaaterskill High Peak Trail, northern trailhead (map 1: B9)

Distances from north junction with Kaaterskill High Peak Snowmobile Trail (3,000 ft.) to
- Kaaterskill High Peak summit (3,655 ft.): 0.4 mi., 650 ft., 30 min.
- Hurricane Ledge (3,550 ft.): 0.7 mi., 650 ft. (rev. 100 ft.), 40 min.
- south junction with Kaaterskill High Peak Snowmobile Trail (3,000 ft.): 1.4 mi., 650 ft. (rev. 550 ft.), 1 hr.

SUGGESTED HIKES

Easy Hikes

Kaaterskill Falls Trail [rt: 0.8 mi., 1:40]. An interesting, short-but-steep climb past Bastion Falls to Kaaterskill Falls, following alongside crystal-clear Spruce Creek.

Mary's Glen Trail [rt: 0.4 mi., 0:25]. A pleasant, level stroll passing a beaver pond to Ashley Falls, most attractive during runoff periods.

Moderate Hikes

Sunset Rock Spur Trail [rt: 2.0 mi., 2:00]. One of the region's most popular and most scenic hikes, with views east and south across the Hudson Valley and southwest into the Kaaterskill Wild Forest. Begin at the North Lake picnic area trailhead.

Huckleberry Point Trail via Kaaterskill Wild Forest Trail [rt: 4.6 mi., 3:10]. A rewarding hike to a high sandstone outcropping at the junction of rugged Platte Clove and the Escarpment. One of the more popular short hikes in the Eastern Catskills.

Strenuous Hikes

Kaaterskill High Peak Trail via Kaaterskill Wild Forest Trail [rt: 8.4 mi., 5:00]. A remote and challenging hike across the summit of a scenic and wild mountain, with close-up views of the Indian Head Wilderness to the south from Hurricane Ledge.

Kaaterskill High Peak Snowmobile Trail [rt: 12.4 mi., 7:00]. Originally marked as a snowmobile trail, this upper-elevation loop makes an interesting and challenging hike or backcountry ski tour. Plan for an all-day outing on skis or foot, and be prepared for the challenge of remote wilderness travel with over 2,000 ft. of cumulative elevation gain. Not for the inexperienced backcountry user!

North Point via Escarpment Trail [rt: 5.0 mi., 3:30]. One of the most popular destinations in the Eastern Catskills, with broad views of the Wilderness areas to the north and south, and panoramic views east across the Hudson Valley into the Taconics, Helderbergs, Berkshires, and beyond. Combine this hike with a visit to Sunset Rock via Sunset Rock Spur Trail.

Section 2
Rusk Mountain Wild Forest

This wild forest, designated in 2008, was formerly a part of the Hunter Mountain Wild Forest, which with additional parcels became the Hunter-West Kill Wilderness. It is bounded on the north by the Schoharie Creek, and on the southwest and east by the Hunter-West Kill Wilderness. At 3,900 acres, it extends westward from Spruceton Trail (aka Spruceton Truck Trail because it was the road used to construct and maintain the Hunter Mtn. fire tower) across a high ridge that includes the trailless peaks of Rusk (3,690 ft.), Evergreen (3,350 ft.), Pine Island (3,100 ft.), and Packsaddle (3,100 ft.) mtns. Many hikers choose to climb Hunter Mt. from Spruceton Trail, since it offers a more gradual approach to this rather large mountain than the easterly trailheads at Becker Hollow and Stony Clove. The Spruceton Valley, through which the West Kill Creek flows, is also a worthy scenic destination in itself. This ingress also offers hikers the opportunity to take the short detour into West Kill Falls (0.8 mi.), an attractive spot to visit during the spring runoff and during the hotter summer months, when, although the flow may be low, a pool beneath the falls provides a popular swimming hole. Ingress from Spruceton Trail also presents hikers with the opportunity for a day or overnight loop hike (camping in tents or lean-tos), traveling in either direction using Diamond Notch Trail, the Devil's Path, and Hunter Mtn. Trail (see Hunter-West Kill Wilderness for trail details).

Spruceton Trail narrows to a 200-ft.-wide corridor at the point where it joins Colonel's Chair Trail, also a part of the Rusk Mountain Wild Forest. This corridor, which will allow for the trail's use by both equestrians and mountain bikers, continues to the summit and fire tower of Hunter Mtn. The Hunter Mtn. fire tower and observer's cabin are set in a wild and remote spruce-fir environment. The tower, the cabin, and the Spruceton Truck Trail itself have been placed on the State and National Registers of Historic Places. The 70-ft. tower was erected in 1917.

Spruceton Trail

Spruceton Trail (blue markers) begins as a flat, wide thoroughfare, following the Old Hunter Road (originally Jones Gap Turnpike, circa 1880). This trail is a popular approach to Hunter summit (4,050 ft.).

From the large trailhead parking area at the east end of Spruceton Road (CR 6), 6.5 mi. from the turnoff at Deep Notch (originally Deer Notch) and CR 42, trailhead signs are located on the left (north) side of the road at a large parking area. The trail begins here. Another parking area, 0.2 mi. farther southeast, acts as overflow parking for the smaller Diamond Notch trailhead parking area at the extreme east end of Spruceton Road.

From the northeast corner of the designated parking area, Spruceton Trail follows blue markers around a barrier gate and within moments Hunter Brook appears on the left (west). This is also a horse trail (yellow markers). Within a short distance, the trail crosses a bridge and begins to ascend. Cross a small stream, hiking uphill and traveling east. Several more stone culverts pass beneath this wide, grassy, well-constructed road. Restricted views of West Kill Ridge, North Dome, and Sherrill open up to the right (southwest). At 1.5 mi., the trail reaches an intersection where Old Hunter Road continues straight ahead (north), descending into Taylor Hollow onto private lands in the Schoharie Valley. Avoid this unmarked trail. The blue Spruceton Trail turns right here.

Bearing right at the intersection, the trail begins to climb the steepest section of Spruceton Trail. At 2.1 mi., two large, flat rocks and a hitching post to the right (south) mark a short spur off the main trail, leading 100 yd. to a spring.

Continue past the John Robb lean-to at 2.2 mi. on the left (north) at 3,500 ft. Across the trail is a flat, open area with views of Rusk, Evergreen, West Kill, North Dome, and Sherrill. Located in an attractive setting, the lean-to is well positioned to take advantage of the prevailing southwesterly winds. At 2.4 mi., the Colonel's Chair spur trail departs to the left (north), descending to the Hunter Mtn. Ski Area and summit lodge. Spruceton Trail continues straight (east), ascending gently into a dense boreal (evergreen) forest zone.

Flattening out, the trail tends to retain standing water here for several days after periods of rain. A pure spruce forest yields to birch as the trail climbs, leveling again where standing, dead spruce snags loom over a lush, vigorously reproducing forest. The trail straightens, bearing right (south), soon revealing the shoulder of Hunter Mtn. On the left (northeast) a lookout frames the Blackhead Range. The trail crosses more rocky flats before it begins its final ascent to Hunter's summit, where it increases notably in angle and ascends over surfacing bedrock. Just before this incline (approximately 3.0 mi.) a spur leads left (east) 1,500 ft. to an unreliable spring.

At 3.2 mi., Spruceton Trail arrives at Hunter's open summit, the location of the fire tower and observer's cabin. Trail signs are obvious on the right (west). Just ahead on the right is the power line right of way, heading downhill (this is not a view spur trail). The panoramic view from Hunter's fire tower is among the most arresting and far-reaching in the Catskills. The western 180 degrees looks very similar to the view from the lookout near the old summit, a 10-minute stroll to the south on Spruceton Trail (see Becker Hollow Trail for details). To the west are Rusk and Evergreen, Colonel's Chair, and the ski trails of Hunter. To the north are Windham High Peak and the Blackhead Range.

Continuing south are Stoppel Point, North Mtn., Pine Orchard, and South Mtn. North Lake and its beach area are visible, and slightly below and to the right, the great Amphitheater and double cascades of Kaaterskill Falls can just be seen with the naked eye. The Kaaterskill Wild Forest and Indian Head Wilderness Area are visible. Far beyond on a good day it is possible to observe the Taconics, Berkshires, and Green Mtns. In the west, the mountains of the Big Indian Wilderness and hundreds of lesser peaks, named and nameless, crowd the horizon. Although your compass will be rendered useless by the fire tower's steel frame, if you're fortunate enough to arrive while an observer is present, the original map and alidade will help to identify the landmarks.

Spruceton Trail continues straight (south) along the western edge of the clearing, entering the woods through an enchanting section of spruce-fir forest, reaching the old fire tower site and the junction of Becker Hollow and Hunter Mtn. trails at 3.5 mi. Trail signs are posted here at the end of Spruceton Trail. Creative opportunities for (expert) backcountry ski touring are possible using this trail, possibly combining an ascent of Hunter's summit with a day's telemarking at the Hunter Mtn. ski area. It is not uncommon (given a good base and, ideally, a fresh snowfall) for seasoned skiers to follow Hunter Mtn. Trail to Devil's Acre, descending the Devil's Path west to Diamond Notch and a shuttle car. The level of ability required to ski this terrain is in direct correlation to both snow depth and freshness. The deeper the base and the new snowfall, the easier it is to ski on steep terrain.

Spruceton Trail (map 1: B7–B8)

Distances from Spruceton Road (CR 6) (2,083 ft.) to
- John Robb lean-to (3,500 ft.): 2.2 mi., 1,400 ft., 1 hr. 50 min.
- Hunter Mtn. summit (4,050 ft.): 3.2 mi., 1,950 ft., 2 hr. 35 min.
- Becker Hollow Trail and Hunter Mtn. Trail (4,010 ft.): 3.5 mi., 1,950 ft. (rev. 50 ft.), 2 hr. 45 min.

Colonel's Chair Trail

Beginning 2.3 mi. from the start of Spruceton Trail, the Colonel's Chair spur trail descends from a point just uphill (east) from the John Robb lean-to. It's easy to miss the junction, because at present signs are not ideally placed for hikers coming uphill on Spruceton Trail. Colonel's Chair Trail itself is well marked with yellow trail markers, and signs are posted 20 ft. uphill and beyond (east from) the junction. The views from "The Chair" (the northern spur of Hunter Mtn.) itself are outstanding, offering an unusual contrast to those from Hunter's fire tower. If time allows, this interesting side trip will prove very worthwhile.

At Colonel's Chair trailhead on Spruceton Trail, a trail sign is located near the spur. The Chair was named for Colonel William Edwards, a tanlord who founded Edwardsville (circa 1817), later to become Hunter.

Descending north from the junction with Spruceton Trail, within ten minutes the trail bears right at the trail register near the edge of a ski trail. Trail signs are scarce hereafter, but the trail is self-guiding until the (discontinued) summit cross-country ski-touring trails begin to confuse things somewhat. These trails are marked with numbers, and occasional signs point to the summit lodge. The trail goes straight (north) and is frequently traversed by multi-terrain service vehicles. Tree cover is predominantly stunted hardwood. Descending, the trail approximates a woods road, passing a gravel pit on the left (west), where Rusk's trailless summit can be seen to the west. The trail levels, passing ski lifts on the left (west) side.

Soon, the view opens up, and the otherworldly, concrete summit lodge appears, as the trail emerges from the woods near the top of an infamous ski trail. Known as K27, it boasts the steepest vertical drop of any commercial ski area in the East. From this ridge—the Colonel's Chair—are views of Hunter's summit and the fire tower. The best views from the Colonel's Chair are from this vicinity, from the picnic tables outside the lodge, from the lodge itself, and from the small gazebo near the top of the chairlift in front of the lodge (the Archer Winsten Monument). The views are far-reaching. From the rustic Winsten seat, the long, flat mountain straight ahead (northeast) is North Mtn. The hump to its left is Stoppel Point. Coming down off North Mtn. is South Mtn., and the lowest point between the two is Pine Orchard, the location of the erstwhile Catskill Mountain House. Moving left (north) is Blackhead Range, followed by Onteora Mtn. and Jewett Range. Kaaterskill High Peak and Roundtop are in the right (eastern) foreground.

It's possible to take the Hunter Mtn. chairlift in either direction in order to "cheat" on this hike, an outing that would still require a moderately strenuous 3.8 mi. return hike with nearly 1,000 ft. of vertical rise (allow 4 hr.). The lift runs on some weekends in June, most days in July and August, and on Saturdays and Sundays in September and October from 10 A.M. to 4 P.M. (and in times of adequate snow cover). The summit lodge is open for refreshments during these periods.

Colonel's Chair Trail (map 1: B8)

Distance from Spruceton Trail (3,630 ft.) to
* Hunter Mtn. summit lodge (3,100 ft.): 1.0 mi., 0 ft. (rev. 550 ft.), 30 min.

SUGGESTED HIKES

Easy Hike:

Diamond Notch Falls (West Kill Falls) via Diamond Notch Trail, Spruceton Road trailhead [rt: 1.6 mi., 1:00]. A short, level walk into the westerly watershed of Southwest Hunter Mtn. and the Devil's Path Junction. These attractive falls provide a shady swimming hole. (See Hunter-West Kill Wilderness for Diamond Notch Trail description.)

Strenuous Hikes

Hunter Mtn. via Spruceton Trail [rt: 6.4 mi., 7:30]. A steep climb up an old roadbed to the Catskills' second-highest summit. Many outstanding scenic treats await the hiker, culminating in the 360-degree viewshed from the summit fire tower.

Hunter Mtn. ski area summit lodge via Spruceton Trail, Colonel's Chair Trail [rt: 6.3 mi., 5:00]. An interesting ascent to Colonel's Chair Trail, which leads downhill to the ski area's summit lodge, open to hikers in the summer and fall. Also, consider the chairlift as an alternate means to approach Hunter's summit (see Colonel's Chair Trail).

SECTION 3
HUNTER-WEST KILL WILDERNESS

This rugged, steep, and scenic wilderness area contains 27,000 acres. It is bounded by NY 42 to the west, the Shandaken Wild Forest and NY 28 to the south, NY 214 to the east, and CR 6 to the north. Due south and across NY 214, it is bordered by the Phoenicia-Mount Tobias Wild Forest, and to the east across Stony Clove lies the Indian Head Wilderness Area, which abuts the wilderness and is connected to it by the Devil's Path. There are two lean-tos in the wilderness area, in Diamond Notch (along Diamond Notch Trail), and the Devil's Acre lean-to, on the Devil's Path. The lean-to on Spruceton Trail, in the former Hunter Mountain Wild Forest (John Robb lean-to), is now a part of the newly designated extension of the Rusk Mountain Wild Forest. Within the Hunter-West Kill Wilderness are the named peaks of Hunter Mtn., Southwest Hunter Mtn., West Kill Mtn., North Dome, Mt Sherrill, and Balsam Mtn. The wilderness area contains 18 mi. of foot trails, and has a minimum elevation of 920 ft. and a maximum of 4,040 ft. (Hunter Mtn.). The spruce-fir-clad summits of West Kill, North Dome, and Sherrill lie within the Catskill High Peaks Bird Conservation Area, and provide important habitat for the Bicknell's thrush and the blackpoll warbler.

Many hikers approach Hunter Mtn. (4,050 ft.), the Catskills' second-highest peak, from the Hunter Mtn. ski area, using the chairlift and Colonel's Chair Trail to enjoy a significant distance and elevation advantage over other trailheads. This detail makes the trails around Hunter attractive to backcountry skiers and, on occasion, mountain bikers.

A fire tower is located on Hunter Mtn., north of the true summit. Renovated in 1999 and reopened to the public, it provides an exceptional panoramic view. The Department of Environmental Conservation has been staffing the tower on weekends during the hiking season with volunteer stewards, at which times the public may have access to the tower's cab. The fire tower steward program is actively seeking volunteers at this time.

The easterly portions of this wilderness area were the center of the Catskill tanning industry, which later gave way to furniture factories and their requisite sawmills. Quarrying, although present, has not been as ambitious here as in the east-lying northern Catskills. Hikers may see evidence of upper-elevation logging operations, especially in the area around Devil's Acre. Extractive resource enterprises in this area gave way to the tourism industry in the Hunter area, as the railroads made an increasing number of rooming houses and small hotels possible. The ski industry is "the mountain top's" largest industry and began with the 1960 construction of the Hunter Mountain Ski Bowl, which has been both an economic boost and an environmental challenge to the area.

Becker Hollow Trail

The fastest, steepest approach to Hunter Mtn., this 2.3-mi.-long trail rises abruptly out of Stony Clove, making a beeline for the (old) summit and climbing over 2,200 vertical ft. If you want to go the quick way up Hunter, this is it—but it is not recommended for a season opener.

The trailhead parking lot is well identified on the west side of NY 214, 1.2 mi. south of NY 23A, and 1.5 mi. north of Devil's Tombstone public day-use and picnic area at Notch Lake. At this large forest preserve access site, wild-forest signs and trail information are posted. This wooded route to the Hunter summit enters Becker Hollow before rising steeply into the west. Some of the Catskills' best views lie ahead—the first are seen from the lookouts to the west of the true summit (2.05 mi.), and then from Hunter's fire tower, a short walk to the north of the true summit on Hunter Mtn. Trail.

The trail passes between the columns of a stone archway at the entrance to the old Becker property, crosses open fields, and enters a hemlock woods. It then spans a footbridge, passing an unnamed (private) trail to the right (north). Ahead, off a short, unmarked path to the left (southeast) is an interesting, small concrete dam across Becker Hollow Brook—an irrigation pond for the old Becker farmstead. Following next to the creek, through small hemlock stands, the trail ascends into hardwoods, gradually at first over the rocky base of a tanbark road (once used to reach trees felled to support the leather-making industry's demand for tannins), and then very steeply. Pass through a small stand of very large spruce trees, with a deep ravine (Becker Hollow) visible to the left (south). At 1.8 mi., pass Fire Tower Spur Trail on the right (north).

The trail continues to ascend straight ahead (west) for about ten minutes to the Hunter Mtn. Trail junction. This trail intersection (the end of Becker Hollow Trail) is where an observation tower and lean-to once stood. Straight (west) through the junction, a presently unmarked spur leads 300 ft. to a ledge providing a 180-degree westerly view, from north to south. This lookout is not to be missed. Some hikers claim to prefer this lookout's views to the fire tower's. The lookout is the place to practice landmark identification using a map and compass (accurate bearings are not possible from the steel fire tower).

To the south, the Shawangunks are clearly visible, including Sky Top, Eagle Cliff, and Minnewaska State Park. Ashokan High Point is seen in the Sundown Wild Forest. The high peaks lie close to the southwest—Rocky, Lone, Wittenberg, Cornell, Table, Peekamoose, Slide (you can see the slide), Giant Ledge, and Panther Mtn. Diamond Notch and Southwest Hunter lie in the foreground. Tremper Mtn.'s fire tower can be seen at 214 degrees. Balsam Lake Mtn.'s fire tower can be spotted with binoculars. Doubletop and Graham are also visible. In the foreground are the mountains and ridgeline of the Big Indian Wilderness. Directly in front of you is West Kill with its distinctive pyramid-shaped crown.

Better views, although lacking the solitude of the lookout, are available from the fire tower. To reach the fire tower, return to the junction of Hunter Mtn., Spruceton, and Becker Hollow trails and turn left (north), arriving within ten minutes' time (see Hunter Mtn. Trail, Spruceton Trail for details).

Becker Hollow Trail (map 1: B8)

Distances from NY 214 (1,830 ft.) to
- Fire Tower Spur Trail (3,800 ft.): 1.8 mi., 2,000 ft., 1 hr. 55 min.
- Hunter Mtn. Trail and Spruceton Trail (4,010 ft.): 1.9 mi., 2,200 ft., 2 hr. 10 min.
- Hunter Mtn. summit (4,050 ft.) via Spruceton Trail: 2.2 mi, 2,250 ft., 2 hr. 15 min.

Hunter Mtn. Trail

This upper-elevation connector trail joins the Devil's Path to Hunter Mtn. summit and Spruceton and Becker Hollow trails. Hikers wishing quick access to the mountain from Stony Clove will find Becker Hollow Trail (north of the Devil's Path) the fastest route (and also the steepest), unless they elect to take the Hunter Mtn. ski lift to Colonel's Chair Trail to climb Hunter from Spruceton Trail. However, a loop hike can be taken by combining the Devil's Path, Hunter Mtn. Trail, and Becker Hollow Trail if hikers are willing to walk the scenic 1.5-mi. road distance on NY 214 in order to close the loop. Begin from the trail junction of the Devil's Path and Hunter Mtn. Trail and turn northeast onto the latter.

The trail is an old, rocky road, ascending easily through a forest of knee-high ferns under birch and spruce-fir. Starflower and Canada lily are common along the trail. Following a pair of switchbacks at 0.9 mi., the trail turns northwest and levels on the narrow summit ridge. At 1.3 mi., the trail arrives at the junction with Becker Hollow Trail (right). Don't miss this outstanding lookout at the end of the spur to the left (west). See Becker Hollow Trail for more details.

Hunter Mtn. Trail (map 1: B8)

Distances from Devil's Path (3,530 ft.) to
- Becker Hollow Trail and Spruceton Trail (4,010 ft.): 1.3 mi., 500 ft., 55 min.
- Hunter Mtn. summit (4,050 ft.) via Spruceton Trail: 1.6 mi., 500 ft., 1 hr.

Fire Tower Spur Trail

Located to the north of the fire tower on Hunter Mtn., in the northeastern corner of the tower clearing, this spur trail provides a shortcut to Becker

Hollow Trail. The spur is marked with yellow disks, but is not signed and may take a moment to locate. The trail proceeds on the level through dense balsam, shortly switches back to the north, and drops steeply. Three stone steps are followed by another three, then more as the path swings back to the southeast, passing a large, flat boulder covered with trees. Sparse seasonal views are visible to the left across Stony Clove, as are a few old tin trail disks. Expansive birch woods characterize the trail. Large fir along the trail give way to groves of paper birch and fern, where a few small trickling streams are crossed before the junction with Becker Hollow Trail is reached.

Fire Tower Spur Trail (map 1: B8)

Distance from Hunter Mtn. summit (4,050 ft.) to
• Becker Hollow Trail (3,800 ft.): 0.3 mi., 0 ft. (rev. 250 ft.), 10 min.

Diamond Notch Trail

This historical road climbs into the densely forested realms of Diamond Notch, passing scenic Diamond Notch Falls and crossing the Devil's Path, and then joins Spruceton Road in the north.

This trail was developed in 1937 as a backcountry ski-touring trail, but because of slides and forest encroachment, it is a good deal narrower than it was originally, and casual skiers expecting even terrain—or anything resembling a tracked surface—will be sorely disappointed. This is the backcountry—rugged, rocky, unforgiving terrain—but hikers will have no problem following the established trail. Expert backcountry skiers will find this route superb during periods of good snow cover, and can ascend from Spruceton for a loop ski over Hunter Mtn. (overnight recommended).

To reach Diamond Notch Trail, turn left onto Diamond Notch Road five miles north of Phoenicia on NY 214. Trailhead parking requires travel over a difficult rocky section, nearly impossible for two-wheel-drive vehicles, especially in winter conditions. Adding to the difficulty, a landowner at the road's end has posted private No Parking signs. According to town and state police, Diamond Notch Road is a town road, and hikers are legally entitled to park anywhere along it provided they are not "obstructing movement" along the road. You cannot park off the side of the road on any private land. If conditions allow, drive into the woods at the end of Diamond Notch Road. An unposted lot appears to the left and another farther on, which is the designated trailhead parking area. Here you will find the trail register.

The trail, an old road, follows Hollow Tree Brook on the right. After crossing a wooden bridge, the trail ascends easily, soon crossing another bridge, followed by a steep flight of twenty stone steps that were placed here to avoid a washout. As the trail ascends, the creek is on the left.

Ledges appear on the right as the trail gains elevation, and the sense of entering the notch increases dramatically as the trail crosses a relatively treeless slide. Acres of talus appear uphill and down, and the trail is reinforced on the downhill side, having been rebuilt time and again. At an open area mid-slide are views south-southwest of Slide (4,190 ft.), Table (3,847 ft.), Lone (3,721 ft.), Peekamoose (3,843 ft.), Cornell (3,870 ft.), and Ashokan High Point (3,080 ft.).

An old road descends sharply into the ravine on the trail's left (west) side. The trail approaches its highest point 1.7 miles into the notch, where West Kill (3,890 ft.) and Southwest Hunter (3,750 ft.) come so close that you can touch them both simultaneously (in theory). In *The Catskills, from Wilderness to Woodstock*, Alf Evers has joked that "a man who wants to make the effort can stand today with one foot on West Kill Mtn. and the other on a supporting ridge of Hunter Mtn. [Southwest Hunter was not yet recognized as such] so that he may boast ever afterward that he once stood on two mountains at the same time."

Across the notch, on the West Kill side, conifers appear, mostly red spruce. Now the trail crosses the notch, peaks, and begins to descend slightly. Diamond Notch disappears in the scabrous geology of Southwest Hunter Mtn., at a spot near the hemlock-shrouded Diamond Notch lean-to, on the right (east) at 1.8 mi. The shallow, upper elevations of the notch lie in front of the shelter. The trail descends and at 1.9 mi. arrives at Buttermilk Falls (Diamond Notch Falls, West Kill Falls) on Spruceton Brook. It passes the Devil's Path to West Kill Mtn. (3,890 ft.) on the left (southwest) before the bridge, and passes it again on the right (northeast) after crossing the creek. In the past, this charming swimming and picnic spot has been overused, but the DEC's suspension of all camping in the immediate area has resulted in its recovery.

Diamond Notch Trail continues beyond the notch itself, following the blue trail along a dirt road for 0.9 mi., with a creek to the left, arriving at the Spruceton Road trailhead to Hunter Mtn.

Diamond Notch Trail (map 1: B7)

Distance from Diamond Notch Trailhead (1,700 ft.) to
- Devil's Path (2,300 ft.): 1.9 mi., 1,000 ft. (rev. 400 ft.), 1 hr., 30 min.
- Spruceton Rd. (2,100 ft.): 2.7 mi. 1,000 ft. (rev. 200 ft.), 30 min.

SUGGESTED HIKES

Easy Hike

Diamond Notch Falls (West Kill Falls) via Diamond Notch Trail, Spruceton Road trailhead [rt: 1.6 mi., 1:00]. A short, fairly level walk into the westerly watershed of Southwest Hunter Mtn. and the Devil's Path Junction. These attractive falls provide a shady swimming hole. This is an easy snowshoe or cross-country ski trip.

Strenuous Hikes

Hunter Mtn. via Becker Hollow Trail [rt: 3.8 mi., 4:30]. Becker Hollow Trail provides the fastest, steepest access to this scenic summit. Don't miss the views from an isolated ledge just west of the trail's junction with Hunter Mtn. Trail (see Becker Hollow Trail).

Buck Ridge Lookout [rt: 4.5 mi., 4:30]. Beginning at Spruceton Road, this scenic hike rises 1,650 ft. in elevation to an outcropping on the easterly slope of West Kill Mountain. Continue another 0.1 mi. to West Kill summit and views to the west (see the Devil's Path).

West Kill Summit via Diamond Notch Trail, Devils Path, Spruceton Road trailhead [rt: 8.0 mi., 7:00]. Beginning 3.6 mi. east of West Kill from the intersection of NY 42 and CR 6 (Spruceton Road), the Devil's Path (western terminus) gains 2,000 ft. to the summit of West Kill Mtn. (3,890 ft.). Scenic outlooks appear on the main summit, but the best views can be enjoyed 0.1 mi. east of the summit at Buck Ridge Lookout.

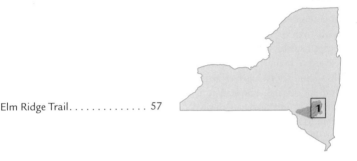

This small (1,335 acres) wild-forest area lies at the northernmost boundary of the Catskill Forest Preserve in Greene County. It was created within the updated Catskill Park State Land Master Plan to provide for increased use by off-road bicyclists. It contains only 2.2 mi. of foot trails—Elm Ridge Trail, and the northernmost 1.4 mi. of the Escarpment Trail (see Kaaterskill Wild Forest for trail description). Aside from its popularity for the purposes of thru-hiking the Escarpment Trail (the trip is traditionally undertaken from south to north, beginning at Kaaterskill Wild Forest trailhead), both the northern Escarpment trailhead as well as Elm Ridge Trail are the two most popular trailheads for hikers headed to Windham High Peak (3,524 ft.). This wild forest is bordered on the east by the Windham-Blackhead Range Wilderness, on the north by NY 23, and in the south and west by the hamlets of Maplecrest and Hensonville, respectively. Elevations are from 1,700 ft. at NY 23 to 2,400 ft. on Elm Ridge, which lies southwest of the Elm Ridge Trail/Escarpment Trail junction.

Elm Ridge Trail

Elm Ridge Trail, in the Elm Ridge Wild Forest, offers the shortest, most attractive route to Windham High Peak via the Escarpment Trail. From the village of Maplecrest, follow CR 40 to CR 56 (Big Hollow Road). Turn left (west) onto Peck Road and follow the trail signs (posted at the intersection) 0.8 mi. to the trailhead parking area. Signs are posted here.

The trail leaves from the north side of the parking lot and passes the trail register. It enters the woods, follows yellow markers, and proceeds north on a dirt road, passing a residence off to the right. A spruce plantation to the right (east) has reclaimed the site of an early settlement area, a situation that continues as stone walls and a foundation appear. Ascending easily over bedrock and dirt, the trail gradually gains elevation and passes a piped spring to its immediate right (east). A vague, unmarked dirt road leaves the main trail to the left (west). Elm Ridge Trail continues straight ahead and shortly arrives at the trail junction at 0.8 mi. (see Escarpment Trail for details). The lean-to is 500 ft. to the right. Elm Ridge Trail ends here. Go right (east) to climb Windham High Peak on the Escarpment Trail. Many hikers who are up for a longer day's outing have hiked a loop over Windham High Peak and the very scenic Burnt Knob Mtn. (3,190 ft.), returning on Big Hollow Road (CR 56) and Peck Road rather than backtracking—a jaunt of just over 9.0 miles.

Elm Ridge Trail (map 1: A8)

Distances from Peck Road trailhead (2,070 ft.) to
- Escarpment Trail (2,310 ft.): 0.8 mi., 250 ft., 30 min.
- Windham High Peak summit (3,524 ft.) via Escarpment Trail: 2.9 mi., 1,450 ft., 2 hr. 15 min.

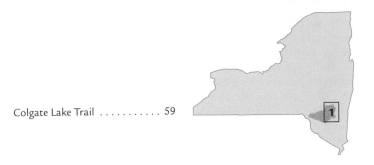

Created to accommodate off-road cyclists, the Colgate Lake Wild Forest is 1,500 acres in area. A primitive bicycle corridor runs from the trailhead of Colgate Lake Trail to Stork's Nest Road at the eastern end of the Dutcher Notch Trail (see Windham-Blackhead Range Wilderness for trail descriptions). This is a unique wild forest in that it is almost completely surrounded by the Windham-Blackhead Range Wilderness, with private lands lying to the west. The unit is named for Colgate Lake, which is popular with paddlers and anglers. The average elevation of this relatively flat wild forest is 2,100 ft.

Colgate Lake Trail

This historical trail, part of the old East Jewett-Catskill Turnpike, penetrates the dense Windham-Blackhead Range Wilderness, passing open fields, beaver ponds, and the site of an abandoned settlement. It provides unusually scenic vistas of the Blackhead Range. The trail is used frequently by cross-country skiers and occasionally by mountain bikers. As a result, Colgate Lake Trail and Dutcher Notch Trail to Stork's Nest Road have been designated as a primitive bicycle corridor.

Colgate Lake Trail is most easily reached from Tannersville. Heading north on CR 23C, pass the elegant historical summer colony houses and gardens of Onteora Park, where Mark Twain summered at the height of his literary fame. At the intersection with CR 25 (by the elegant little stone Onteora Chapel), where there are good views of the Devil's Path mountains to the south, bear left (northwest).

Turn right (east) 3.1 mi. from Tannersville, onto CR 78 in East Jewett. At 4.6 mi., pass Colgate Lake (public, state-owned), and a large white pine forest to the right. At 5.0 mi., the forest preserve access parking area is on the left (north) of CR 78. Trail signs are prominent.

The trail heads north out of the parking lot through an open field with outstanding views of the Blackhead Range and the southwestern slopes of the Escarpment. Soon the East Jewett Range, Onteora, and Parker Mtn. come into view. The trail enters the woods 1,000 ft. from the parking area, passing the trail register and evidence of old farmstead stone walls and foundations. The trail becomes wide and flat, gradually turning to the east. White birch gives way to dense second-growth pioneer trees (which spring up after logging or fire), with stands of skinny hardwoods appearing throughout this logged-over tract. Watch yellow arrows closely as the trail turns left, skirting a private inholding (lands completely surrounded by state land) at 1.2 mi. and crossing the small inlet that feeds Lake Capra (private). After crossing the creek, the trail rises out of a shallow ravine and crosses a woods road, turning left (north) as it joins another woods road at 2.4 mi. and a junction marked by a yellow trail arrow. The trail ascends slightly and swings 90 degrees to the right (east, trail arrow) at the edge of a small clearing. It then descends as it turns southeast to skirt a wet area before entering groves of large oak mixed with maturing hemlock.

The trail remains level and continues well marked, crossing a footbridge that spans a large beaver pond in dense hemlock over the East Kill. The atmosphere is wild and remote. Following to the south of the wetland the trail again crosses the East Kill over a bridge, soon thereafter passing a ruined, disused stone-arched bridge to the left of the trail. The trail bends to the right here, through a sugar maple stand, passing the wreckage of a vintage automobile. At 3.0 mi., at the edge of an open field and the reclaimed orchards of old East Jewett, the trail passes the site where a small but thriving farm community once existed. Views from the clearing are good, including Arizona Mtn., Dutcher Notch, Blackhead, Black Dome, and Thomas Cole.

The trail turns hard to the right (east), following the old road, and begins to climb through pine and maple woods, passing a little glen and mini-waterfall on the right (south). Scree slopes and mossy rock ledges follow as the trail climbs gradually up to the four-way intersection with the Escarpment Trail and Dutcher Notch Trail in Dutcher Notch (2,550 ft.) at 4.1 mi. This trail has proven popular with backcountry skiers over the years, and is perhaps most attractive in winter, when it is possible to explore the beaver meadows and look for signs of bobcat, which are plentiful just west of the notch. Hundreds of footprints can be seen after snowfalls. It is possible that lynx (introduced) may also be present.

An 8.2 mi. round trip, this is a serious day outing for both hikers and skiers, the latter of whom enjoy the steep descent of this historical road as it continues along on Dutcher Notch Trail, dropping 1,400 ft. in 1.7 miles to provide a fast, narrow, and demanding ski tour. This requires expert-level ability, metal-edged backcountry skis, and the usual cautious winter preparations, as well as a shuttle car placed on Stork's Nest Road.

Colgate Lake Trail (map 1: B9)

Distances from CR 78 parking area (2,100 ft.) to
- view of beaver meadow (2,200 ft.): 2.5 mi., 250 ft. (rev. 150 ft.), 1 hr. 25 min.
- site of old East Jewett (2,210 ft.): 3.0 mi., 250 ft., 1 hr. 40 min.
- Dutcher Notch (2,510 ft.): 4.1 mi., 550 ft., 2 hr. 20 min.

SECTION 6
WINDHAM-BLACKHEAD RANGE WILDERNESS

This wilderness showcases rugged, steep terrain with a group of peaks that include the third-, fourth-, and fifth-highest in the Catskills (Black Dome at 3,990 ft.; Blackhead at 3,950 ft.; and Thomas Cole at 3,950 ft., respectively). Additional peaks in excess of 3,000 ft. are Windham High Peak (3,524 ft.), Stoppel Point (3,430 ft.), Burnt Knob (3,190 ft.), and Acra Point (3,110 ft.). There are also six unnamed peaks in excess of 3,000 ft. in this wilderness area, which contains 17,000 acres, 30 mi. of foot trails, and two lean-tos. It is bounded to the south by the Escarpment Trail, to the west by the Elm Ridge Wild Forest, and to the north by the boundary of the Catskill Park lying south of NY 23. To the south it abuts Kaaterskill Wild Forest. The minimum elevation is 980 ft. and the maximum is 3,990 ft. (Black Dome). The higher elevations of the Blackhead Range contain extensive old-growth forests, which add to the rugged appeal and wilderness character of the area. Opportunities for both extended backpacking trips and challenging day hikes are outstanding.

The two most popular day-hike routes in this wilderness area are to Windham High Peak from Elm Ridge Trail and to Blackhead, Acra Point, Burnt Knob, or other scenic points accessible from Black Dome Range Trail. Day hikes originating from the western trailhead of Black Dome Range Trail are not as popular because of the relatively long hike to Thomas Cole and Black Dome mountains, neither of which can compete with the outstanding views of Windham High Peak or Blackhead. Those with limited time are encouraged to hike Blackhead from the Black Dome Valley. It is perhaps the area's most popular and scenic day hike. These peaks are distinct landmarks from many of the Southern and Central Catskill trails, as well as from the northern part of the state and the surrounding states, forming the unmistakable skyline silhouette that has been likened to a camel's back. The two smaller peaks to the west on Black Dome Range Trail are accordingly called the Camel's Hump and the Caudal (the tail). From the trails of the Windham-Blackhead Range Wilderness, hikers can see the Green Mtns., the Berkshires, and even the White Mtns. of New Hampshire.

There are two lean-tos in the Windham-Blackhead Range Wilderness, one lying west of the Escarpment Trail on Batavia Kill Trail, and the other at the intersection of Elm Ridge Trail and the Escarpment Trail. Opportunities for camping below 3,500 ft. are unlimited. Impact on the ridge's more scenic ledges has been a problem in the past, but increased management has resulted in their partial and continuing recovery. The Escarpment Trail is very popular with college outing clubs and scout troops, and during the late summer months hikers will encounter large groups of campers staging in the vicinity of Dutcher Notch and Colgate Lake, many of them having arranged shuttles at either end of the trail, or from its middle miles via southerly Colgate Lake and Dutcher Notch trails.

Deer and bear reside in this area, as well as the mammals typically found in the northern hardwood forests and spruce-fir summits of the Catskills, including the reintroduced lynx. Critical habitat identification for threatened or endangered plant and animal species is ongoing. Ridgetop hiking in both the Windham High Peak and Blackhead Range areas is remote and dry. Hikers are advised to plan accordingly.

Dutcher Notch Trail

This trail begins at the intersection of Colgate Lake Trail and the Escarpment Trail. Part of the original turnpike from the site of old East Jewett to markets in Catskill, the Dutcher Notch Trail descends from Dutcher Notch into the east, providing the quickest egress from the Escarpment Trail's remote middle miles. It is also the fastest access (and one of few easterly approaches) to Dutcher Notch and the Escarpment Trail from the

Hudson Valley. The eastern trailhead access point on Stork's Nest Road is seldom used by day hikers, but it does offer a vigorous hike to a scenic lookout point on the Escarpment Trail, 0.5 mi. north of Dutcher Notch (see Escarpment Trail for details). Trail signs will be found in Dutcher Notch. No services whatsoever are available in the vicinity of the trailhead on Stork's Nest Road. The trail is used frequently by cross-country skiers and occasionally by mountain bikers, and as a result, it has been designated a primitive bicycle corridor, in conjunction with a portion of Colgate Lake Trail to the west.

From Dutcher Notch, the trail descends along the dirt roadbed, within 0.3 mi. passing the obvious Dutcher Spring on the right. The flow may be sluggish, but this spring is considered to be very reliable. Be advised not to drink directly from the basin, and remember that the state recommends that all water drawn from any source be treated or filtered. The trail continues downhill, becoming severely washed out as it turns to the northeast, leaving state land and crossing directly in front of a private residence to the trailhead parking area (small, space is limited) on the right (south) side of Stork's Nest Road at 1.7 mi. Signs are posted here. Stork's Nest Road can be reached from Palenville by traveling north on Boart Road bearing left at the fork with Pennsylvania Avenue, continuing onto Castle Road (leaving Mountain Turnpike Road and Sleepy Hollow horse trail to the left), and left again onto Game Farm Road. Bear right onto Polly's Rock Road (dirt; winter maintenance varies), and straight on Floyd Hawver Road. Turn left onto Stork's Nest Road and go to the end. Trailhead parking is on the left before a private drive. The book's map (East) will provide only basic navigation.

Dutcher Notch Trail (map 1: A9)

Distances from Escarpment Trail (2,510 ft.) to
- Dutcher Spring (2,200 ft.): 0.4 mi., 0 ft. (rev. 300 ft.), 10 min.
- Stork's Nest Road trailhead (1,110 ft.): 1.7 mi., 0 ft. (rev. 1,100 ft.), 50 min.

Blackhead Mtn. Trail

This short trail (yellow markers) begins in Lockwood Gap at an intersection with Black Dome Range Trail and rises to the east between Blackhead and Black Dome mtns. to the summit of Blackhead (3,950 ft.). There are no destination signs for Blackhead in the gap at this time (see Black Dome Range Trail for additional information).

Heading east, the trail begins to ascend immediately out of Lockwood Gap (seldom named on maps), soon becoming steeper through a section of scenic terraces, arriving at a popular lookout with broad views to the west that are considered among the Catskills' very best by knowledgeable hikers. West Kill Mtn. (3,890 ft.) is at 248 degrees, seen rising over the top of the Hunter Mtn. ski slopes. Hunter's fire tower is visible. The high peaks, including Slide, Table, Cornell, and Wittenberg, are seen. To the east of Hunter, the terrain drops steeply into Stony Clove Notch, rises to Plateau Mtn., drops again into Mink Hollow (where Mt. Tobias rises in the distance), then surveys Sugarloaf, Pecoy Notch, Twin, Indian Head, and Overlook. Roundtop and Kaaterskill High Peak and the mountains of the Indian Head Wilderness Area lie to the south. For those interested only in scenery, there is no use in proceeding any farther to the viewless summit of Blackhead. The trail climbs steeply, relenting above the 3,700-ft. mark where balsam becomes thick. Blueberry bushes and lilies gone to seed appear here in late summer, where red clusters of bunchberry give the trail a festive appearance. The summit is a small, viewless bald enclosed by a dense evergreen pocket about 20 ft. square. Here the Escarpment Trail goes north to the Batavia Kill and south to Dutcher Notch.

Blackhead Mtn. Trail (map 1: A9)

Distances from Black Dome Range Trail at Lockwood Gap (3,430 ft.) to
  • Blackhead lookout (3,700 ft.): 0.4 mi., 250 ft., 20 min.
  • Blackhead summit (3,950 ft.): 0.6 mi., 500 ft., 35 min.

Batavia Kill Trail

The Batavia Kill Trail provides access to the Escarpment Trail and the Blackhead Range. It is most frequently used by hikers to complete a loop hike over Blackhead. The trail, like others in the vicinity, is characterized by steep climbs and deep forest cover. The area is very popular with backpackers and day hikers.

Batavia Kill Trail is also used for its lean-to and for completing the popular loop hike over Blackhead. Both approaches (the Escarpment Trail from this point, and Black Dome Range Trail via Lockwood Gap) are extremely steep in their upper elevations.

From CR 40 in the village of Maplecrest, turn right (east) onto Big Hollow Road (CR 56), passing farms and scattered orchards. At 2.2 mi., the road turns to dirt, soon after which a section of Black Dome Range Trail leaves to the left (north). Continue another 100 ft. to the end of the public section of Big Hollow Road to the trailhead parking area. Trail signs are comprehensive and the trail system is very well marked. For the first 0.5 mi., Batavia Kill Trail and Black Dome Range Trail share the same route. Signs are posted in the Batavia Kill trailhead parking area.

Red and yellow markers lead into the woods to the east. Pass the trail register on the right and cross the Batavia Kill. Ascend easily along the imprint of a dirt road through mixed hemlock and hardwood forest. Soon the trail ascends away from the kill, narrowing to the character of a footpath. Cross the kill again and shortly thereafter arrive at a junction and the confluence of creeks where Black Dome Range Trail comes in from the southwest.

Cross the kill, bearing left on yellow markers. Maturing hardwoods, large maple, fern, and oxalis characterize the trail to the lean-to, positioned near the headwaters of the Batavia Kill. This kill is frequently running at this elevation (or slightly lower) late into the summer. Continuing above the lean-to (0.7 mi) the trail assumes a more alpine character, where spruce and painted trillium appear. The trail levels at its junction with the (blue) Escarpment Trail.

Batavia Kill Trail (map 1: A9)

Distances from Black Dome Range Trail (2,390 ft.) to
- Batavia Kill lean-to (2,670 ft.): 0.7 mi., 300 ft., 30 min.
- Escarpment Trail (2,870 ft.): 0.9 mi., 500 ft., 40 min.
- Blackhead summit (3,950 ft.) via Escarpment Trail: 1.7 mi., 1,600 ft., 1 hr. 45 min.

Black Dome Range Trail

Coming south from Maplecrest on CR 40 (or north from Tannersville on CR 23C to CR 40), turn east onto Barnum Road (Elmer Barnum Road) just south of the village of Maplecrest. The trailhead parking area is on the right (southwest) at 1.0 mi., at the end of Barnum Road. The trail begins adjacent to a private residence on the left (northeast) side of Barnum Road and heads southeast.

Following a washed-out dirt road uphill, the trail crosses several seasonal creeks in a hardwood forest. Marking is good. Within 0.2 mi., the trail turns northeast (left) at a poorly marked junction where an old dirt road continues east (don't follow it). In a stand of white birch, the trail register and signboard stand to the left at 0.2 mi. Aster appears in profusion as the trail begins to ascend over red-silt soil, rising over ledges and gaining elevation, sometimes steeply. Nearing 3,200 ft., the ascent relaxes considerably as you approach the Caudal (the Camel's Tail), soon flattening on the Caudal itself (viewless) at 0.1 mi. before descending briefly into a saddle at 3,250 ft. The trail turns to the east now, through thick vegetation and a canopy of beech and sugar maple, where spotted touch-me-nots are common.

The trail climbs to the 3,500-ft. mark (signed) and levels for a very short distance onto the Camel's Hump at 1.5 mi. (3,550 ft.). As the trail attains level ground, avoid a short spur on the right (southeast) that leads to obstructed views, and watch for an unmarked spur just ahead, immediately to the left of a flat-topped, west-facing boulder. This short spur off the main trail leads to a rock with excellent views to the north and southwest, which include Albany, and to the right a few degrees, Equinox Mtn. (3,816 ft.) and the cluster of mountains around Emerald State Park, among them Woodlawn Mtn. (3,072 ft.). Farther to the south, in clear conditions it is possible to see Stratton Mtn. (3,936 ft.) and the associated peaks in the Green Mountain National Forest—Mt. Snow, Glastenbury, Bald, and Haystack. Still farther south and closer to the west are Mts. Williams and Greylock in the Mt. Greylock State Reservation, north of Pittsfield, MA—all views that are common to the north-facing Escarpment Trail lookouts during periods of clear weather. Windham High Peak and Burnt Knob sit in the northeast. The low-lying hills in the western foreground are Red Hill and Van Loan Mtn. (the latter named for the early mapmaker and author Walter Van Loan).

The trail descends briefly to a spruce-fir-and-blueberry bald that characterizes the saddle between the Camel's Hump and Thomas Cole Mtn. As the trail ascends, a small lookout to the right offers good views to the south of the Jewett Range, West Kill, Hunter and its fire tower, Rusk, and Evergreen. Down through Stony Clove Notch over the back side of Carl Mtn., distant Samuel's Point, in the Slide Mountain Wilderness, juts eastward.

The trail steepens as viburnum, wood sorrel, bunchberry, and balsam suddenly appear. The grade then flattens onto the summit of Thomas Cole Mtn., named for the founder of the Hudson River School of painting, at 2.6 mi. (3,950 ft.). Today, it is viewless. Previously named Mt. Kimball by Arnold Guyot (founder of the National Weather Service), this peak appears on some old maps as "Black Tom"—for its profuse evergreen peak (which looks black from a distance), a characteristic common to each of the three summits in the range. Among woodsmen and foresters, this spruce-fir cover is commonly referred to as "black growth."

At or slightly beyond the actual summit, a spur trail leaves to the right to a treed-in view. The tallest hikers may be able to see Kaaterskill High Peak, Roundtop, Indian Head, and Twin, and those continuing east can enjoy views from Black Dome (looking in the same direction). The trail follows flat over the remainder of the summit and descends into the high saddle on the approach to Black Dome, where views of the Devil's Path notches and peaks materialize to the south through the trees. Sparse seasonal views take shape to the left (northwest). The ascent barely levels as Black Dome's summit (3,990 ft.) is achieved at 3.3 mi., offering spectacular views south from an idyllic, flat rock shelf.

Ugly graffiti surrounds a few interesting pieces from the mid- to late 1800s, most notably the well-done 1889 caricature by F.E. Elitt. Here are views of the interior high peaks in the Slide Mountain-Panther Mountain Wilderness beyond the Devil's Path mountains, through Stony Clove Notch. Hunter, its fire tower, the ski slopes on Colonel's Chair, West Kill, and peaks to the west are also visible. In front of you are Onteora, Parker, and the Jewett Range. The long ridge running west from Stoppel Point is West Stoppel Point. The villages of Tannersville (best seen at night) and East Jewett lie below, with Colgate Lake east of Lake Capra (private).

The trail continues east, descending, turning south briefly to cross the top of a ledge where an obvious spur leads a few feet to excellent views east across Lockwood Gap. Blackhead commands the middle ground. Included here are views of North Mtn., Stoppel Point, the Hudson River, and the northeastern ranges and lowlands. The trail drops down sharply below the ledge and continues the descent to Lockwood Gap junction, arriving at 3.8 mi.

A poorly situated, designated campsite exists to the northeast of the junction, a short distance beyond two closed sites. The only tent site is on a slope. Camping opportunities, especially for larger groups, improve only at lower elevations. A fairly reliable spring, rising near the middle of a brook and easily overlooked, is located 0.3 mi. downhill from Lockwood Gap on Black Dome Range Trail.

(NOTE: Hikers wishing to take a short side trip in order to see one of the Catskills' best views should leave Black Dome Range Trail here and go east following yellow markers toward Blackhead. See Blackhead Mtn. Trail for details.)

Black Dome Range Trail continues left (north), descending very steeply. From this point (Lockwood Gap) the distance to the Batavia Kill Trail is 1.0 mi.; the Batavia Kill parking area in Black Dome Valley (Big Hollow Road) is at an additional distance of 0.5 mi. Continue descending to the junction with the Batavia Kill Trail, crossing a seasonal creek through maple-and-hemlock woods. Ordinarily there is water at this confluence, restricted to the main bed of the Batavia Kill itself during dry periods.

Bearing left (northwest), cross the kill on a footbridge. The trail improves, descending an eroded roadbed. A few large spruce trees appear as the trail widens, again crossing the kill on a footbridge. The trail passes the register and trail signs, arriving at the trailhead parking area at 5.3 mi. Black Dome Range Trail continues from a point 100 ft. west of the trailhead parking area at the east end of Big Hollow Road. From this point it provides the shortest and fastest access to the Escarpment Trail and the scenic destinations of Burnt Knob and Acra Point. Hikers with limited time will appreciate the fact that Burnt Knob Mtn. (3,190 ft.) is both closer and considerably more scenic than Acra Point. Signs are posted here.

Locate the red markers and trailhead signage that mark the continuation of Black Dome Range Trail. Within 200 ft. of the road, the trail passes the register and crosses the Batavia Kill on a footbridge at 5.3 mi., heading north. The trail climbs next over mineral soil to a tributary into a hemlock woods, ascending through a stand of spruce on the left (west) side of the trail. Hemlock increases as the trail follows alongside the creek and then crosses it. This is the nearest water to the junction and the most reliable water in proximity to the long stretch of the Escarpment Trail between the Batavia Kill and Elm Ridge. The trail passes through a flat, grassy area ideal for camping, shortly thereafter arriving at the ridge and the Escarpment Trail at 6.3 mi. Go left (northwest) to reach Burnt Knob (see Escarpment Trail for details).

Black Dome Range Trail (map 1: A8–A9)

Distances from Barnum Road trailhead (2,110 ft.) to
- Camel's Hump (3,550 ft.): 2.0 mi., 1,550 ft. (rev. 100 ft.), 1 hr. 30 min.
- Thomas Cole Mtn. summit (3,950 ft.): 2.6 mi., 2,050 ft. (rev. 100 ft.), 2 hr. 15 min.
- Black Dome Mtn. summit (3,990 ft.): 3.3 mi., 2,300 ft. (rev. 200 ft.), 2 hr. 45 min.
- Blackhead Mtn. Trail at Lockwood Gap (3,430 ft.): 3.8 mi., 2,300 ft. (rev. 550 ft.), 3 hr. 5 min.
- Batavia Kill Trail (2,390 ft.): 4.8 mi., 2,300 ft. (rev. 1,050 ft.), 3 hr. 35 min.
- Big Hollow Road (2,170 ft.): 5.3 mi., 2,300 ft. (rev. 200 ft.), 3 hr. 50 min.
- Escarpment Trail (2,770 ft.): 6.3 mi., 2,900 ft., 4 hr. 35 min.

SUGGESTED HIKES

Easy Hike

Elm Ridge Trail to Elm Ridge lean-to [rt: 2.0 mi., 1:30]. An easy walk through an old settlement area, of which only stone walls and vagrant apple trees remain. Ideal for an overnight, this trail passes a piped spring and leads to a quiet lean-to in an area of mature forest and lichen-covered ledges. (See Elm Ridge Wild Forest for trail description.)

Moderate Hike

Burnt Knob via Black Dome Range Trail, Escarpment Trail, CR 56/ Black Dome Range Trailhead [rt: 2.5 mi., 2:30]. An enjoyable short, gentle then steep hike (950 ft. elevation gain) that follows the northern section of Black Dome Range Trail to the Escarpment Trail. Bearing north, the trail climbs steeply, leveling out as it heads to Burnt Knob. A small scenic overlook on the left of the Escarpment Trail is reached by a short spur. Views include the Black Dome Valley and the encompassing high peaks. For a vigorous day's outing (strenuous), complete a loop by continuing north, summiting Windham High Peak, descending Elm Ridge Trail, and walking Black Dome Valley Road back to the Batavia Kill trailheads (total, 9.0 mi.) (See Kaaterskill Wild Forest for Escarpment Trail description.)

Acra Point via Black Dome Range Trail, Escarpment Trail, CR 56/ Black Dome Range Trailhead [rt: 3.6 mi., 2:10]. A fairly easy hike to a quiet and private lookout with rugged and intimate views of the interior Northern Catskills. (See Kaaterskill Wild Forest for Escarpment Trail description.)

Strenuous Hikes

Windham High Peak via Black Dome Range Trail, Escarpment Trail, CR 56/Black Dome Range Trailhead [rt: 6.8 mi. 5:00]. An all-time favorite of many hikers, this outing features dense plantations of Norway spruce and many views of the Hudson Valley and Catskills from outcroppings in all directions.

Blackhead via the Black Dome Trail, Blackhead Mtn. Trail, CR 40/ Black Dome Range Trailhead [4.2 mi., 4:00]. A stiff hike with a 1,750-ft. rise to the westerly and scenic shoulder of Blackhead. Alternate: Continue the loop over Blackhead summit joining the Escarpment Trail, turn north, and descend on the Batavia Kill Trail (total loop distance 4.5 mi.). (See Kaaterskill Wild Forest for Escarpment Trail description.)

SECTION 7
INDIAN HEAD WILDERNESS AREA

The scenic Indian Head Wilderness Area lies between the Hudson River Valley on the east, where the Escarpment rises suddenly from an elevation of 750 ft. to 2,500 ft. (the average altitude of the Escarpment), and extends westward to Stony Clove, crossing five major peaks: Plattekill (3,110 ft.), Indian Head (3,573 ft.), Twin (3,650 ft.), Sugarloaf (3,810 ft.), and Plateau (3,850 ft.) mtns. It contains 16,800 acres, with a minimum elevation of 900 ft., to a maximum of 3,840 ft. (Plateau Mtn.). The area has 24 mi. of foot trails as well as 5.6 mi. of designated cross-country ski trails. There are three lean-tos (Mink Hollow, Echo Lake, and Devil's Kitchen) and ten designated campsites.

Collectively known as the Devil's Path Range, these mountains and notches of the Indian Head Wilderness Area are host to one of the Catskills' most renowned and difficult hiking trails—the Devil's Path. It is an area of steep ascents and descents with varying and rugged terrain. Its notches, carved into soft sandstone by ancient rivers, deepen as hikers travel west, leading to increasing vertical rises through steepening terrain. Although day hikers frequently climb these summits from the feeder trails that primarily enter the range from the north (Mink Hollow, Pecoy Notch,

Jimmy Dolan Notch, and CCCD trails emanating from the Platte Clove Preserve), and less often from the longer southerly approaches on Overlook Mtn., Southern Mink Hollow, and Warner Creek trails, few but the most determined backpackers travel the entire Devil's Path from east to west rather than vice versa. For hikers, the result of this user pattern is a good deal of wilderness solitude and the opportunity to experience extended periods of isolation at higher altitudes.

Quarrying, tanning, glassmaking, sawmilling, the charcoal industry, and the ensuing tourist development have left their mark on this now silent and lonely wilderness. Many old roads, primitive paths, bluestone quarries, and dugways (trenches made in slopes that acted as log or stone chutes) exist in the area. Hikers will see the remnants of early industry and will often notice hand-tooled stones on the trails that fell from ox-drawn quarry wagons during the early 1800s. Although decimated by the notoriously wasteful tanning industry, the Indian Head Wilderness Area is still densely populated with hemlocks, where difficult terrain has protected isolated, virgin stands. Extensive northern hardwood forest covers the lower elevations, and summits are often clad in dense, nearly impenetrable fir called "cripplebrush."

Much of the preserve lands were acquired in the early twentieth century, with trails being constructed by the state and the Civilian Conservation Corps in the 1930s. Today the trails are maintained largely by volunteer organizations such as the New York-New Jersey Trail Conference, the Adirondack Mountain Club, and the Appalachian Mountain Club.

It is believed that fishers populate this area along with the typical big-game species found in the Catskill ecozone. During the 1800s, wolves were common in the area, and elk were common before that time. Today campers will often hear packs of howling coyotes that can sound chilling to the uninitiated, although these animals are not known to approach humans. Packs of a dozen or more animals may "sing" for several minutes at a time. They are shy, wary, relatively small, and rarely seen. The only natural lake in this wilderness area is the 12-acre Echo Lake, a glacially dammed, shallow pond with a small and fickle population of brook trout. Other ponds in the area are seasonal beaver impoundments, existing primarily at middle elevations and often seen from trails. In general, the area is very popular with backpackers, and Echo Lake (best avoided on nice weekends) draws more than its share of campers.

Devil's Path

The Devil's Path has a double meaning, deriving its name not only for the Devil whom Dutch settlers believed lived in the deep, wild hollows and jagged cloves of the Catskills, but also for its demonic and unforgiving ascents, its rugged and punishing peaks, and particularly in the summer, its fiendish lack of water. Next to the Escarpment Trail, the Devil's Path is perhaps the most popular and challenging trail for extended backpacking and day hiking in the Catskills, offering several peaks and loop hikes in beautiful forests with sensational mountaintop scenery. All hikers are advised to take things easy on this difficult trail, planning cautiously and keeping daily mileage quotas reasonable (a ten-mile day on the Devil's Path is like a twenty-mile day elsewhere). Backpackers will average little more than 1.0 MPH over such highly variable terrain. Even day hikers traveling light will find the vertical rises and rocky ledges daunting and should plan for sudden changes of weather with corresponding drops in temperature and possible high winds and windchill along exposed ridges.

The Prediger Road trailhead marks the official beginning of the Devil's Path, although the Devil's Path is frequently reached from many other locations and is often hiked via Overlook Mtn. Trail from Meads Mtn. Road, with the first ascent being Overlook Mtn. Although Overlook is a fairly stiff first ascent, it is hardly the demanding terrain one can expect from the ensuing mountains. Regardless of how it is hiked, the Devil's Path offers one of the most scenic and challenging thru-hikes in the northeast.

Located off CR 16 (Platte Clove Road), the Devil's Path trailhead is best reached from NY 23A in Tannersville. From the light in the center of town, travel 0.25 mi. east on NY 23A, turning right (south) onto Spring Street (CR 16), which becomes Platte Clove Road. At 5.7 mi., find Prediger Road on the right (south) side of CR 16, marked with state-trail signs. Follow Prediger Road 0.4 mi. south to the trailhead parking area. The trail is a level woods road, leading in 0.4 mi. to a lively creek and the intersection with Jimmy Dolan Notch Trail.

Bearing left to the east over level ground through hardwood forests, the trail narrows into a footpath. This section of the trail is a poor yet designated ski trail, which receives little or no use by skiers. The trail is suitable (though not very interesting) for accomplished backcountry skiers, but it is by no means diagonal striding terrain. Considerable base is necessary to cover the trail's many rocks, blowdowns, and short, steep pitches. This section is also designated as a primitive bicycle corridor that continues south on Overlook Trail once the two paths meet.

The trail leads east over hillocks and across small seasonal rills, one of which has a very well-made stone step bridge. Many locations along the trail are flat and convenient for camping, and those headed for the popular Devil's Kitchen lean-to (located on Overlook Trail) on a busy weekend might consider this option. There are also tent sites near the lean-to, where there is water.

At 1.8 mi. the Devil's Path joins Overlook Trail. This junction is not well identified. Turn right (south) and within 200 ft. turn right (west) again to continue toward Indian Head Mtn. This trail leaves Overlook Trail from the right (west) side of the Old Overlook Road, turning back to the southwest and climbing gently but steadily uphill. Initially the trail climbs and levels through a grove of hemlocks, some of them very large. Through the years, these groves have proven to be popular bivouacs, and far off the trail it is not uncommon to find old fire rings. An open forest follows as the trail gains elevation in small doses amid moss-cloaked boulders and large, exposed roots. This pattern of climbing and leveling continues as views appear to the north (provided there are few leaves). Views improve dramatically ahead. A northern hardwood forest predominates until the trail narrows and steepens, becomes grassy, turns east, and descends slightly to an expansive lookout at 3.2 mi. An exposed rock, it faces northeast. This is Sherman's Lookout, named for Civil War hero General William Tecumseh Sherman, commading general of the Union Army under General Ulysses S. Grant and an 1890 visitor to the Catskill Mountain House. With this last bit of elevation gain, small balsam fir marks the beginnings of a nearly ⚠ contiguous Canadian boreal forest. *This is a dangerous ledge with substantial vertical drop—stay ahead of youngsters at this point.*

On a clear day, the views from Sherman's Lookout are extensive. The monolithic mountainside close on your right is the western face of Plattekill Mtn. (3,100 ft., trailless). Just on the other side of that ridge running north–south at 2,600 ft. is Overlook Trail. Roundtop (3,440 ft.) and Kaaterskill High Peak (3,655 ft.) are the two closest mountains to the north, directly in front of you. On the right, sloping downhill and to the southeast from the long shoulder of Kaaterskill, above Platte Clove on the rocky ramparts of the escarpment, is Huckleberry Point (84 degrees). Continuing to the right is a piece of the Hudson River (North Germantown Reach) where several cement plants, stacks, and industrial silos around Duck Cove and Inbocht Bay impose upon the otherwise pastoral valley landscape. Across the Hudson, hikers can identify Bash Bish Gorge in the Taconics. The Bash Bish falls themselves are not visible.

The most impressive and informative view of all is heavily dissected Platte Clove itself and the adjacent, deeply eroded streambeds that join it from the north. These clefts run parallel to the direct line of descent and are accordingly labeled "parallel drainage" by geologists. Platte Clove was formed by the retreating Wisconsin Ice Sheet about 15,000 years ago; the difference in what we see today is merely cosmetic. The most notable difference is perhaps the loss of the hemlock trees. In the days before the tanbark period, stands were thick and covered much of the landscape.

The trail curves to the south. *Be cautious near another vertical drop on* *the left, very close to the trail.* Swinging away from the ledge, the trail climbs easily, nearly tunneling over with balsam as it curves around to the northwest. A limited view appears on the left, just before the trail's best southerly vantage. At 3.4 mi., the trail is now level and narrow as thick stands of spruce-fir suddenly give way to phenomenal views of the central high-peaks area and the lowlands between, from the Hudson River to the Ashokan Reservoir, and west across the high summit skyline, taking in most of the major peaks from Ashokan High Point to Slide and beyond, toward the Delaware Valley.

The Devil's Path now approaches pure boreal forest on the Indian's long, oblate chin. Off the trail, the dense, scrubby evergreen cover is nearly impenetrable cripplebrush. The trail descends gently. Ahead and uphill, the Indian's "eyebrow" (as it appears from the north) looms directly overhead. A short scramble follows through a steep, heavily impacted, and eroded crevice beneath the high rock overhang of the eyebrow. Roots and rocks provide handholds, but the pitch requires careful footing, especially in icy conditions. At 3.6 mi., the trail reaches an open view from a small, dangerously exposed flat outcropping over a substantial vertical drop. *Keep* *your children behind you as you approach the rock, and use extreme caution! If it is icy, stay off the shelf completely.*

There are minimal views upriver to the north from this point. More imposing are those to the south, most immediately of Overlook Mtn. and the Sawkill Valley. Overlook's cellular tower caused a large but unsuccessful public-resistance effort, and for the few hikers who do not use cellular phones, it serves only as a convenient marker for the surrounding, somber gray ruins of the ill-fated Overlook Hotel. Equidistant between the eyebrow and the long ridge of Overlook and Plattekill mtns. are the thickly oak-forested, south-facing slopes and headwaters of the Sawkill, which drain through unnamed tributaries to the southwest, filling Cooper Lake, the city of Kingston's water supply. The strip of water to the right and beyond the cell tower is the Ashokan Reservoir (often it is mistaken for the Hudson, which lies farther to the east), and to its westerly extreme the first big peak is Ashokan High Point. Following into the west are the Catskills' highest peaks. The Tibetan Buddhist monastery appears at 208 degrees in the saddle between Overlook and Guardian mtns. in Meads. Finally, off to the south-southwest at 219 degrees and nearly as far as the eye can see even with good binoculars is High Point, New Jersey's highest point at 1,803 ft., with its distinctive war monument. The Appalachian Trail goes through that section of High Point State Park and turns east toward Harriman State Park and the Hudson Highlands, which can be seen to the southeast.

A series of short, steep climbs follows through ledgy, virgin spruce-fir terrain that becomes a nearly homogeneous and impenetrable fir canopy, tunneling over flat, mossy rock.

At 3.8 mi., an overstory of large, dead and dying red spruce characterizes the balsam-clad summit, and the trail is sparsely decorated with mountain ash and paper birch. The remaining red spruce, which were originally damaged in a 1950 hurricane, have suffered the effects of exposure and drought. There are no views until the westerly descent to Jimmy Dolan Notch begins, and these are of neighboring Twin Mtn. and the Blackhead Range to the north.

Like most of the saddles between the Devil's Path summits, the descent into Jimmy Dolan Notch is moderately steep, although short (elevation drop, 500 ft. from summit). At 4.2 mi., the trail intersects with the (blue) Jimmy Dolan Notch Trail in the notch itself.

From Jimmy Dolan Notch, the trail rises steeply to the west on the approach to Twin Mtn., quickly gaining 500 ft. in elevation. The trail relaxes, heading southwest briefly. A cut view appears east of the trail, providing views of Indian Head Mtn. (3,573 ft.), Overlook Mtn. (3,150 ft.), Kaaterskill High Peak (3,655 ft.), and Roundtop Mtn. (3,440 ft.). A beautiful stone trail follows, lined with blueberry bushes, spruce, and fir.

The state's practice of cutting vistas has drawn criticism from many outdoor groups and enthusiasts, who maintain that it is not in keeping with the Forever Wild mandate of the state constitution. The state, pointing to a loophole in management language, continues the practice, to the delight of many hikers.

At 5.1 mi., the trail reaches the south peak of Twin Mtn. (3,580 ft.) and an expansive view southward, one of the Devil's Path's finest. From the eastern side of this open area, Overlook Mtn. and its fire tower can be seen. Most of the Ashokan Reservoir is seen, as well as Cooper Lake in the foreground. To the left of Ashokan High Point are Sky Top and Eagle Cliff in the Shawangunks' Mohonk Preserve and the Mohonk Mountain House. In the Slide Mountain-Panther Mountain Wilderness Area are the Catskill high peaks, showing Slide Mtn. (4,190 ft.), Cornell (3,870 ft.), and Wittenberg (3,790 ft.), with Terrace Mtn. (2,360 ft.) tapering down to the right. Over the top of Giant Ledge the landscape blurs into the vaporous peaks of the Big Indian-Beaverkill Range Wilderness Area. Panther Mtn. (3,730 ft.) appears to the right of Giant Ledge. Tremper Mtn. (2,740 ft.) can be spotted in the middle ground—with binoculars you can see the fire tower. The north shoulder of Twin is immediately to the west, as well as Sugarloaf (3,810 ft.) at 320 degrees, and to the left, Plateau Mtn.'s long ridge (3,850 ft.), from which Olderbark Mtn. (3,450 ft.) projects south.

The trail proceeds west, descending easily, and varies in composition from sandy loam and moss-margined rock to densely foliated spruce-fir as it rises to Twin's northerly summit (3,650 ft.). Slightly below this point are a rock outcropping and a view that provides a more northerly vantage than the last, showing the previously unseen Hunter Mtn. (4,050 ft.) and its fire tower, and giving a good look at Table (3,847 ft.) and Peekamoose (3,843 ft.). The trail drops downhill through a crack to the left of an overhanging rock that has been abused by careless campers. This is the 3,500-ft. mark. The trail's surface is covered in broken slabs over roots as it descends through ledges, passing a conspicuous boulder on the right. An extensive boulder field covers the well-marked trail and provides for open views to the north of the Blackhead Range and of Sugarloaf Mtn., immediately west. This appealing rocky terrain continues through scrubby hardwood forest and nearly into Pecoy Notch, where the terrain relaxes in the saddle at 5.6 mi. (2,800 ft.). There are no views. Opportunities for camping in the tangled, dense underbrush are limited; one overused site was recently closed. Pecoy Notch Trail leads north and downhill to the Roaring Brook trailhead parking area (this is the fastest egress). The Devil's Path continues straight ahead (west) toward Sugarloaf Mtn.

The Devil's Path swings north for a short distance before switching back to the southwest and climbing steeply into an 850-ft. vertical rise to the summit of Sugarloaf. Increasingly clear views of Twin and its terraced, sedimentary geology are visible to the east across Pecoy Notch. A few ledges require light hands-on work. As higher elevations are achieved, natural vantage points appear, each of them looking easterly. The trail begins to level, passing the 3,500-ft. mark, and a long, flat, boreal ridge follows, nearly tunneled over in thick spruce and fir trees. At 6.5 mi., the trail reaches the summit of Sugarloaf, which lies in the vicinity of a short spur trail that leaves left (south) a few hundred feet to a lookout featuring the Catskills' high peaks, (those of the Burroughs Range), Giant Ledge and Panther, the Ashokan Reservoir, and the Hudson Highlands to the south. The Shawangunks are clearly visible, and to the west are the hills and peaks of the Big Indian-Beaverkill Range Wilderness Area.

The trail descends over a grassy treadway, passing a lookout facing Plateau Mtn., and thereafter views to the north of the Blackhead Range appear. The hulking spires of large, dead spruce trees loom overhead as the trail descends over broken ledges with some steep drop-offs (which are potentially dangerous), at one point passing beneath an unstable precipice of loose, overhanging rock. The trail passes beneath a natural rock bridge at one point and continues its descent into hardwoods when, at 7.2 mi., Mink Hollow Trail to the Roaring Kill parking area appears on the right (northeast) at 2,500 ft. in elevation. (Don't confuse this trail with the abandoned Mink Hollow Trail that leaves to the north from the intersection straight ahead.) The trail shortly arrives at the junction with the southern section of Mink Hollow Trail at 7.3 mi., where a lean-to is situated.

The abandoned Mink Hollow Trail descends on a woods road to the north. It remains the fastest egress from the Devil's Path in case of emergency. To the left (south) is the lean-to. Thru-hikers should be aware that the nearest provisions are in Tannersville, a long walk from the trailhead. There are no provisions or services in Lake Hill to the south—only a post office. Woodstock is the nearest village.

The Devil's Path continues straight ahead (northwest) to climb Plateau Mtn., the westernmost peak of the Indian Head Wilderness Area, from which the Devil's Path drops steeply into Stony Clove. Once called Stony Mtn., its boreal summit ridge is long and flat, averaging 3,800 ft. This section of the Devil's Path was built by the Civilian Conservation Corps in 1935. Plateau is a remote and attractive peak, offering solitude and far-reaching scenery.

The trail heads northwest and flattens through hardwoods, providing sparse views of Mink Hollow and Sugarloaf Mtn. to the east. Climbing steeply, through rocky, ledgy terrain, the trail passes through a stand of very large red spruce trees and continues to ascend until leveling out near 3,700 ft., where views to the north reveal Kaaterskill High Peak (3,655 ft.), Roundtop (3,440 ft.), and neighboring Sugarloaf Mtn. (3,810 ft.) to the east. Soon afterward, the trail arrives at the (viewless) true summit at 8.0 mi. The ridge narrows, the trail becomes soft duff, and hikers will sense the abyss on either side of the mountain as they travel west.

A long, nearly level hike along the summit ridgeline follows the actual summit on the southeast side of the mountain. Thick, often impenetrable stands of large spruce trees thin as the trail heads west. To the north (right) a nameless lookout shows Roundtop and Kaaterskill High Peak sloping down into Platte Clove. Use caution at this fairly steep drop. The trail wanders along the flat ridge, where it has been worn into the soft soil. Within fifteen minutes or so, the trail passes a more significant lookout on the right (east), where a large boulder is etched with the image of a rising sun. This rock has long been known as Danny's Lookout. Visible far (80 mi.) to the northeast at 58 degrees is the Green Mountain National Forest. Although the individual peaks are difficult to isolate, among them are Bald Mtn. (2,865 ft.), Glastenbury Mtn. (3,748 ft.), and beyond it, Stratton Mtn. (3,936 ft.), with Mt. Snow to the east of Glastenbury. Moving south are the Taconic Range and Mt. Greylock State Reservation. Roundtop, Kaaterskill High Peak, and Sugarloaf are still with you—beyond them are long views of the eastern Hudson Valley. Thomas Cole (3,950 ft.), Black Dome (3,990 ft.), and Blackhead (3,950 ft.) are easily identified to the north-northeast, along with Arizona Mtn. (3,400 ft.) southeast of Blackhead, where the Escarpment drops down into Dutcher Notch.

The trail continues north along the flat ridge, speckled with a forest floor of mottled yellow trout lilies, until reaching Orchid Point (aka Plateau Mtn. Lookout), where another startling gulf of valleys, ridges, and mountains presents itself. Stony Clove is carved into the landscape below. Across it stands Hunter Mtn. (4,050 ft.) and its fire tower, with West Kill and Southwest Hunter to the south. Slide Mtn. is obvious at 220 degrees, and interestingly its namesake landslide can be seen, especially when residual snow cover sticks in the surrounding forest. Many other peaks in the Slide Mountain-Panther Mountain Wilderness Area are prominent. This fascinating view ranks among the most interesting from any of the northeastern Catskill vantage points.

The trail descends, leaving spruce-fir for stunted birch, passing a shallow rock overhang, and at 3,400 ft. swinging into the south across a flat, wet area with large, flat stones, before switching back and descending again. Spring beauty, Dutchman's breeches, and purple trillium (John Burroughs's wake-robin, a carrion flower) appear among the now isolated spruces. A stand of pure white birch signals the final steep descent, as the trail drops into Stony Clove. The tree type changes to beech as the trail makes a sharp turn from south to west. Ahead to the southwest you can see Slide and Wittenberg. A nameless tributary of Edgewood Stream runs down the clove to the left (south). Finally reaching Stony Clove, the trail crosses the footprint of the old Stony Clove & Catskill Mountain Railroad, which brought tourists from as far as Philadelphia to the Catskill Mountain House and the Hotel Kaaterskill. A short walk on to the south of the trail will reveal some remaining railroad ties.

The trail continues straight ahead, descends a flight of wooden stairs, and, at 11.0 mi., crosses NY 214 at Notch Lake, a point 0.3 mi. north of Devil's Tombstone Public Campground. Here there are a parking area, trail signs, picnic tables, and fireplaces. This steep and attractive trail penetrates the Hunter Mountain Wild Forest to the northeast shoulder of Southwest Hunter Mtn. before descending into Diamond Notch. Thru-hikers should note that there are no showers at the Devil's Tombstone Public Campground. The nearest provisions are in Hunter or Tannersville to the north, or in Phoenicia to the south.

The Devil's Path continues at the south end of Notch Lake, crossing a wooden bridge and rising to the trail register. The rocky trail ascends steeply, switching back and forth through a dense sugar maple forest. Within fifteen minutes it passes a moss-covered ledge on the right of the trail, at the corner of which is a shallow rock overhang. The trail continues steeply through ash-and-maple stands and up a short flight of rock steps, switching back into a hemlock grove and turning north for a moment, ascending at a more relaxed pace.

Beech appears as the trail levels, the forest type changing to include birch and cherry trees, with a ground cover of oxalis and moss. Soon the trail assumes a course along a southeastern slope of Southwest Hunter Mtn. (3,750 ft.), allowing obscure summer views across Stony Clove and beyond. Bright white birch appears and the trail turns from rock to dirt, becoming flat. Striped maple saplings hang into the narrow trail, and little stands of red spruce dot the woods. This is the headwater slope of Myrtle Brook, which the trail crosses. The trail remains level for some time as it turns west, at 12.9 mi. arriving at the junction with Hunter Mtn. Trail (yellow).

The Devil's Path bears left (west), following red markers, within moments coming upon the lean-to. Because it has been ravaged by porcupines, the privy is fully encased in hardware cloth. The lean-to, although very old, is in good condition, with a broken concrete fire ring campers have improved upon with piled-up rocks. Just beyond the lean-to the trail crosses a brook. At a point just beyond this, the trail makes a right-angle turn across the same shallow brook, while prior to this turn, an unmarked trail (easy to mistake for the main trail) goes left a few hundred feet to an appealing, established, and legal campsite. Birch trees tower above a vast understory of fir as the main trail follows a slope heading west, climbing easily. As the terrain flattens, an unmarked but obvious path leaves to the left (south) and is cairned with small rocks to alert the hikers of the Catskill 3500 Club that this is the bushwhack route to Southwest Hunter Mtn. This interesting trail follows a reinforced, graded bed that most likely served as a horse-drawn log railway in the early 1900s.

The trail descends, becoming rocky as it turns north and relaxes, remaining generally flat as it follows along a ridge amphitheater above Diamond Notch. A short spur trail to the left of the main trail leads a few feet to views of Southwest Hunter (3,750 ft.) and West Kill (3,890 ft.) mtns. and into Diamond Notch. *This is an extremely dangerous ledge—a* *fact that is not apparent until its edge is reached.* Return to the Devil's Path, which passes a few overused and discontinued campsites. The trail becomes somewhat muddy, catching runoff from the steep westerly slopes of Hunter Mtn., only 0.5 mi. uphill to the east (not visible). A long, steady downhill follows through dark, majestic stands of tall sugar maple, with an attending undergrowth of stinging nettle crowding the trail. The trail crosses several runoff trickles and a larger tributary of the West Kill before it arrives at the grassy, open field adjacent to West Kill Falls (aka Buttermilk Falls, Diamond Notch Falls) and the energetic West Kill Creek at 15.0 mi.

Sign in at the trail register (cleverly contained in a section of PVC pipe to protect it from porcupines) at the intersection of Diamond Notch Trail (blue) and the Devil's Path (red). Diamond Notch itself is a short distance to the south along the blue Diamond Notch Trail. The Devil's Path continues to the left, crosses the bridge, and immediately turns right. The trail initially passes beside the falls. The large pool at their base is a popular swimming spot. Following the West Kill Creek for a few hundred feet, the trail turns uphill to the southeast, ascends over a varied surface from mineral soil to rock, and turns to the southwest, passing a spring to the left of the trail (2,900 ft.). The path turns rooty, offering only wintertime views of Rusk Mtn. (3,690 ft.) and Evergreen Mtn. (3,360 ft.) to the right (north). Broad sheets of bunchberry and oxalis (wood sorrel) cover the forest floor. At 3,420 ft., the forest assumes a more alpine character, and the trail levels and turns to the west, becoming muddy in spots. The trail passes a shallow rock overhang mid-trail at 3,490 ft., where illegal fires have scarred the rock. Just above this ledge, the 3,500-ft. sign appears. Birches become gnarly and stunted now, then there begins a long, level stretch with an understory of small balsam fir beneath even-aged stands of larger fir.

At 3,700 ft., open space is visible to the left and right, but no views appear. Descending slightly to 3,600 ft., the trail passes a spur trail that drops downhill to the left (south) to a treed-in view. (This once-cut vista has recovered, but the trail's sensitive vegetation hasn't.) Don't be distracted by tantalizing spurs that lead nowhere (there are several); the scenic reward lies ahead at Buck Ridge Lookout at 17.1 miles. After a brief ascent the trail flattens and without warning arrives at Buck Ridge (3,740 ft.). The view is beyond expectation—one of the Eastern Catskills' best. Hunter Mtn. (4,050 ft.) and its fire tower are at 94 degrees. Across Diamond Notch is Southwest Hunter (3,750 ft.); and across Stony Clove is Plateau Mtn. (3,850 ft.), with Olderbark jutting south. Just over the lowest point between Plateau and Olderbark mtns. (3,440 ft.) is Overlook (3,150 ft.) and its fire tower. Conspicuous in the east-northeast is the entire Blackhead Range, as well as Windham High Peak (3,524 ft.) and Burnt Knob

(3,190 ft.). The open ski slopes of Hunter Mtn. West are obvious to your left. The enormous easterly ridge of West Kill lies directly to the east. On a good day you can see sailboats in the Hudson River. Moving to the right (south) across the Rondout Valley in the Shawangunks appear Sky Top, Eagle Cliff, and the Trapps. Then, the Shawangunk Ridge in Minnewaska State Park cuts west. The large pointy mountain to the left of Sky Top and in the foreground is Mt. Tobias (2,550 ft.), and to its left, back in the Shawangunks again, is Bonticou Crag. The fire tower of Tremper Mtn. (2,740 ft.) can be seen at 190 degrees. Wagon Wheel Gap in Sundown Wild Forest can be seen directly over the top of the tower. The central high peaks are visible, including Slide and Wittenberg.

The trail continues west. A spur immediately to the right (north) leads to a rock with northerly views of Huntersfield, Tower, Cave, the Blackhead Mtns., and the townships of Lexington, Halcott, Roxbury, Conesville, Prattsville, Ashland, Windham, and Durham. You can see a piece of the Schoharie Reservoir in the north-northwest. The trail continues to the flat summit of West Kill Mtn. (3,890 ft.) at 17.2 mi., which is enclosed in balsam fir, and passes through a wet area dense with cow parsnips and Solomon's seal. The westerly shoulder of the mountain provides curious hikers with additional lookouts to the west, toward North Dome (3,610 ft.) and Sherrill (3,550 ft.). The trail descends from the boreal zone and walks level through hardwoods. At 3,300 ft., it climbs steeply again, through a short stretch of tilted, slippery slabs. Although self-guiding and adequately marked, the trail is faint in places, showing considerably less use than the much shorter easterly approach. At 3,400 ft., from a false summit, are seasonal westerly views across Mink Hollow to the eastern slopes of North Dome. Descending steadily, the trail arrives at the margin of a wetland in Mink Hollow, where it turns sharply to the right (north).

The trail descends through Mink Hollow. Nettle and sugar maple go hand in hand, leading to a dense hemlock forest where a private parcel is posted to the right. A trail arrow alerts hikers to a sharp left turn. As the Devil's Path begins its final descent to Spruceton Road, the trail register is reached on the right among large white pine. State-land wilderness area signs are posted here. At 21.4 mi., the trail ends at the parking area and the western Devil's Path trailhead. Signs are posted here, just across Spruceton Road.

Devil's Path (map 1: B9–B7)

Distances from Prediger Road trailhead (1,970 ft.) to
- Jimmy Dolan Notch Trail, lower junction (2,100 ft.): 0.4 mi., 150 ft., 20 min.
- Overlook Trail (2,230 ft.): 1.8 mi., 350 ft. (rev. 50 ft.), 1 hr. 10 min.
- Indian Head Mtn. summit (3,573 ft.): 3.8 mi., 1,850 ft. (rev. 150 ft.), 3 hr.
- Jimmy Dolan Notch Trail, upper junction (3,110 ft.): 4.2 mi., 1,850 ft. (rev. 450 ft.), 3 hr. 15 min.
- Twin Mtn. summit (3,580 ft.): 5.1 mi., 2,500 ft. (rev. 100 ft.), 4 hr. 5 min.
- Pecoy Notch Trail (2,810 ft.): 5.5 mi., 2,500 ft. (rev. 850 ft.), 4 hr. 25 min.
- Sugarloaf Mtn. summit (3,810 ft.): 6.5 mi., 3,500 ft., 5 hr. 35 min.
- Mink Hollow Trail, east junction (2,610 ft.): 7.2 mi., 3,500 ft. (rev. 1,200 ft.), 6 hr.
- Plateau Mtn. summit (3,850 ft.): 8.0 mi., 4,750 ft., 7 hr. 20 min.
- Stony Clove Notch (NY 214) (1,990 ft.): 11.0 mi., 4,800 ft. (rev. 1,900 ft.), 8 hr. 55 min.
- Hunter Mtn. Trail (3,530 ft.): 12.9 mi., 6,350 ft., 10 hr. 45 min.
- Diamond Notch Trail (2,330 ft.): 15.0 mi., 6,350 ft. (rev. 1,200 ft.), 11 hr. 45 min.
- Buck Ridge Lookout (3,740 ft.): 17.1 mi., 7,900 ft. (rev. 1,650), 13 hr. 30 min.
- West Kill Mtn. summit (3,890 ft.): 17.2 mi., 8,000 ft. (rev. 100 ft.), 13 hr. 40 min.
- Spruceton Road trailhead (1,790 ft.): 21.4 mi., 8,250 ft. (rev. 2,350 ft.), 16 hr. 15 min.

Jimmy Dolan Notch Trail

Jimmy Dolan Notch Trail is a popular route, used often for loop hikes of Indian Head Mtn. (3,573 ft.) in concert with the Devil's Path or as an out-and-back ascent of Twin Mtn. (3,650 ft.), also employing the Devil's Path. While the notch itself provides little in the way of scenery, its proximity to these two neighboring peaks in the Indian Head Wilderness Area makes it a useful and attractive alternate route for scenic day outings.

This trail begins at the 0.4 mi. point on the Devil's Path (which begins at the Prediger Road trailhead). At the junction of the Devil's Path and Jimmy Dolan Notch Trail, signs are posted.

Jimmy Dolan Notch Trail turns right (west) here, passing through stands of hemlock and soon a pure beech forest. Several seasonal capillaries of the Schoharie Creek will be encountered, but they are unlikely to be evident in summer or early autumn. The trail is rocky, even, and often grassy as it follows the abandoned road. Storybook hemlock forests occupy the middle realms of the trail at 0.5 mi., yielding to sparse hardwood cover as the terrain steepens into the south, with a lively creek to the right (west) through the woods some distance. Late-arriving parties will find many attractive places to camp along this section of trail (there are no established sites), in proximity to the upper Schoharie Creek; stopping here is preferable to camping near the notch, which is difficult to do legally.

The trail climbs steeply but briefly beyond the hemlock stands and into the notch (3,100 ft.) at the junction of the Devil's Path. The notch is named for Jimmy Dolan, who kept a tavern here in the late nineteenth century.

Jimmy Dolan Notch Trail (map 1: B9)

Distance from lower junction with Devil's Path (2,100 ft.) to
- upper junction with Devil's Path (3,110 ft.): 1.4 mi., 1,000 ft., 1 hr. 10 min.

Roaring Kill Trail

Locate the Roaring Kill parking area and trailhead off CR 16, roughly 3.0 mi. from Tannersville where the yellow-marked Roaring Kill Trail goes south. From NY 23A, take Spring Street (CR 16, at the east end of the village), bearing right onto Elka Park Road at roughly 2.0 mi; the trailhead can also be reached from Platte Clove Road (also CR 16) via Dale Lane, 1.0 mi. west of Prediger Road (the Devil's Path trailhead). A signboard is located at the trailhead. The Roaring Kill, lying in view a short distance to the west of the parking area, makes for a worthwhile visit. It flows north and joins the Schoharie Creek headwaters. The area is heavily wooded. Elka Park Road is dirt here, and is not maintained by the town during winter, although it is generally passable. Across Elka Park Road is a section of wild forest that could be used for late-arrival, low-impact camping (legal, undesignated, unestablished). Camping is also possible and close at hand in the flat areas above the trail's initial ascent, in the wilderness area itself. Observe the 150-ft. law to select a legal site.

The trail enters the woods, briefly ascends, and then continues level through mixed hardwood and hemlock over roots and duff soil. Within five or ten minutes, arrive at the junction of Mink Hollow (blue) and Pecoy Notch (blue) trails at elevation of 2,100 ft. Roaring Kill Trail ends here.

Roaring Kill Trail (map 1: B8)

Distance from Roaring Kill parking area on Elka Park Road (1,970 ft.) to
- Pecoy Notch Trail and Mink Hollow Trail (2,100 ft.): 0.3 mi., 150 ft., 15 min.

Pecoy Notch Trail

From the junction of Roaring Kill and Mink Hollow (northern section) trails, Pecoy Notch Trail leaves to the south to join the Devil's Path between Sugarloaf (3,810 ft.) and Twin (3,650 ft.) mtns.

The trail ascends, moving across slope through open hardwoods until reaching an obvious quarry pit, where it levels. A few large stone "flags" are leaning against the mined face just inside the quarry. The trail remains level through sugar maple-and-ash woods and is self-guiding, providing minimal summer views to the east. Uphill to the right (west) is a steep and rugged talus field of fragmented rock and tangled vegetation. Becoming increasingly dense, sugar maple shades the ground cover of spring beauty and trout lily.

The trail enters a shady hemlock stand, at the eastern edge of which is a closed campsite. Additional, legal sites exist on this fairly flat plateau, farther to the south. The trail turns immediately to the left (northeast) after entering the hemlocks (this 90-degree turn is not obvious) and turns east again as it descends to a large, open talus field at 0.7 mi. Excavated from an extensive quarry, the massive stone heap provides open views to the north and east at 2,300 ft. This is Dibble's Quarry. Hikers have assembled a variety of stone art here in fascinating druidic configurations, including a pair of comfortable seats surrounding an arch druid's throne. Such seats are traditional among the better-known quarries of the Catskills, but this is the gold standard of the art form, established to take advantage of the extraordinary view over Platte Clove and Huckleberry Point. As a rule of thumb, always keep in mind that rattlesnakes like quarries too, although they are found primarily in proximity to oak woods.

Twin Mtn. appears across Pecoy Notch on the right. The building with the terra cotta roof is the Hutterian Bruderhof. Kaaterskill High Peak and Roundtop are in the upper-elevation foreground. The trail turns to the right, into the south. Slightly below the trail on the quarry's left (east) side is a large rock overhang, sufficient to shelter several people, but technically illegal (nonconforming) for camping. Hikers will see more tables and chairs of stone in the inner quarry, surrounded by overgrown tailing hillocks and crumbling hut foundations. Standing water near the quarry's faces sometimes encroaches upon the trail. The trail continues straight ahead (south) until once again entering hardwoods, at 1.0 mi. crossing a footbridge over a nameless tributary of the Schoharie Creek. The trail ascends thereafter, turning left (east) along the edge of an open marsh and beaver pond/meadow at 1.3 mi., with views of the northern face of Sugarloaf Mtn. (3,810 ft.) to the right (south).

Turning south and becoming steeper, the trail penetrates the heavily wooded notch. There are no views, except for the shoulder of Sugarloaf to the right (west) and sparse winter vistas to the north and south. Camping possibilities are poor in this rugged terrain, improving both east and west along the Devil's Path, ahead. The trail reaches the notch at 1.5 mi. The only suitable campsite within the notch itself is closed permanently (impacted, nonconforming). Pecoy Notch was named for a glassmaker named Pecor who operated in the Plains (called the "Glass Plains," because the broken, discarded glass reflected in the sunlight and appeared as a plain from the mountain) of the upper Sawkill Valley on the south side of the Devil's Path range. The word's transformation to Pecoy was a typographic error.

Pecoy Notch Trail (map 1: B8)

Distances from junction with Roaring Kill Trail and Mink Hollow Trail (2,100 ft.) to
- Dibble's Quarry (2,300 ft.): 0.7 mi., 300 ft. (rev. 100 ft.), 30 min.
- Devil's Path at Pecoy Notch (2,810 ft.): 1.5 mi., 800 ft., 1 hr. 10 min.

Mink Hollow Trail (south of Devil's Path)

This trail is popular with day hikers, cross-country skiers, and backpackers who are headed for the craggy Devil's Path. It is not scenic with vistas, but it features extremely attractive forest, imparting the rugged, deep-woods motif of the Indian Head Wilderness with its steep, rocky scree and ledge slopes.

The trail is used frequently by cross-country skiers and occasionally by mountain bikers, and as a result, it has been designated a primitive bicycle corridor.

The trail begins at the top of Mink Hollow Road in the hamlet of Lake Hill, a few miles west of Woodstock off NY 212. From NY 212, drive 2.9 miles to the end of Mink Hollow Road. Parking is good at the trailhead, where a kiosk displays forest preserve information. Be careful to avoid private property, access to which is shared briefly by the trail. The distance from the parking lot to the lean-to is 2.4 mi., with 1,100 ft. of elevation gain. The trail leaves the parking lot to the north and passes around a barrier gate by the trail register, in moments crossing a brook, and continues along the stream's edge. Ascending, the trail crosses the stream again near a small, crumbling abutment, which could date to the road's construction in the late 1700s (perhaps the earliest road built in the interior Catskills).

The trail steepens. Hemlock pockets and large, isolated hardwoods lead to extensive stands of beech as elevation is gained. The ledgy terrain makes excellent habitat for bear and bobcat, which are sometimes seen (or heard). Most of the hollow is a deer winter-concentration area owing to its protected, south-facing slope; it has also been identified as important habitat for the northern water shrew, which likes good ground cover near cold water. Birds and other wildlife abound, and the hollow is a good place to listen for them. It is possible that you might see the hairy woodpecker.

As the trail approaches the saddle, it steepens dramatically before leveling again on its final approach to the height-of-land where the lean-to is located. You'll wonder how oxen could have pulled their heavy burdens of passengers and uncured hides over the mountain to the tanneries in Hunter.

The area surrounding the Mink Hollow lean-to (2,680 ft.) is marked with No Camping signs as the result of previous, heavy impact. There is little in the way of suitable group tent space nearby. The setting is forested with stocky beech, birch, and maple trees. A small colony of common burdock (sunflower family) grows in front of the lean-to. Within view of the lean-to to the north is the Devil's Path intersection, so there is frequently foot traffic close by. The hollow's southerly aspect provides sunlight until late afternoon, dramatically illuminating the craggy western slopes of Sugarloaf. Strong winds will tunnel through the hollow noisily, lending to the remote atmosphere—and the windchill factor.

Mink Hollow Trail (south of Devil's Path, map 1: B8–C8)

Distance from end of Mink Hollow Road (1,510 ft.) to
  • Devil's Path (2,610 ft.): 2.4 mi., 1,100 ft., 1 hr. 45 min.

Mink Hollow Trail (north of Devil's Path)

Enter Mink Hollow Trail from Roaring Kill Trail, which begins at the Roaring Brook parking area on Elka Park Road (seasonally maintained).

Locate the Roaring Kill parking area and trailhead off CR 16 roughly 3.0 mi. from Tannersville, where the yellow-marked Roaring Kill Trail goes south. From NY 23A, take Spring Street (CR 16, at the east end of the village), bearing right onto Elka Park Road at roughly 2.0 mi., and look for the trailhead on the right (south) side of the road. The trailhead can also be reached from Platte Clove Road (also CR 16) via Dale Lane, 1.0 mi. west of Prediger Road (the Devil's Path trailhead). The trail is used frequently by cross-country skiers and occasionally by mountain bikers, and as a result, it has been designated a primitive bicycle corridor,

A signboard is located at the trailhead. This is the longer of the two options for climbing Sugarloaf Mtn. from the north (the shorter is Pecoy Notch Trail). Each trail is interesting and many hike Sugarloaf as a loop, using both. At the trail junctions of Roaring Brook, Pecoy Notch, and Mink Hollow trails, bear right (west).

The trail is flat through a maple woods with ledges and scree along the northerly slopes. The forest type shifts to mixed hardwood as, off to the northeast, Roundtop Mtn. (3,440 ft.) and the Blackhead Range can be seen (seasonally). The trail follows an early quarry road that washes out occasionally. Talus piles are seen, heaped with forest litter, along with quarry pits and a few identifiable hut foundations. The high ridges of Sugarloaf Mtn. come into view during the leafless months. Hemlock pockets take hold in the mossy, ledgy terrain as a larger, well-preserved quarry is encountered at 0.6 mi. (2,500 ft.) at a bend in the trail. Here an old dirt road leaves to the right (west) onto private property, over which the original quarry road descended through the Roaring Kill Valley to Mink Hollow Road. Turning left (east) here, the trail rises through wind-ravaged terrain, where blowdowns are common, and swings into the south as the long ridge of Plateau Mtn. (3,850 ft.) and Spruce Top (3,380 ft.) appear immediately to the northwest. A shallow rock overhang appears along the trail at 2,800 ft., where yellow-paint blazes denote the state-land boundary, and a lookout point appears on the right (northwest) looking across Mink Hollow, directly at the eastern ramparts of Plateau Mtn. and beyond into the Schoharie Valley. The route turns back on itself nearly 180 degrees here. Descending, in continuous view of Plateau Mtn., you turn to witness Sugarloaf's western ridge, looming ahead as the trail flattens. At 2.2 mi., in a bowl formed by the head of Roaring Kill Hollow, cross a rustic handmade footbridge, the stringers of which were cut from a solitary grove of virgin, standing hemlock (you might still see the flat-sawn stump in the streambed downhill) that would have outlived the bridge itself by decades. Sadly, this shallow creek does not require such an elaborate—and, in terms of labor, costly—construction. The original bridge with its still-visible bluestone abutments was necessary only for wagons carrying heavy loads.

Ascending now, you approach the hollow. Arrive at the junction with the Devil's Path in dense hardwoods at 2.3 mi. Bear right (west) on the Devil's Path (red), 0.2 mi. to the junction with the southern section of Mink Hollow Trail, and the Mink Hollow lean-to (see Mink Hollow Trail, south of Devil's Path).

Mink Hollow Trail (north of Devil's Path, map 1: B8)

Distance from junction with Roaring Kill Trail and Pecoy Notch Trail (2,100 ft.) to
 • Devil's Path (2,610 ft.): 2.3 mi., 700 ft. (rev. 200 ft.), 1 hr. 20 min.

Catskill Center for Conservation and Development (CCCD) Trail, Platte Clove Section (Platte Clove Preserve)

This trail begins at the CCCD's Platte Clove Preserve on Platte Clove Road, a few hundred feet west of the small cabin that the CCCD uses for its artist-in-residence program. The preserve is located on Platte Clove Road (CR 16). Travel southwest off NY 23A onto Spring Street from the east end of the village in Tannersville, 0.25 mi. east of the light. At 1.9 mi., CR 16 turns into Platte Clove Road, bearing left (southeast). The CCCD Preserve is identified with signs on the right (south) side of Platte Clove Road at 6.4 mi.

This trail is the shortest, prettiest trail in the Indian Head Wilderness Area. It is perhaps the most popular approach to Indian Head summit. Find the Platte Clove Nature Preserve Trail a few hundred feet northwest of the artist's residence on the south side of CR 16 (Platte Clove Road, unmaintained from November 15 to April 15). Parking is poor and often limited on the road's widened south shoulder adjacent to the trailhead, but additional space is available in the Kaaterskill High Peak Wild Forest parking area 0.25 mi. southeast of the preserve off Platte Clove Road (see Kaaterskill Wild Forest).

The trailhead is identified and marked with the CCCD's diamond-shaped green markers. You may also see some of the older markers: green arrows on rectangular silver backgrounds. Destination signage and Long Path blazes are in place at this time. The trail descends slightly to the head-waters of the Plattekill Creek, crossing a bridge. Just across the creek, the trail ascends gently, following to the right of the old road, which is for some distance a deeply eroded drainage ditch, worn several feet deep into the duff and soft silt subsoil. The area is densely foliated with a predominance of hemlock and assorted hardwood cover. Soon the trail assumes the original roadbed, in a very pretty setting where smooth surface bedrock has resisted erosion. A nameless tributary of the Plattekill crosses the stone trail, rarely exceeding a depth of several inches.

Within twenty minutes or so of the trailhead, the trail passes a quarry close on the left (east). Much of the talus has been reclaimed by nature, buried in moss and duff. These tailing piles can be explored easily, but this particular site is inferior (as quarries go) and less accessible than the highly attractive (and scenic) Codfish Point quarry, just ahead off Overlook Trail. Use caution—footing is poor, the ledge pools are often deep and flooded, there are a few substantial pits (as in most quarries), and although they are seldom reported and this is not an identified den site, rattlesnakes prefer this kind of dry, ledgy (but typically more remote) habitat as opposed to the moist surrounding forest.

At 1.0 mi., and a very short distance beyond the quarry, on state land, CCCD Trail ends where the Devil's Path (red) comes in from the right (west) from its Prediger Road trailhead (this junction is poorly marked). The Devil's Path turns right (southwest) to Indian Head only a two-minute walk farther south at the junction of Overlook Trail (which is a continuation of the Old Overlook Road). Devil's Kitchen lean-to (popular, often occupied) is 0.2 mi. ahead on Overlook Trail, situated alongside the Cold Kill (see Overlook Trail for details).

Catskill Center for Conservation and Development (CCCD) Trail, Platte Clove Section (Platte Clove Preserve, map 1: B9)

Distance from Platte Clove Road (1,830 ft.) to
- junction with Devil's Path and Overlook Trail (2,230 ft.): 1.0 mi., 400 ft., 40 min.

Plattekill Falls Trail

This short path leads to a picturesque waterfall at the head of Platte Clove. The Platte Clove Preserve, located at the top of precipitous Platte Clove on CR 16, is owned and maintained by the Catskill Center for Conservation and Development (CCCD), a nonprofit, member-supported conservation advocacy organization (see CCCD Trail, Platte Clove Section). The preserve is posted and well identified. Hikers are permitted to visit the property year-round. The center maintains a cottage on Platte Clove Road that is used seasonally by its artist-in-residence program. There are two trails on the preserve. One goes south from a point just west of the cottage; the other leaves from the roadside 200 ft. west of the cottage.

Follow the old roadbed east, keeping the red CCCD cottage to your right and keeping an eye out for the green, diamond Platte Clove Nature Preserve Trail markers and even some of the older CCCD arrow markers. Within 300 ft., bear right at the first fork (unmarked) and descend into a hemlock forest. As the trail drops steeply, it turns back to the right (west). Avoid the unmarked spur to the left, particularly in winter, because it comes dangerously close to the vertical wall of the clove (it is possible to slide on the steep, icy surface with no means of arrest). The trail follows a slope above the Plattekill, soon arriving at the picturesque falls, which are about 50 ft. high and normally run year-round. This is the end of the footpath.

Plattekill Falls Trail (map 1: B9)
Distance from Platte Clove Road (1,830 ft.) to
  • Plattekill Falls (1,670 ft.): 0.2 mi., 0 ft. (rev. 150 ft.), 10 min.

Echo Lake Spur Trail

Echo Lake is a secluded pond lying to the north of Overlook Mtn. Its lean-to has made it a popular spot for both backpackers heading for the Devil's Path and day hikers coming in from Meads on Overlook Mtn. Trail.

From Overlook Trail (1.3 mi. north of the intersection with Overlook Mtn. Trail), Echo Lake Trail drops downhill into the west (yellow markers). A descent of 450 ft. follows over the next 0.6 mi. The lean-to is situated on the north shore and is sometimes subject to noisy weekend visitors.

Additional (legal) campsites exist to the east, where the trail follows the lakeshore for some distance.

Echo Lake is a fragile and popular spot that is subjected to high-use quotas—staying within the legal parameters of camping will help to preserve this area. Echoes are good and were touted as a tourist attraction here during the heyday of the Overlook Mountain House.

Echo Lake Spur Trail (map 1: C9)

Distance from Overlook Trail (2,530 ft.) to
  • Echo Lake lean-to (2,070 ft.): 0.6 mi., 0 ft. (rev. 450 ft.), 20 min.

Codfish Point Spur Trail

This spur off of Overlook Trail provides the only summer views along the approach to Overlook Mtn. from the north. It is identified by a single yellow trail disk and is barely noticeable from Overlook Trail.

At a point 0.6 mi. above (southeast) the Devil's Kitchen lean-to, just as the trail levels and turns south to follow the eastern edge of Plattekill Mtn., the Codfish Point spur goes east. It is a vague but well-established footpath. Two large, flat puddingstones on the west side of Overlook Trail, in the woods just opposite the spur, act as convenient markers (42° 06.776' N, 74° 04.656' W).

The spur trail begins level and descends slightly along the edge of the quarry, ending above an extensive, treeless talus field with an open easterly view of the Hudson Valley. The Saugerties lighthouse can be seen at 125 degrees. Tivoli Marsh is visible on the east side of the river behind Cruger and Magdalen islands. Far into the east are farms—silos, barns, cultivated hillsides—in Columbia and Dutchess counties. Overlook Mtn. and the fire tower can be seen at 218 degrees; the rock outcropping on the eastern slope is the Minister's Face. The Hudson Highlands (loosely defined by the definitive cut in the river between Storm King Mtn. and Breakneck Point, just north of West Point) appear at 190 degrees. In the Shawangunks you see Guyot Hill and Bonticou Crag.

No Camping signs are posted in the quarry itself, which extends hundreds of feet south. Bits of old crockery, hand-tooled stones, and hut foundations conjure up images of quarrying days. As in many bluestone quarries, abandoned stones show evidence of manual tool work and lie among the piles. Against the vertical, working face of the pits, water gathers in shallow pools. Jim Morton, a lifelong resident of Platte Clove, tells the story of his grandfather, a quarryman who together with his coworkers was snowed in at the quarry for several days in the winter of 1890. Having finished all the tinned food available, they were reduced to the last few crates of salt cod, which they detested. In protest, and to identify the snowed-in quarry road for their "rescue" party, they nailed a piece of codfish crate to a tree. This marker remained in place for years, giving the point its name.

Stones from this quarry and others were used to pave the sidewalks of New York City and other Hudson River towns and were shipped in sailing vessels. Some may well have ended up as far away as Havana, Cuba, a regular destination for Catskill bluestone.

Codfish Point Spur Trail (map 1: C9)

Distance from Overlook Trail (2,530 ft.) to
• Codfish Point Lookout (2,470 ft.): 0.8 mi., 0 ft. (rev. 50 ft.), 25 min.

Warner Creek Trail
(section north of Silver Hollow Notch)

This section of the Long Path was created in 2007 and 2008 by members of the Catskill Mountain Club. The following summer it was improved upon by members of the ADK trail maintenance crew. The trail is a significant and long-awaited improvement for Long Path hikers, who can now save themselves the extra distance and inconvenience of walking the road between Edgewood and Devil's Tombstone. The new trail is the northerly continuation of the existing Warner Creek Trail (see Phoenicia-Mt. Tobias Wild Forest). Silver Hollow Notch Spur Trail provides access from NY 214 to this section of Warner Creek Trail.

In Silver Hollow Notch, trail marking is good (blue markers), with new signage at an otherwise obscure intersection. Striking northeast, the trail switches up the southern slope of Plateau Mtn. through open hardwood and ledgy terrain. It is considerably more self-guiding than the southerly section of Warner Creek Trail because there is less rock. Twenty minutes into the hike the trail levels and views appear to the south. A spur leaves to the right several hundred feet to a lookout point highlighting Tremper Mtn. Wittenberg can be seen (Slide is hidden), as well as Ashokan High Point. Immediately after passing a low, vertical ledge next to the trail, another vista lies 100 ft. to the left, and another is seen on the right, within a fifteen-minute hike. Views improve ahead. The trail levels onto a long saddle as it approaches the ridge. The forest turns subalpine at 3,000 ft., with cherry, balsam, and birch appearing, and becomes more interesting. This mixed scrub gives way to some beautiful, large specimens of red spruce. A dense woods of small, even-aged spruce-fir follows, where the footway is soft, and the trail descends slightly. The ridge of Plateau Mtn. can sometimes be seen ahead. Another vista appears to the right. Ascending again, the hiker encounters the 3,500-ft. marker, where a spring lies to the right, 500 ft. to the east. There tends to be very little standing water here, so filtering is advised. The last (and best) vista is a small open ledge immediately to the right of the trail. This provides a sweeping view to the south, including the high peaks of the Slide Mountain Wilderness Area. A final, steep ascent, followed by a relaxed stroll through boreal woods, leads to the trail junction with the Devil's Path (red markers).

Warner Creek Trail (map 1: B8)

Distance from Silver Hollow Notch (2,350 ft.) to
• Devil's Path (3,810 ft.): 2.9 mi., 1,600 ft. (rev. 150 ft.), 2 hr. 15 min.

Silver Hollow Notch Spur Trail

This yellow-marked spur is the ingress-egress for hikers wishing to reach the Long Path from NY 214. There is no designated trail on the south side of the notch (into Willow). The trail follows a seasonal streambed, intersecting with Warner Creek Trail 1.0 mi. from NY 214. Parking is not very secure, because there is no designated area, and it's therefore not patrolled.

Silver Hollow Notch Spur Trail (map 1: B8)

Distance from NY 214 (1,750 ft.) to
• Warner Creek Trail (2,350 ft.): 1.0 mi., 600 ft., 50 min.

SUGGESTED HIKES

Easy Hike

Plattekill Falls Trail [rt: 0.4 mi., 0:20]. A short, easy descent to a 50-ft. waterfall.

Moderate Hike

Codfish Point Quarry via CCCD Trail, Overlook Trail [rt: 3.6 mi., 3:00]. An interesting and attractive hike through old quarry areas to an easterly lookout over the Hudson Valley. This quarry provides a fairly well-preserved example of a mid-nineteenth-century bluestone quarrying operation. (See Overlook Mountain Wild Forest for Codfish Point Spur and Overlook Trail descriptions.)

Strenuous Hikes

The Devil's Path [ow: 24.45 mi., 2 days]. A difficult and challenging end-to-end hike that is often thru-hiked in two to three days by avid hikers. This scenic and arduous route offers many opportunities for section hiking.

Echo Lake Trail, via Overlook Mtn. Trail [rt: 7.4 mi., 5:00]. A rigorous climb followed by a long descent to one of the Catskills' few natural lakes, a pretty spot with a lean-to and several tent sites. (See Overlook Mountain Wild Forest for Overlook Mtn. Trail description.)

Indian Head Mtn. via CCCD Trail, Devil's Path [rt: 6.0 mi., 4:30]. Excellent southerly views and a rugged, often steep approach over several high, scenic outcroppings has made this summit a very popular destination hike.

Twin Mtn. via Roaring Kill Trail, Pecoy Notch Trail [rt: 4.6 mi., 4:00]. An interesting double summit with fine southerly views across the Catskill high peaks and the eastern Hudson Valley.

Plateau Mtn. via Devil's Path, Stony Clove trailhead [rt: 6.0 mi., 4:30]. This very steep southeastward climb out of Stony Clove switches its way up to a long, flat plateau. The dense spruce-fir forest opens here and there to provide several interesting far-flung views to the east and north.

SECTION 8
OVERLOOK MOUNTAIN WILD FOREST

This small, 590-acre parcel of wild forest is joined to the Indian Head Wilderness Area and lies within the Ulster County town of Woodstock. Overlook's summit (3,150 ft.) and fire tower are the forest's main attraction for hikers, who often continue north to camp at Echo Lake (in the Indian Head Wilderness Area) or gain access to the Devil's Path. The Overlook Wild Forest is also the location of the Overlook Mountain House ruins, which still stand beneath the mountain's summit along the hiking trail.

Overlook Mtn., the large cornerstone peak seen from the NYS Thruway and from areas to the east, forms the southeasternmost limits of the Escarpment. The mountain is often represented in the paintings of Thomas Cole and other members of the Hudson River School, and it is believed that Cole himself gave the mountain its name in 1847 (it was previously called South Peak). Later artists were drawn to the scenic Saw Kill Valley, among them Ralph Whitehead and Hervey White, who founded the Byrdcliffe Summer School of Art in Woodstock.

Overlook's fire tower is stewarded by volunteers and attracts thousands of day hikers each year. Views from the summit are among the best in the Hudson Valley, including the interior Catskills and Shawangunks, the Hudson Highlands, Taconics, Berkshires, and beyond. An equal number of hikers are drawn to the hotel ruins, a hazard the state has considered dismantling. The existing ruin is that of the third and last mountain house at this site. The first mountain house was built in 1871 and burned in 1874. The second (1878) burned in 1924, at which time it was rebuilt with concrete.

The Depression slowed the building's construction, and during the Second World War it was boarded up. The Department of Environmental Conservation advises hikers to stay out of the ruins, parts of which have collapsed.

Overlook Mtn. Trail

Overlook Mtn. Trail provides a simple, moderately strenuous, and very popular day hike to the mountain house ruins and fire tower, with one of the best Catskill Mtn. views available. From the Woodstock village green in the colorful heart of town, turn north off Tinker Street onto Rock City Road. (This spot is 2.8 miles from the forest preserve access parking area at the Overlook Mtn. trailhead.) Within moments the associated ridges of Overlook Mtn. and the Indian Head Wilderness Area appear; Woodstock was settled by artists because of this landscape. Soon Overlook Summit and the fire tower are seen toward the eastern (right) edge of the ridge. At 0.6 mi. from the green, go straight through the four-way intersection of Glasco (glass company) Turnpike, where Rock City Road becomes Meads Mtn. Road. Continue steeply uphill to the trailhead.

The trail begins at the apex of Meads Mtn. Road, opposite the Tibetan Buddhist monastery, Karma Triyana Dharmachakra. At the trailhead, there are close-up views of several mountains—most notably Indian Head—and hikers have a considerable elevation gain already behind them. Now at 1,800 ft., there are only 1,300 ft. remaining to climb Overlook, making this perhaps the easiest hike with such a remarkable scenic payoff in all of the Catskills (with the possible exception of Giant Ledge).

Signs and a map kiosk are located here. Follow the red markers. The trail climbs, following the fire- and radio-tower maintenance road, a road originally pioneered by tanners and quarry workers and improved by the builders of the Overlook Mountain House (1871). Mountain laurel, hemlock, and oak characterize the foliage of this consistent and moderately strenuous ascent. The total elevation gain of 1,300 ft. translates into a 520-ft.-per-mile rise (1,000 ft. per mile and above is considered steep for the Catskills). Hikers may encounter skiers, sledders, walkers, other hikers and backpackers, joggers, mountain bikers, artists, photographers, birders, picnickers, families, forest rangers, tie-dyed members of the Rainbow Tribe—even the Dalai Lama, who has enjoyed walking in the area. This trailhead is often used by thru-hikers headed for the Devil's Path and points west.

Views of the Ashokan Reservoir appear in the southwest as elevation is gained, and Indian Head, among other ridgelines in the neighboring wilderness area, can be seen to the north (all views from the road are dwarfed by those from the fire tower). At 2,900 ft., the trail passes the drab and haunting skeletal remains of the Overlook Mountain House. Adjacent to it is the new transmission tower, against which local residents and environmentalists fought desperately. The open, roofless ruins (and the nearby annex) are in certain areas unsafe, and unit management plans have called for their removal at some point. Inside the main hall, trees reaching 8 to 10 inches in diameter are growing vigorously. Intent upon demonstrating the hotel's visual history, local artists at one point decorated the walls with fascinating printed information and photos. These biodegradable artworks have dissolved (the posters were ingeniously made with fertilizer that fosters tree growth).

Just a few minutes' walk uphill from the hotel site, at 1.8 mi., the trail arrives at the junction with Overlook Trail. Overlook Mtn. Trail bears right (east) at the junction and ascends, passing a number of unmarked spur trails that the Department of Environmental Conservation (DEC) has placed off-limits, then passes a small, strip-mined red-shale pit (it was used for road improvement and paint in the early days). Continuing the easy ascent, the trail wraps around the mountain through ledges, approaching the summit from the southeast. The trail becomes a footpath as it goes past the observer's cabin on the right and continues to the tower. On summer weekends the tower is open and staffed, and the cab can be entered. (For safety, only six people at a time should climb the tower, according to the DEC.) If the cab is closed, visitors can still climb to the highest flight of steps and survey the stunning scenery—easily ranking among the best Catskill views. (There are some views to the west at ground level here, which can be enjoyed by disabled hikers. The state is reviewing extending access plans with the aid of the New York State Office of Advocate for Persons with Disabilities. Handicapped access, according to the DEC, may include the use, under permit, of four-wheel-drive vehicles or ATVs.) A compass won't work here because of the steel superstructure, and there are so many mountains that identifying individuals is difficult.

A piece of the mountain blocks a small easterly valley view. Observers can see bridges spanning the Hudson River from both Kingston and Rhinecliff. The Esopus Meadows lighthouse can be seen with binoculars in a widening of the river south of Kingston. Mills Mansion can be identified to the left of the lighthouse on the east shore. In the Shawangunks, you see the Trapps, Eagle Cliff, Sky Top Tower, Guyot Hill (named for Arnold Guyot, the Princeton geologist and founder of the National Weather Service—he measured all the major Catskill peaks), and Bonticou Crag. Moving west into the high-peaks area, Slide Mtn. dominates a congregation of peaks above and beyond Cooper Lake. The peak just above Cooper Lake and to the right is Mt. Tobias (2,550 ft.). Left of Cooper Lake is Mt. Guardian (two-peaked). To the right of the cellular tower is Carl Mtn. (2,880 ft.) and next to it, Tremper Mtn. (2,740 ft.). Beyond Tremper and to the right is the West Kill Wilderness Area. To the north are close-ups of the Indian Head Wilderness Area, including all of its mountains—Plattekill (3,110 ft.), Indian Head (3,573 ft.), Twin (3,650 ft.), Sugarloaf (3,810 ft.), and Plateau (3,850 ft.). Kaaterskill High Peak (3,655 ft.) and Roundtop (3,440 ft.) in the Kaaterskill Wild Forest are plainly visible in the north, and beyond them are the Blackhead Mtns.

In addition to these views, another scenic, more private area is located at the end of a trail that goes to the right of the observer's cabin and past the outhouse to a ledge looking south. The landscape painter Charles Lanman named this Eagle's Cliff after a legend in which a small Indian child was stolen away from its mother by an eagle (*vertical drops here are very dangerous*). Mt. Everett, at the Massachusetts–New York–Connecticut border, can be seen from here, as can the Slide Mountain Wilderness Area, so this vantage offers sensational, sweeping views even to those who are reluctant to climb the tower. The large beige strip of wetland on the Hudson's east shore at 130 degrees is Tivoli Marsh. You can see the main dam on the Ashokan Reservoir (the last of the handmade dams, circa 1914) and the dividing weir at 228 degrees, with Ashokan High Point rising beyond the west basin.

Overlook Mtn. Trail (map 1: C9)

Distances from Meads Mtn. Road trailhead (1,770 ft.) to
- Overlook Trail (2,950 ft.): 1.8 mi., 1,200 ft., 1 hr. 30 min.
- Overlook Mtn. summit (3,150 ft.): 2.1 mi., 1,400 ft., 1 hr. 45 min.

Overlook Trail

This popular trail connects the Overlook Wild Forest to the trail system of the Indian Head Wilderness, in particular the Devil's Path. Combining the two (with the destination of West Kill summit and beyond) will provide hikers with extended outings of up to 30 mi. in length. The trail is used frequently by cross-country skiers and occasionally by mountain bikers, and as a result, it has been designated a primitive bicycle corridor,

The trail begins at the 1.8-mi. point of Overlook Mtn. Trail, 0.3 mi. below Overlook's summit, and descends gently, passing around a barrier gate onto what is sometimes still referred to as the Old Overlook Road (blue markers), which goes north to Platte Clove Road. Various remains of the Overlook Mountain House's barns and support structures lie in the general vicinity, slowly disappearing into the underbrush. Water, flowing across the trail from a spring on the right side of the trail at 0.4 mi., is absent by early summer. Views of the Indian Head Wilderness Area develop to the northwest as the trail descends and slowly curves around to the east in a northern hardwood forest of sugar maple, beech, and yellow birch. The trail's surface is gravel and stone. Mountain laurel appears and the terrain flattens as the trail turns slowly left to the northeast. At 1.3 mi., the Echo Lake Trail heads downhill to the left (west).

Continue straight as the trail heads due north and levels along the eastern slope of Plattekill Mtn. Summer views of the Hudson Valley are limited. At the point where the trail swings farthest into the west (directly beneath Plattekill Mtn.) it passes Skunk Spring on the left. This spring has been improved somewhat but is very easy to miss unless water is flowing across the trail. The trail soon climbs gently, leveling out again as it passes a vague but established spur trail on the right. A solitary yellow marker exists at this time, indicating the short path to Codfish Point, the only uninterrupted view available from Overlook Trail (see Codfish Point Quarry Spur Trail).

Hereafter the trail descends, turning northwest, at 3.5 mi. reaching the footbridge spanning the Cold Kill, and shortly afterward (in view) the Devil's Kitchen lean-to. The stone remains of a charcoal kiln, the creek's original namesake (Coal Kill), exist on the left of the trail near the lean-to. A large quarry lies against the western slope above the trail as it descends, where remnant foundation corners and moss-laden talus slopes are evident. Below the lean-to and off the trail, the Cold Kill flows northeast into precipitous Platte Clove, first dropping over 100-ft. Black Chasm Falls, a waterfall used by ice climbers and considered dangerous because of its remote location and steep terrain (it has claimed lives in recent years). At 3.6 mi., the Devil's Path is reached at the point where it leaves to the west to ascend Indian Head Mtn. This is the end of Overlook Trail, but the Old Overlook Road continues north 1.0 mi. to Platte Clove Road over the Catskill Center for Conservation and Development (CCCD) Trail. That trail can be found another few hundred feet north, at a point where the Devil's Path joins Overlook Trail, coming in from the east from the Prediger Road trailhead parking area and the beginning of the Devil's Path. To identify the junction, pay close attention—marking is poor.

Overlook Trail (map 1: C9)

Distances from Overlook Mtn. Trail (2,950 ft.) to
- Echo Lake Spur Trail (2,530 ft.): 1.3 mi., 0 ft. (rev. 400 ft.), 40 min.
- Codfish Point Quarry Spur Trail (2,530 ft.): 2.8 mi., 0 ft., 1 hr. 25 min.
- Devil's Path (2,230 ft.): 3.6 mi., 0 ft. (rev. 300 ft.), 1 hr. 50 min.

SUGGESTED HIKES

Moderate Hike

Codfish Point Quarry Spur Trail via CCCD Trail, Overlook Trail

[rt: 3.6 mi., 3:00]. An interesting and attractive hike through old quarry areas to an easterly lookout over the Hudson Valley. This quarry provides a fairly well-preserved example of a mid-nineteenth-century bluestone quarrying operation. (See Indian Head Wilderness for CCCD Trail description.)

Strenuous Hike

Echo Lake Trail, via Overlook Mtn. Trail [rt: 7.4 mi., 5:00]. A rigorous climb followed by a long descent to one of the Catskills' few natural lakes, a pretty spot with a lean-to and several tent sites. (See Indian Head Wilderness for Echo Lake Trail description.)

SECTION 9
PHOENICIA-MOUNT TOBIAS WILD FOREST

There are six mountains with elevations greater than 2,500 ft. in this wild forest, of which Tremper Mtn. (2,740 ft.) is the most prominent and most often hiked. At 7,300 acres, this wild forest is nearly as large as a wilderness area. It includes Tremper Mtn., Mt. Tobias, and Torrens Hook. There are 11 mi. of foot trails and two lean-tos, one on Tremper's summit and the Baldwin Memorial lean-to. Minimum elevation is 780 ft., maximum elevation is 3,000 ft. The wild forest is bounded on the south by NY 28, in the west by NY 214, and in the north by the Indian Head Wilderness. To the east is Silver Hollow Road in the hamlet of Woodstock.

The rerouting of the Long Path through Silver Hollow and more recently to Plateau Mtn. in the Indian Head Wilderness (to save hikers from walking the road miles to Mink Hollow) has made Silver Hollow Mtn. (3,000 ft.) accessible from Tremper's summit, also providing more direct access to the Indian Head Wilderness Area and the Devil's Path. Tremper Mtn.'s fire tower provides a panoramic view that attracts the public year-round, often bringing large numbers of hikers to this relatively low and otherwise viewless summit.

The mountain's two attractively situated lean-tos shelter many backpackers and provide respite for an increasing number of Long Path hikers. Warner Creek Trail (Long Path reroute) provides visitors to this area with one of the few north–south links between the Southern and Northeast Catskills and crosses a high valley in a remote setting where pristine Warner's Creek spans the hollow. Additional trails in the management unit are planned for the Mt. Tobias and Torrens Hook parcels in the near future. An unmarked but increasingly popular old woods road, referred to as the Tanbark Trail by the Department of Environmental Conservation (DEC), follows the Tremper Mtn. ridge above Phoenicia and may be maintained for use under permit by several users.

Tremper Mtn.'s appeal is enhanced by its position in the center of a vast bowl formed by much higher mountains and considerably larger forests and wilderness areas. Slopes in the unit are generally very steep, but the trails follow old tanbark, quarry, and fire tower maintenance roads that switchback frequently and allow easy but steady climbing through the transitional hemlock, white pine, and northern hardwood forests.

Mt. Tremper Corners, situated at the southeastern extreme of the wild forest area at the crossroads of NY 212 and CR 40, was the site of an early fortification of the Continental Army (Great Fort Shandaken, 1779). Placed at a strategic location in the narrow flats of the upper Esopus Valley between Tremper Mtn. and Romer Mtn., the fortification guarded against surprise raiding parties of British soldiers, Tories, and their Mohawk allies who used such easily traveled lowland routes to raid the Hudson Valley settlements from the north and west. After the Revolutionary War, the area followed development patterns typical of the Catskill Mountains, giving rise to sawmills, tanneries, bluestone quarries, and, later, furniture factories and railroads.

Hikers can examine the remnants and scars left by the quarry mines of yesteryear but are advised to use caution while exploring Tremper Mtn.'s quarries, one of which lies close to the trail. According to the DEC, this quarry has one of the largest documented timber rattlesnake concentrations on the southern slopes of the Catskills. These otherwise shy and reclusive creatures are most active on sunny and warm spring days, when they can be found lying among the warm rocks and slabs in the quarries. Hikers are more likely to see deer, bear, wild turkeys, ground squirrels, snowshoe and cottontail rabbits, and—with any luck—bobcats. Hikers who enjoy fishing are advised to come prepared—the Tremper Mtn. trailhead is located next to the Esopus Creek in an area of easy public access. Supplies are available in Phoenicia, 1.7 mi. west on CR 40.

Phoenicia Trail

Tremper Mtn. (2,740 ft.) has long been a popular climb because of its fire tower and easy access from the nearby tourist towns of Phoenicia and Woodstock. As a result of its increasing use, the trailhead has been moved farther east along CR 40 (between Phoenicia and Mt. Tremper Corners), where a large parking area is located. The addition of a Long Path link accessible from the summit, running from Carl Mtn. through Silver Hollow and joining the Devil's Path in the Indian Head Wilderness (created so hikers could avoid walking the road miles along NY 212), is an attractive hike in itself and will host a growing number of thru-hikers.

Tremper Mtn. has the "feel" of a large mountain, as many hikers have noted of its stiff southwestern approach, long known as Phoenicia Trail. The mountain can also be climbed "the back way," up the path less taken from Jessop Road in the town of Willow, a more interesting hike involving less vertical rise but more distance (see Willow Trail). Hikers often arrange for shuttles to enable a loop hike of both trails, although parking is problematic at Willow Trail trailhead. Phoenicia Trail provides the most direct and practical route for the visiting day hiker. The fire tower, without which there are only limited easterly views from Tremper Mtn., assures the mountain's popularity with day hikers, and two lean-tos and a spring contribute to its practical appeal as an overnight destination.

Enter the trail from CR 40, a mile or so southeast of Phoenicia and 2 mi. northwest of Tremper Corners. Romer Mtn. (2,240 ft.) can be seen to the southwest from the parking lot. The trail begins next to the road and sign kiosk, where two wooden bridges lead to a string of stone steps. The path levels as it heads north-northwest to join the truck trail at 0.5 mi. The trail then turns right (northeast) at the trail register, following along a flat section through hardwood forest, where rocks have been laid across the road to check seasonal runoff, a system that appears to be working well at this time. Large isolated hemlocks (the trail was originally a bark road) and a few giant oaks break the overstory of sugar maples as the trail climbs steadily to the first of a series of switchbacks, turning a long gradual arc into the south. Ledges appear uphill, and the large talus pile of an early quarry is evident on the left (north), its original roadbed visible. This side path can be followed to a high, right-angled rock face where the slabs were removed. The DEC has documented the existence of rattlesnake dens in this quarry, something hikers might want to consider before exploring it.

Phoenicia Trail continues to ascend, switches back again, and relaxes somewhat, becoming grassy as it travels through beautiful, open hardwood forest and winds its way past the Baldwin Memorial lean-to on the right (southeast) at 2.0 mi. (2,150 ft.). There are no summer views from here. A short distance uphill on the left at 2.1 mi. is a piped spring, after which the trail bears slowly around into the northeast, maintaining its bearing uphill as the down slope forest cover turns to a welcome stand of evergreens. At 2.85 mi., the Tremper Mtn. lean-to is reached, and at 2.9 mi. is the summit, where the tower stands in a small open patch of grass and rock enclosed by red oak trees. At the tower's base is the original cornerstone of the long-gone observer's cabin, bearing the initials AA and CB, and the number 27—denoting the builders and the year of its construction, 1927. The summit was joined to the forest preserve in 1901.

The tower has been rebuilt using materials carried up the truck trail by ATV. The cab, the tower's enclosure, is sometimes staffed by volunteers on weekends and is open only during those times. But the top flight of stairs will provide the same promised views, a bit of wind, and respite from the blackflies in late spring.

From the higher stages of the tower it is possible to look out over the canopy at dozens of peaks. Plattekill, Indian Head, both summits of Twin, and Plateau Mtns. in the Indian Head Wilderness Area lie to the northeast (Olderbark Mtn. is blocking your view of Sugarloaf Mtn.). Continuing left (west) are Blackhead and Black Dome in the far distance, and (closer) Hunter (looking carefully, you can find Hunter's fire tower with binoculars), Southwest Hunter, West Kill, and the seemingly endless array of peaks in the Central Catskills, including Belle Ayr and Balsam among a complex of hills (remember, the Catskills have 100 peaks higher than 3,000 ft. in elevation). To the south are Ashokan High Point, bits and pieces of the Ashokan Reservoir, and several high peaks including Wittenberg and Slide. To the right of Slide are Giant Ledge and Panther. To the east is Cooper Lake (Kingston's water supply), as well as Overlook Mtn. Sky Top and Eagle Cliff are seen in the Shawangunks to the south, with the Hudson Highlands beyond. At this point, Phoenicia Trail ends, but the trail itself continues northeast as Warner Creek Trail and the Long Path.

Phoenicia Trail (map 1: B8–C7)

Distances from CR 40, Old Route 28 (750 ft.) to
- Baldwin Memorial lean-to (2,150 ft.): 2.0 mi., 1,400 ft., 1 hr. 40 min.
- Tremper Mtn. summit (2,740 ft.): 2.9 mi., 2,000 ft., 2 hr. 25 min.

Warner Creek Trail

Completed in 2000, Warner Creek Trail provides a Long Path link that was designed to eliminate the need for thru-hikers to walk additional road miles between Willow and Lake Hill. Because it is relatively young and covers a great deal of rock, the northern section of the trail (around Silver Hollow Mtn.) is not entirely self-guiding, and hikers are advised to pay close attention to trail markers. This is a well-designed, interesting trail that explores Warner Creek and Silver Hollow, some of the quietest country in the Catskills.

From the summit of Tremper Mtn., the trail follows blue markers along the heavily wooded and remote northwest ridge. Oak provides the dominant forest type here as the trail steadily and easily descends through ledges and circuitously around bedrock humps to Willow Trail junction. Sparse winter views linger as the trail hugs the eastern ridge, which curls among hemlocks and low ledges. This exposed section of the ridge is often ravaged by high winds, and cherry trees, especially, are often blown down from their tenuous grasps in the shallow soils.

The trail continues northeast, descending 400 ft. along the imprint of an old roadway before leveling out on the western slopes of Carl Mtn. (2,880 ft.) at 2.3 mi. and 2,000 ft. The trail descends, switching back into the northeast through the long, steady drop into Silver Hollow. During leafless months, views of West Kill Mtn. (3,890 ft.) open up to the left (northwest) across Stony Clove. The ridge slopes away steeply to the left as ledgy terrain rises to the right (east) and the grade relents. From a small flat rock with a northerly exposure at 2,100 ft., views across Silver Hollow reveal both West Kill and, now, Plateau Mtn. (3,850 ft.) to the northeast. At 3.0 mi., the trail descends very steeply into the hollow, approaching an eroded streambed while switching back along its left (west) bank. Marking becomes scarce at times, but the trail remains within audible distance of the creek, soon crossing it above the site of two small bluestone quarries on the right (east) of the stream. Tailings strewn into the creek bed mark the excavations, which can be explored east of the trail, and bits of tooled stone can be seen in the trail as it descends straight ahead (northeast). The trail now follows the treadway of the original quarry road, and the grade relaxes as it arrives in Silver Hollow, passing the foundation ruins of a house and barn on the right (east).

The trail turns right (east) here, following picturesque Warner's Creek, where several ideal camping locations present themselves in the hemlock woods beyond the 150-ft. legal camping distance from the creek. Drawing close to Warner's Creek, the trail switches back 180 degrees to ford it and follows east (right) again on the north side, on an old road. Within a few minutes' walk, cross a small tributary and watch to the left for the point at which the trail turns left into the north, following an eroded and sometimes vague path as it ascends through a sugar maple forest over rocky footing. Large oaks follow, and hemlocks appear as the trail cuts across a slope, rising briefly into the northwest through boulder-strewn forest. Leveling at 5.1 mi. (2,700 ft.), onto a ridge where small wet areas flood flat pockets of woods, hemlocks appear in isolation. At 6.0 mi., the trail descends, following next to a low ledge on the left (northwest) before rising slightly onto the northerly corner of the ridge at 2,700 ft. A small, very old fire ring that significantly predates the trail sits near an open ledge among tufts of reindeer moss. Limited views exist to the northeast of Olderbark and Plateau mtns. Skirting ledges to the right (north) and descending, the trail enters the Silver Hollow Notch at 6.9 mi., joining a disused section of Silver Hollow Road at 2,300 ft. There are trail signs at this four-way intersection. The trail continues into the Indian Head Wilderness from here.

Hikers wishing to park at this (north) end of the trail can do so from NY 214 north of Phoenicia, coming south onto Notch Inn Road, where it is possible to park legally only along the roadside just north of the Long Path trailhead. Limited legal roadside parking is also available on the section of Silver Hollow Road south of the trailhead (the middle 1.5 mi. of Silver Hollow Road is not drivable). Pullover parking on both sides of the notch requires some walking to Warner Creek trailhead. The southerly access point, while a legal ingress, is unofficial and unmarked. The area is heavily hunted, and like many places where state and private lands abut, boundaries may be inaccurately posted to discourage otherwise legal public access on this old town road.

Warner Creek Trail (map 1: B8)

Distances from Tremper Mtn. summit (2,740 ft.) to
- Willow Trail (2,390 ft.): 2.0 mi., 150 ft. (rev. 500 ft.), 1 hr. 5 min.
- Warner Creek (1,450 ft.): 3.8 mi., 150 ft. (rev. 950 ft.), 2 hr.
- Silver Hollow Notch (2,350 ft.): 6.9 mi., 1,750 ft. (rev. 650 ft.), 4 hr. 20 min.

Willow Trail

This is the less popular of the two traditional approaches to Tremper Mtn. (2,740 ft.). It follows the route of an old road, penetrating Hoyt Hollow into a remote section of the Phoenicia-Mt. Tobias Wild Forest.

From NY 212 in Willow, take Van Wagner Road north 0.3 mi. to Jessup Road, turn left, and find the trailhead at 1.5 mi. There is no trailhead parking area provided, and a private party has posted the road access. It is legal to park on the side of the road before this point, and to walk on the public easement to the trailhead, 0.3 mi. ahead.

The trail begins on the left (southwest) side of the road in a small clearing and immediately climbs, turning to the northwest at 1,550 ft. Here it ascends against the steep northeast wall of Hoyt Hollow, allowing only seasonal views of Olderbark and Little Rocky. Leveling briefly and again climbing, the trail makes its way to the shallow saddle at 2.6 mi. (2,400 ft.) between Carl Mtn. and Tremper Mtn., where it joins Warner Creek Trail, which departs northward toward Silver Hollow. Warner Creek Trail turns left (southwest) toward Tremper Mtn.

Willow Trail (map 1: C7–C8)

Distances from junction of Jessup Road and Van Wagner Road (1,090 ft.) to
- end of Jessup Road (1,250 ft.): 1.0 mi., 150 ft., 35 min.
- Warner Creek Trail (2,390 ft.): 2.6 mi., 1,300 ft., 1 hr. 55 min.
- Tremper Mtn. summit (2,740 ft.) via Warner Creek Trail: 4.6 mi., 1,800 ft. (rev. 150 ft.), 3 hr. 10 min.

SUGGESTED HIKE

Strenuous Hike

Tremper Mtn., via Phoenicia Trail [rt: 5.8 mi., 4:50]. This trail rises out of the Esopus Valley, switching back along an old road to a fire tower and lean-to. Views are available only from the tower itself.

Section 10
Bluestone Wild Forest

This attractive 3,000-acre wild forest lies just 3 mi. west of exit 19 of the New York State Thruway on the north side of NY 28, on the eastern border of the Catskill Forest Preserve, occupying a dozen or so parcels and inholdings in the towns of Ulster, Kingston, Woodstock, and Hurley. Many hikers are unaware of this forest because of its relative newness and its close proximity to the more popular upper-elevation trails of the nearby wilderness areas. It was also among the last parcels to be annexed to the Catskill Park when its boundaries were expanded. Additionally, those seeking a heightened sense of wilderness may be put off by the extensive impact of early industry (bluestone quarrying), which was perhaps the most intensive in the Catskills between 1820 and 1880. Although the Bluestone Wild Forest area was heavily impacted by these strip-mining operations, most of the evidence is well concealed under layers of forest duff. Long piles of rubble and small quarry ponds dot the area, and a good deal of the trail system utilizes the old dirt roads over which horse-drawn wagons took stone to docks along the Hudson River.

Onteora Lake, a narrow, shallow (20 ft. at its deepest), mile-long body of water draws many visitors to Bluestone Wild Forest as it supports a population of warm-water game fish, among them the tiger muskellunge, largemouth bass, and chain pickerel. Many smaller species are also present.

The fact that "muskies" may be taken in wintertime has made Onteora Lake a popular ice fishing destination. Anglers and hikers alike make use of the several primitive, designated (walk-in) campsites along the western side of the lake a short walk from the parking area. Hikers coming to the interior Catskills from long distances can readily bivouac in these free campsites for the purpose of staging early starts into the high-peaks area. Local day hikers, dog walkers, and joggers are more regularly enjoying this area, with its recently created loop trails among beautiful late-second-growth, maturing forests and Onteora Lake.

Elevations here are low, lying roughly between 400 ft. on Yellow Loop Trail at Onteora Lake and 600 ft. on Wintergreen Ridge Loop Trail, and the trails are fairly level with no difficult ascents. Soils are thin and dry. The forest cover is an attractive mix of oak, white pine, and pitch pine, with occasional pure, dense stands of hemlock and some extensive, pure pine woods. Views are obscure and seasonal.

The Onteora Lake section of the forest is the most accessible and visited, with three well-marked loop trails. To the east in the less frequented Jockey Hill section, Wintergreen Ridge Loop Trail is the longest of the trails. Though the trails in the Onteora section are relatively short, hiking the three loops will take little more than a full day; Wintergreen Ridge Loop Trail can be hiked in a matter of two or three leisurely hours.

Mountain bikers frequent this area and the trails are marked accordingly, but management plans specify that they are pedestrian trails first, and cycling is monitored for both user conflicts and ecological impact. So far, both user groups are far below the trails' carrying capacities and there have been no reported conflicts. There is a strong local cycling community, which contributed to the development of this trail system and also helps to maintain it. Snowmobiles and horses are not permitted at this time. The trails are suitable for snowshoeing and backcountry skiing.

In addition to the historical significance of the bluestone industry, which sent flaggings for buildings and sidewalks to many eastern US cities and others as far away as Havana, Cuba, the Bluestone Wild Forest contains several native archaeological sites of the Munsee. This subtribe of the Lenape was one of three principal divisions of the Delaware Nation. The Munsee were a warlike group who were among the first tribes to encounter (and resist) Europeans. They were forced to cede their homeland to the colonies by way of the 1677 Andros Treaty.

Yellow Loop Trail

This trail begins at the kiosk on a gravel footway next to the Onteora Lake (lower) parking area. It is the most scenic of the loops, as it features the lake for much of its distance. When the access gate is closed, hikers must begin at the upper overflow parking lot and walk 0.3 mi. to the trailhead parking area.

From the lower parking area the trail follows an old quarry road along the west side of the lake among hardwoods, first passing the boat launch area and soon entering the woods. Several designated campsites appear on both sides of the trail. A trail register appears on the right.

The trail descends, and at 0.6 mi. crosses a plank bridge following the swampy northern realms of the lake, turning south and climbing slightly through a hemlock-shrouded quarry area that is largely reclaimed by nature. Close attention is required to identify the junction at which the returning Yellow Loop Trail appears to the right (trail signage is needed here). Access to the returning section is here, but continue to the better-marked junction ahead at 0.7 mi. At the junction of Red Loop Trail and Yellow Loop Trail, bear right following yellow markers amid a forest of even-aged oak and isolated, tall white pines.

The trail is undulating to flat up to a point at which it descends slightly and turns north, following the edge of Pickerel Pond at 1.1 mi. There is a well-established beaver house here, and eagles and osprey frequent the area. The trail soon rises away from the lake and follows the edge of a ridge on its eastern side, entering an enchanting hemlock forest at 1.7 mi., where Onteora Lake is seen to the left. At 2.0 mi., the loop is closed at a point just north of the junction with Red Loop Trail. Bear left, retracing familiar ground back to the parking area, arriving in another 0.7 mi. for a total hike of 2.7 mi.

Yellow Loop Trail (map 1: D9)

Distances from trailhead (400 ft.) to
- Red Loop Trail (500 ft.): 0.7 mi., 100 ft., 20 min.
- Blue Loop Trail, via Red Loop Trail (550 ft.): 1.1 mi., 35 min.

Red Loop Trail

Red Loop Trail begins at its junction with Yellow Loop Trail as described above, 0.7 mi. from the Onteora Lake lower parking area. At the junction, bear left following red markers.

The trail begins heading north following an old road on easy terrain, rising to an elbow atop a ridge as it turns into the east passing an erratic boulder at 0.3 mi. At 0.4 mi., bear left at a Y.

Young white pines struggle beneath a dominant overstory of white oak, but soon establish dominance on a plateau where they have reached maturity, appearing in an extensive, pure stand. At the northern end of the pine forest, the trail descends, passing a vernal pond to the left at 0.6 mi. The trail turns south, following sections of flat but rooted old road, passing the trailhead of Blue Loop Trail at 1.4 mi., and returning to the Y again at 1.6 mi.

Rejoining the loop, the trail returns to the junction with Yellow Loop Trail for a total of 2.0 mi. Bear right, following Yellow Loop Trail 0.7 mi. to the parking area.

Red Loop Trail (map 1: D9)

Distances from trailhead to
- around loop (500 ft.): 2.0 mi., 250 ft., 50 min.
- to Blue Loop Trail (550 ft.): 580 ft., 1.4 mi, 150 ft., 35 min.

Blue Loop Trail

Follow Yellow Loop Trail to Red Loop Trail (0.7 mi), and bear right at the Y on Red Loop Trail (0.4 mi.). Blue Loop Trail begins here.

Bear right as the trail winds its way downhill, following an old road amid quarry faces and rubble piles. The trail heads north, and at 0.3 mi. turns through the north and east before heading south. It then follows the edge of a steep, wet ravine, where ledges become vertical in places, following along the tops of quarries. This is one of the most attractive areas in the Bluestone Wild Forest. Signs of bobcat are present, and deer, turkey, and bear inhabit the area. The trail rises through mixed woods to meet Red Loop Trail at 0.8 mi.

Blue Loop Trail (map 1: D9)

Distances from trailhead to
- around loop (550 ft.): 0.8 mi., 200 ft., 45 min.

Wintergreen Ridge Loop Trail

The trail begins in the Jockey Hill section of the Bluestone Wild Forest. The trailhead is reached from the Sawkill Road exit off of US 209 (north of NY 28). Drive 1.5 mi. the turn left onto Hill Road. After 0.8 mi., turn left onto Jockey Hill Road and follow it 0.3 mi. to the end of the pavement. Follow the dirt road to the small designated parking area on the left. (Winter access to the trailhead can be problematic because of the built-up berm of plowed snow at the end of Hill Road.) At this point the trail is a dirt road and gated to frustrate ATV use (mountain bikes are permitted), although there is still some snowmobile and ATV evidence. State-trail marking is poor or absent at this point of the trail but improves dramatically on the loop section. Efforts to curb illegal dumping in this area have been successful but are ongoing, illustrating some of the difficulties the state faces with the management of wild forest areas, and new acquisitions in particular.

Crossing a seasonal brook, the trail heads southeast. Several unmarked side trails enter the woods from both sides. At 1.1 mi., at a prominent Y, bear left following yellow state-trail markers. This section of trail utilizes old quarry roads.

Cross a shallow brook and climb easily. The trail splits at a Y. Bear left. The trail levels above a tributary of the Sawkill Creek, which runs at the bottom of a scenic ravine to the west. Hemlock persists in pure stands here, yielding as the trail rises onto a plateau of sparse hardwoods at 1.8 mi. Red and white oak and hickories appear above small white pines. Quarry rubble appears here and there, although not with the regularity of the Onteora Lake trails. The trail makes a small loop in the north before heading south and soon turns west, passing through an isolated stand of pitch pine and blueberry ground cover. The trail reaches the junction at 3.4 mi. and arrives at the parking area at 4.4 mi.

Wintergreen Ridge Loop Trail (map 1: D9)

Distances from trailhead to
- beginning of loop (450 ft.): 1.1 mi., 50 ft., 25 min.
- around loop (450 ft.): 2.3 mi., 300 ft., 1 hr. 20 min.

PART 2

SOUTHERN CATSKILLS

The Southern Catskills include the region bounded by NY 28 and NY 28A in the north and northeast, respectively; by Big Head Indian Hollow (CR 47) to the west; and by CR 3 and NY 55 in the south. Because of the concentration of high peaks in such a vast and scenic wilderness setting, the Southern Catskills—comprising the Slide Mountain Wilderness Area, the Sundown Wild Forest, Shandaken Wild Forest, and the Willowemoc Wild Forest—are the Catskills' most popular hiking destination and claim the highest mountain (Slide, 4,190 ft.). There are many marked trails, lean-tos, designated campsites, trout streams, rugged peaks, and much expansive scenery here. Opportunities for extended backpacking trips are plentiful. Several rigorous day hikes can be arranged from most of the trailheads.

The wild forest areas to the south and west of the central high-peaks wilderness area offer hikers another kind of experience, one with far fewer hikers and deeper, quieter forests of less challenging terrain. Together these areas (the Willowemoc and Sundown wild forests) offer the best backcountry ski-touring trails and the best mountain-biking trails the Catskills have to offer. The rest of the terrain in the southern region is self-limiting to these sports.

The Southern Catskills are also the headwaters of important streams such as the Neversink River, Esopus Creek, and Rondout Creek, each of which contributes to New York City's water system. The southern watersheds themselves have drawn a great deal of tourism to the area, mostly composed of anglers. A good deal of championship-level kayak racing has been conducted on the Esopus as well. Born on the slopes of Slide Mtn., the Esopus is well known for its spring run of rainbow trout. The fish winter in the Ashokan Reservoir and run upstream to spawn in early spring, often becoming record catches. Hikers are advised that swelling spring waters produce good upper-elevation fishing for wild strains of native trout.

The Southern Catskills have been important to the proliferation of the state's most harvested big-game animal—the whitetail deer. Hikers are advised to take precautions when traveling afield during hunting season. Check with the forest ranger in the area where you expect to travel and, when possible, wear brightly colored clothing (ideally blaze orange).

SECTION 11
SUNDOWN WILD FOREST

The most interesting areas to hikers of this 30,000-acre wild forest are the 4,100-acre Kanape section's trail to Ashokan High Point; the 8,600-acre Vernooy Kill Falls section with its matrix of snowmobile, hiking, skiing, and bike trails; and Red Hill Trail, with its fire tower. The forest comprises low mountains and ridges, with ten mountains higher than 2,000 ft. This wild forest has a wilderness feel as the result of the neighboring Slide Mountain Wilderness Area to the north and the 14,900-acre Willowemoc Wild Forest to the west. To the northwest, along the section of Peekamoose Road at Bull Run, it is bordered by Peekamoose Valley, which is popular for its primitive camping areas.

The geologic centerpiece of this lonely, mostly trailless group of quiet hills—collectively known as the Ashokan Catskills—is the huddle of crowns around High Point itself. The area's lower elevations once supported bluestone quarrying and water-powered milling. Berry harvesting as well as the gathering of wintergreen (for oil) were confined to upper elevations.

Sundown's floral diversity is perhaps the most fascinating feature of this wild forest area, which is in many ways typical of the rest of the Catskills. Although there are no threatened or endangered floral communities in the Sundown Wild Forest, it is interesting to note that the globally rare small whorled pogonia orchid was identified here by the botanist Herbert Denslow in the 1920s. It has not been rediscovered since. The three birds orchid, another of Denslow's finds, was rediscovered here by Henry Dunbar in the 1950s.

Among the most fanciful references to this area is the account of a lost, secret hideaway near Ashokan High Point's summit. Outlined in Dewitt Clinton Overbaugh's *The Hermit of the Catskills* (1900), this hermit cave was lavishly appointed with animal skins, rustic furniture, and lamps fueled by bear fat. The hermit and his mate, a beautiful native princess, had played host to such dignitaries as George Washington and the murderous Mohawk chieftain Joseph Brant (presumably not at the same time—Brant's military cunning was on behalf of the British). Still, both of their portraits hung on the cavern's walls.

Hikers will also find the Vernooy Kill Falls area of interest. A high plateau, hemlock forests, and extensive wetlands surround a matrix of roads connected by hiking trails that are suitable for mountain biking and backcountry skiing. The most popular destination is Vernooy Kill Falls, a series of low cascades and shallow pools.

Several excellent primitive campsites can be found off Vernooy Kill Falls-Bangle Hill trailhead. Located in four distinct areas—the Upper, Middle, Lower, and Trailer fields—these sites are managed by forest rangers. Permits are required for trailer camping and for stays of more than three nights (tent campers included).

Ashokan High Point Trail

Ashokan High Point (3,080 ft., alternately called High Point, Shokan High Point, and Ashokan High Peak), while smaller than many trailed summits in the Southern Catskills, is unusually scenic. It is also more easily accessible from NY 28 than the neighboring Catskill high peaks, and although it requires a rigorous climb, is easier than most of them. The mountain is within a wild forest, but it conveys a true wilderness feeling because it is joined physically to the Slide Mountain Wilderness Area, of which hikers will enjoy intimate and spectacular views. Ashokan High Point is an ideal destination for a satisfying overnighter, especially for the small family new to backpacking or for the inexperienced hiker seeking a moderately challenging route. It is also a popular trek among day-hiking parties interested in the kind of close-up, big-mountain scenery that is typically a feature limited to the interior Catskills' highest (and busiest) peaks, and for those who want to pick over one of the few former commercially viable blueberry crops in the Catskills.

The trail begins deep in the rugged, densely wooded valley of Peekamoose Clove. The recommended (road) route from the east is from Winchell's Corners in Shokan on NY 28, coming south across the Ashokan Reservoir's dividing weir (0.3 mile). The weir offers perhaps the best view of the Catskill peaks and Ashokan High Point from anywhere in the eastern Esopus lowlands, a spectacle that ranks easily among the most impressive views in the Hudson Valley. (This particular vantage of High Point inspired the 1853, pre-impoundment landscape of the same name by Asher B. Durand, who cofounded the Hudson River School with Thomas Cole.)

Those using this particular route to the trailhead will cross the weir dividing the reservoir's western and eastern basins and turn left at the T onto Monument Road. From the T, Ashokan High Point stands slightly to the right in the southwest. Bear right onto NY 28A toward Olivebridge, skirting the edge of the posted buffer zone's extensive evergreen forests. Five miles beyond the T, bear left onto Watson Hollow Road (CR 42) toward Sundown, and follow it gradually uphill along the winding Bush Kill into Peekamoose Clove.

Four miles uphill into the clove on CR 42, turn right (north) into the Kanape Brook trailhead parking area. A map kiosk and outhouse are present here. On the south side of the road and downhill 200 ft., enter the trailhead (red markers) on a wooden bridge spanning Kanape Brook. The trail is self-guiding, an old road used by early settlement farmers to reduce travel time between here and the Rondout Valley. In 1930 the road was improved by the Civilian Conservation Corps, and it remains in excellent condition with the help of a local scout troop. The surrounding forest is primarily a second-growth mix of birch, maple, and ash, but the Kanape itself is thick with hemlock.

The trail passes the register on the left and climbs slightly. Stone heaps, wall remnants, culverts, and the ramparts of a small bluestone dam (perhaps used to power a mill) appear along the trail and in the surrounding woods (these were part of Watson's farm, for which Watson Hollow is named). Little Rocky (3,015 ft.) emerges through the forest canopy to the right (south), and neighboring Mombaccus (2,840 ft.) soon appears. Laurel hems the trail and Norway spruce is evident singly and in isolated stands.

The trail levels as a designated campsite is reached at 1.5 mi., where a broken fire ring stands in an open clearing of grass adjacent to the Kanape and to a dense, boreal glen of Norway spruce. Aside from the summit balds, this is the optimal campsite. Backpackers can expect to reach this site in under an hour from the trailhead. Should the campsite be in use, many more legal (though undesignated) camping opportunities exist in the extensive Norway spruce plantation in proximity to the brook (observe the 150-ft. rule and use the designated site, if possible, to limit impact). It is also possible to camp near the saddle ahead.

The trail erodes and ascends, steepening through a hardwood forest with a few very large oak, ash, and hemlock trees. A hemlock understory develops as the saddle is approached, where the terrain levels into a grassy, open woods. Note the trail arrow at the T and the obvious summit trail to the left (north) at 2.6 mi., before resting at the saddle 300 ft. beyond, where a large, open campsite (legal, undesignated) and fire ring exist adjacent to private land at 2,100 ft. At this point the old road descends into Samsonville (Marbletown), becoming Freeman Avery Road. There is no legal access from the south at this time.

At the previous T, the trail turns northeast toward Ashokan High Point, within 150 ft. passing the vague and poorly marked loop trail on the left (northwest), which is the longer approach to the summit. Continue straight ahead (northeast) as the trail turns from road to footpath, quickly gaining elevation into an oak-and-laurel forest. Water bars are frequent as the trail terraces, rising in sometimes steep shelves between easier pitches. An obvious but unmarked short spur to the right (south) leads to poor southerly views. The trail continues to ascend at a 30-degree incline, while views to the southwest open up. The summit is attained at 3.6 mi., with its restricted scenery to the south. Other peaks in the area showcase views to the south in a much grander fashion (in particular, Wittenberg), but the views from High Point of the southeast-facing slopes of the Burroughs Range to the northwest are among the most striking to be found anywhere, and these will be encountered a very short distance farther along the trail.

From High Point summit, several significant landmarks are visible, however. Sky Top Tower of the Mohonk Preserve, Eagle Cliff, and the Mohonk Mountain House itself are visible at 165 degrees magnetic, across the Rondout Valley. The Hudson Highlands (to the right of Sky Top and far south) are roughly 45 mi. away (between Storm King and Breakneck Mtn. a small section of the Hudson can be identified). The city of Kingston and the seemingly unbroken woodlands of Hurley, Rochester, Marbletown, and Wawarsing lie below. The ridge horizons to the south (following right from Sky Top) are the lands of Minnewaska State Park. Given a clear day, you can see into the ridges of New Jersey's Kittatinny Mountains to the thin tower on the state's highest point, High Point. Views of the Ashokan Reservoir, to the east, are very limited.

The Samson No. 1 and No. 2 USGS benchmarks are embedded in the summit, as well as the anchor bolts for a dismantled triangulation tower. There is some poorly scribed graffiti, dating to 1878. Just beneath the summit is a rock overhang that might shelter a hiker or two from the rain and a flat area that has been significantly damaged by (illegal) camping. The trail continues to the north. It is marked, but not immediately obvious, and leads a short distance to several southwesterly vantage points, the first of which again shows the Kittatinny's High Point tower at 220 degrees and Little Rocky in the immediate foreground. In the west, fine views begin to take shape, first of Peekamoose and Table Mtns. This north-facing area of the summit is a nearly continuous bald of late lowbush blueberry (*Vaccinium angustifolium*), possibly the best blueberry patch on any of the Catskill peaks. Blueberries were deliberately encouraged here, and both intentional and rare natural fires have kept the summit open, the soils thin, and the berries prolific. It will prove very worthwhile to visit during berry season, which is roughly two weeks behind the normal season at sea level (toward late July is the typical harvest time).

Consuming vistas will tempt hikers off the trail and onto the russet, open balds, especially during berry season. Off the berry patches in the scrubby hardwood margins it is possible to camp legally. Views of the Ashokan Reservoir can be had by foraging east through the woods. The low knob to the east is Little High Point (2,800 ft.). Half of the knob is privately owned. The state has shown some interest in acquiring that parcel for the ultimate construction of a larger loop that would descend to the north, cut west across South Hollow, and connect with the Kanape Trail.

Three small but conspicuous boulders sit in an area to the north of the trail where sandstone bedrock surfaces in small patches. From a position roughly in the center of these open fields are Slide Mtn. (4,190 ft.), at 330 degrees, and Balsam Cap. Moving left from Slide is an unnamed peak (3,446 ft.), then Rocky (3,508 ft.), Lone (3,721 ft.), Table (3,847 ft.), and Peekamoose (3,843 ft.) follow. To the right of Slide are Friday (3,694 ft.), Boggart (3,870 ft.), and Wittenberg (3,790 ft.). The Burroughs Range is the birthplace of the Rondout Creek, which winds around to the west and east again, emptying into the Hudson in Kingston. The Devil's Path mountains (Indian Head Wilderness Area) stand to the northeast, and to the right of Wittenberg are the rural uplands of Lexington, Hunter, and the rugged West Kill Wilderness Area, including Hunter Mtn. (4,050 ft.).

Following the loop adds an hour to this hike. If the weather deteriorates or darkness approaches, hikers are advised to return the way they came. The trail continues along the western slope of the mountain. Although it would seem that the trail might proceed to the north here (following herd paths across the balds), it in fact goes off to the left (west), so watch carefully. Because trees and rocks are scarce here, so are trail markers and paint blazes.

Backtrack if necessary to regain the trail. The trail turns into the forest to the north-northwest, toward Slide Mtn., and drops downhill through a section that is not adequately marked.

Continuing on the loop, the trail travels up and down gently through a mixed hardwood forest. Views are limited. At 4.1 mi., the trail turns 90 degrees to the left (south) and is not adequately marked at this time. Without the aid of a GPS device, it is possible to miss it entirely (41° 55.807' N, 74° 17.985' W). Although the trail has been difficult to follow in places so far, it becomes (and remains) self-guiding after the turn. Where the terrain opens to northwesterly views, ignore an established path to the right as the main trail bears left. The route swings southwest and descends gradually, changing direction 180 degrees from northwest to southeast, and back into the southwest again toward Mombaccus Mtn. and the saddle (where the summit ascent began at the 2.6-mi. point). Parts of the descent are steep and rubble-strewn. At 5.8 mi., the loop is completed, and the trail turns right (west), reaching the saddle in a few hundred feet. The trail turns right (northwest) and descends to the trailhead at 8.4 mi.

Ashokan High Point Trail (map 1: D7)

Distances from trailhead on Peekamoose Road (1,110 ft.) to
- loop junction (2,090 ft.): 2.6 mi., 1,000 ft., 1 hr. 50 min.
- Ashokan High Point summit (3,090 ft.) via east loop: 3.6 mi., 2,000 ft., 2 hr. 50 min.
- loop junction (2,090 ft.) via west loop: 5.8 mi., 2,200 ft. (rev. 1,200 ft.), 4 hr.
- for complete loop and return to trailhead: 8.4 mi., 2,200 ft., 5 hr. 20 min.

Vernooy Kill Falls-Bangle Hill Trail

Vernooy Kill Falls has become a popular destination for hiking and ski touring, and the surrounding matrix of roads and snowmobile trails provides the most rideable mountain biking terrain in the forest preserve. This section of the Long Path crosses Bangle Hill into the Slide Mountain Wilderness, where it continues over Peekamoose Mtn. Marking in this section needs improvement, and relatively few recreational hikers—other than those using the Long Path—hike in the area north of Vernooy Kill Falls. (At some point in the future the Long Path will be rerouted through the Lundy Parcel at the north end of Lundy Road.) GPS coordinates are provided for aid in identifying the several key trail junctions in this section of the Sundown Wild Forest.

The trailhead is located off Upper Cherrytown Road. From NY 209, 0.6 mi. north of the traffic light in Kerhonkson, take Samsonville Road (CR 3) left (northwest) for about 3.5 mi. from NY 209, bearing left onto Upper Cherrytown Road where Ridgeview Road comes in from the north. Continue bearing left. At a three-way junction, bear right onto Upper Cherrytown Road and continue 3.0 mi. to the Department of Environmental Conservation trailhead parking area on the right (east) side of the road. The trail leaves immediately across the road from the parking area, following a marked (multiuse) hiking and snowmobile trail into a white pine-and-oak woods. Signs are posted on Upper Cherrytown Road at the trailhead.

At 0.25 mi., the trail crosses a footbridge over Mombaccus Creek, ascending steadily through a burned-over area to the left of the trail, with a substantially damaged understory of maple saplings. According to forest rangers, an 850-acre fire was started by a careless hiker in May 2001. Pulling away from the creek, the trail ascends, passing a woods road that veers left. Continue straight, still climbing. The trail soon levels and descends gently, passing a designated campsite to the left before arriving at Vernooy Kill Falls at 1.6 mi. The falls are small, appearing mostly upstream of the bridge in several tiers. A narrow chute flows under the bridge, and the creek flows past the single intact wall of a gristmill built in the 1700s by Cornelius Vernooy.

A few herd trails explore the general area, upstream and down. The trail continues to the right (northwest) of the bridge and uphill a very short distance (300 ft.), following the snowmobile trail's north loop. The south loop continues across the bridge and goes on to Greenville.

Long Path blazes are not evident through this section (or the remaining distance to Peekamoose Road), but blue state-trail disks appear consistently. From this point forward, there is no destination signage. The trail ascends slightly and levels, following a dirt road. Watch carefully, for at 2.65 mi., the trail turns left (41° 53.027' N, 74° 21.756' W) and ascends gently. To the right 0.2 mi. are Vernooy Kill Road, a trailhead parking area, and two designated campsites on a creek.

Climbing gently to the north-northeast, at 3.9 mi. the trail turns to the left (west) again, where it joins another, more established woods road (41° 53.884' N, 74° 22.049' W). Cross an auto bridge and continue as several side trails appear, crossing another, smaller plank bridge at 4.6 mi. The forest is dense hemlock with mountain laurel beneath. Water is abundant and the sandy road is typically wet and potholed. Pass a rustic hunting camp to your right (north), and soon thereafter a dirt road leaves to the left at 5.35 mi. Continue straight, watching to the right for a pair of poorly built cairns that mark the trail at 5.6 mi. The trail (now a footpath) turns right here (41° 53.713' N, 74° 23.628' W) and climbs to another dirt road. Turn left (southwest) at 5.9 mi. (41° 53.784' N, 74° 23.907' W).

(NOTE: To the right this road curves uphill slightly and ends at the site of a small stone shack. Hikers who have reached this point have gone too far and must backtrack a few hundred feet, watching for the markers, which are placed above eye level and are easy to miss.)

At 6.1 mi. the trail turns right (north) and goes uphill (41° 53.682' N, 74° 23.992' W). Ascend easily. Within a few hundred yards the trail turns sharply to the left (west-northwest) and climbs to a height-of-land before descending easily, passing through thin hemlock stands, crossing a rocky creek (dry in late summer), and another smaller but usually flowing trickle. The trail ascends to Bangle Hill, arriving at 8.5 mi. (2,350 ft.). It is heavily wooded—there is no view. Following a steep descent down the north side, the trail turns west, nearly leveling as it traverses a steep slope and follows a seasonal streambed downhill to join a woods road in a homogeneous sugar maple forest. Now the trail descends very steeply, passing two skid roads to the left (west) and a deep gully to the right, at 9.0 mi. arriving at Peekamoose Road.

A small trailhead parking area is located across the road. The extensive Sundown Primitive Campsite on the north side of Peekamoose Road offers dozens of good tent sites. From here, West Shokan is 11.0 mi. to the northeast along CR 42. The Long Path continues from the north side of Peekamoose Road (CR 42), 0.4 mi. to the east.

Vernooy Kill Falls-Bangle Hill Trail (map 1: D6)

Distances from trailhead on Upper Cherrytown Road (1,226 ft.) to
- Vernooy Kill Falls (1,670 ft.): 1.6 mi., 550 ft. (rev. 100 ft.), 1 hr. 5 min.
- connector to Vernooy Kill Road (1,790 ft.): 2.7 mi., 650 ft., 1 hr. 40 min.
- upper reaches of Vernooy Kill (1,950 ft.): 4.6 mi., 950 ft. (rev. 150 ft.), 2 hr. 45 min.
- Bangle Hill (2,350 ft.): 8.5 mi., 1,500 ft. (rev. 150 ft.), 5 hr. 5 min.
- Peekamoose Road (1,190 ft.): 9.0 mi., 1,500 ft. (rev. 1,150 ft.), 5 hr. 35 min.

Red Hill Trail

Large, fallow potato fields remain in this high, exposed country above Claryville, lying south of the Big Indian and Slide Mountain wilderness areas, at the confluence of the Neversink River's east and west branches. Here, an alluring blend of upper-elevation pasturelands abut the deep, mixed forests of the Southwestern Catskills. Red Hill marks the watershed divide of the Hudson and Delaware rivers.

The trail begins on Dinch Road (aka Coon Road). Take NY 55 from NY 209 north of Ellenville, or from NY 17 in Liberty. Take CR 19 6.5 mi. to Claryville and turn right onto Red Hill Road. In 3.2 mi., go left onto Dinch Road, 1.5 mi. to the trailhead parking area on the left. Claryville is reached from the north by Slide Mtn. Road (West Branch Road on its westerly side) and from the east on Peekamoose Road.

The trail begins innocently, working its way across a tributary of the East Branch, rising through broken ledges amid hardwoods. It remains level for some time; the footway is soft soil, following through thick mats of wood fern as it circles the northerly slope of Red Hill. Club moss, shining pine, and ground cedar mark the way through even-aged stands of sugar maple. The trail turns southwest and begins to climb steeply, leveling on a grassy flat on Red Hill's summit. A picnic table and observer's cabin are on the site.

The tower, built in 1920, is 60 ft. high, and the cab is open and staffed on most summer weekends. This tower also served as a communications tower before the existence of radio repeaters in the Catskills and was the last operating tower in the Catskills. The 360-degree views are a highlight of the hike. From Ashokan High Point, look north through the Catskill high peaks, including Table and Peekamoose, only 5.0 mi. distant. Slide and Panther are seen, as well as the summits of Doubletop and Graham, with its abandoned TV station tower. You will see Balsam Lake Mtn. and its fire tower, and in the south lies the Shawangunk ridge, showing Sky Top and Eagle Cliff. The compound below, on Denning Road, is Frost Valley's (YMCA) education camp.

Red Hill Trail (map 2: D5)

Distance from trailhead on Dinch Road (2,160 ft.) to
• Red Hill summit (2,990 ft.): 1.2 mi., 850 ft., 1 hr.

SUGGESTED HIKES

Easy Hike

Vernooy Kill Falls Trail [rt: 3.2 mi., 2:30]. This popular hike visits a small cascade (Vernooy Kill Falls) near the site of an early Dutch gristmill, possibly the first of its kind in the state. Some remains are evident.

Moderate Hike

Red Hill Trail [rt: 2.4 mi., 2:00]. A flat approach to a short, steep ascent brings hikers to a fire tower on this small but isolated western summit with sweeping views of the Western Catskills.

SECTION 12
SLIDE MOUNTAIN WILDERNESS AREA

The Slide Mountain Wilderness Area is the Catskills' largest, most popular wilderness. At 47,500 acres, it contains the Catskills' highest summit (Slide Mtn., 4,180 ft.) and an extensive trail area making trips of several days' duration possible. Located in the northwestern corner of Ulster County, the tract forms the watersheds of Esopus Creek, Rondout Creek, and Neversink River. The terrain is rugged and scenic, encompassing a group of trailed and trailless peaks, boasting thirteen named mountains higher than 3,000 ft. in elevation.

Hikers visiting the Slide Mountain Wilderness Area will be presented with many options for challenging single- and multiday outings. The most popular of these is Wittenberg-Cornell-Slide Trail (Burroughs Range Trail), a skyline trail named for the Catskills' naturalist and guardian, John Burroughs. It can be hiked in a single day by avid hikers in good condition (who have spotted a car on each end of the trail), but the preferred method for many is an approach of two separate day hikes, allowing time to be spent enjoying the views from Wittenberg and Slide (Cornell's view is limited).

In the north of this area is the tremendously popular Giant Ledge, an easy day outing with significant scenic attractions. Panther Mtn. is less frequently hiked as a destination in itself, but it is used as a thru-trail for extended hikes from the south. Slide Mtn. is the area's most popular destination by merit of its height, but most hikers do not consider its views to be as good as Wittenberg's. Still, the allure of Slide is great: its summit view includes nearly 70 named Catskill peaks as well as a wide vista of the Hudson Valley, Ashokan Reservoir, Green Mountains, Berkshires, Taconics, Hudson Highlands, and Shawangunks. This is the same view that State Forest Commissioner, Townsend Cox, climbing Slide in 1886, pronounced to be "every bit as fine as anything to be seen in the Adirondacks."

In the 1980s, New York State geologist Ingvar Isachsen discovered that a meteorite impacted the area around what is today's Panther Mtn. some 375 million years ago. His discovery, which had originally been received with a good deal of skepticism in the scientific community, was backed up by his recovery of spherules—tiny iron droplets of condensed gas that proved his theory. Satellite images clearly show the circular crater, defined by the circuitous route of the Esopus Creek, which hikers can make out by studying their map.

The mountains in the Slide Mountain Wilderness are cloaked in spruce-fir rocky summits and mountain spruce-fir forest (3,000 to 4,000 ft.), the latter of which is very rare in New York State. Northern hardwoods persist at lower elevations. Hikers will find many wildflowers and ferns common to the area, and they will find that this wilderness contains the largest continuous old-growth forests in the Catskills, with several virgin tracts. Wildlife abounds, and there are significant deer-wintering areas and important bear habitats. Porcupines may visit hikers for lunch or try to investigate backpacks on summits. A distinct species of thrush that depends on boreal forest (Bicknell's thrush) was discovered by E.P. Bicknell in 1881 and is believed to inhabit several peaks in the wilderness area.

Public use has caused significant impact in this wilderness area. Trailhead registrations show Slide Mtn. with the greatest number of visitors annually, with Giant Ledge attracting similar numbers. The fewest hikers come in from Fox Hollow in the north. Average yearly totals run upward of 35,000 visitors, most arriving between mid-May and mid-October. The area's capacity to withstand use has been challenged with the steadily rising number of visitors each year and the Department of Environmental Conservation (DEC) asks for strict compliance in order to avoid deterioration of the wilderness character of this area. Trail maintenance is ongoing by the DEC, the New York–New Jersey Trail Conference, the Adirondack Mountain Club, and other groups. Hikers can do their part by using backpacking stoves instead of building fires, by camping in designated areas only, by staying on marked trails, and by employing the principles of Leave No Trace.

(Note: At the time of publication, work on an extensive rerouting of the Long Path over Romer Mtn., Mt. Plesant, and Cross Mtn. was not yet complete, but the New York–New Jersey Trail Conference anticipated it would open in Fall 2013. The Map 1 (C7) in this text shows the proposed route of this trail from its junction with Wittenberg-Cornell-Slide Trail to its terminus at Lane St. in Phoenicia. For more current information, please visit outdoors.org/amcbookupdates.)

Wittenberg-Cornell-Slide Trail (Burroughs Range Trail)

This is the Catskills' most popular interior-forest hiking route, traversing the Slide Mountain Wilderness Area and providing hikers with a scenic and memorable wilderness experience. The area is fragile and sensitive to the many visitors it has endured over the years.

The trail begins at the Woodland Valley trailhead parking area at the end of Woodland Valley Road, just east of the state campground's main gate (see Phoenicia–East Branch Trail for directions from Phoenicia). A minimal day-use fee is collected for each parked car during the months of the campground's operation. Consult the map and information kiosk in the parking area. Cross the road and go left (east), with the campsite on the right (south). Trail signs are posted on the right, in view of the parking area.

In addition to blue state-trail markers, the aqua blazes of the Long Path appear here. (These will be removed when the trail is rerouted over Cross Mtn.) The trail leaves from within the campground, between campsites 45 and 46, and heads left toward the creek, turning downstream and crossing a footbridge.

The trail heads left (east) after crossing the creek and ascends over a rocky, well-maintained treadway, passing the trail register. The scratches visible on the rocks here are from crampons. Moss-covered ledges and talus slopes under a canopy of mature forest characterize the steep ascent to a rocky hemlock knoll (2,000 ft.). The trail ascends the lower north-western extremity of Wittenberg—today an unnamed hill, but known in the late 1800s as the Big Knoll, from which bits of Hemlock (3,240 ft.), Spruce (3,390 ft.), and Fir (3,630 ft.) mtns. can be observed, especially in winter. The trail relaxes now. This area, including the high peaks, was a part of the Hardenburgh Patent that became the private property of Robert Livingston.

Passing many picturesque rock formations, at 0.5 mi. the trail levels through a hemlock grove with a large bedrock monolith in its center. To the left (east) as the trail flattens, a small rock outcropping offers limited views to the south and east. Wittenberg, to the hard right (south), is among these, easily identified by its boreal green—or in varied light, black—summit. This area is legal for camping (beyond 150 ft. of the trail), but it is fragile. Mosses, over which old fire rings were built, have never recovered. A shallow ravine follows on the left as the trail bears right (south).

Fern, violet, and trout lily are dominant on these hardwood subslopes, blooming profusely in the spring. The trail ascends through a northern hardwood forest and crosses a small seasonal creek, soon switching back hard to the left (southeast) at a point where an early roadway continues southwest, eventually disappearing. The existence of a herd path here suggests that many hikers have missed this turn and continued straight ahead. Stay alert.

Penetrating a talus slope tangled with hemlock, the trail soon cuts up 90 degrees to the right (south), turns left (east), ascends, descends, and passes a number of hemlock stands before crossing a seasonal creek. The trail descends slightly after the kill, following along the edge of a slope and offering scant summer views to the north. Several nameless and seasonal brooks and rills follow before the trail turns right (southeast) and uphill at 2,600 ft., topping out on a flat where the vegetation type changes to beech and scrubby maple, with small spruce trees beginning to appear. Views of Wittenberg up to the right (west) appear as the junction with Terrace Mtn. Trail is reached at 2.3 mi., where trail signs appear. (This is the time to consider a short, very worthwhile detour to Terrace Lookout. See Terrace Mtn. Trail.)

Turning right (west), the trail ascends moderately toward Wittenberg. Climbing around to the north of Wittenberg's steep eastern slopes, a long rock outcrop offers some good views—views that are redundant to those from Wittenberg's summit. Included are Overlook Mtn. (3,150 ft.), Plattekill (3,110 ft.), Indian Head (3,573 ft.), Sugarloaf (3,810 ft.), Plateau (3,850 ft.), and Hunter (4,050 ft.). Hunter's fire tower can be seen by looking very carefully with binoculars at 42 degrees. Stony Clove, Diamond Notch, and West Kill Mtn. (3,890 ft.) are also seen.

At 3,000 ft., the forest type transitions to spruce-fir. The trail ascends steeply now, with one ledge requiring all fours, reaching 3,500 ft. at the site of an ideal but illegal campsite. The forest is now homogeneous spruce-fir and the trail continues climbing, switching back through ledges and flats until the summit is attained at 3.9 mi. (3,790 ft.). This open, east-facing ledge has attracted thousands of hikers annually. Fortunately, the summit is exposed bedrock and has proved resistant to the scars of high impact. (Arguably, some of the exposed bedrock is the result of intensive use.)

In the opinion of many seasoned Catskill hikers, this is the region's premier scenic hike. Samuel's Point stands to the east. To the right of Samuel's Point is Friday Mtn. (3,694 ft., trailless), showing the scar from a May 1968 landslide. Balsam Cap (3,623 ft., trailless) follows, with Peekamoose (3,843 ft.) and Table (3,847 ft.) to the right. Back to the north, the Blackhead Range is seen. Tremper Mtn. (2,740 ft.) and its fire tower and all of the Devil's Path peaks can be identified. Ashokan High Point in the south and Sky Top in the Shawangunks' Mohonk Preserve are visible. The Ashokan Reservoir (built from 1907 to 1916) is the showpiece of this view. Its multi-arched bridge over the dividing weir, and Brown Station, the location of the aerating plant (and the beginning of the Catskill Aqueduct to New York City), are seen. A bit more to the right is the West Dike, and then the main dam (among the last of the handmade dams ever built) beyond Samsonville Cove. The straight railroad right of way running east and west along the north shore is the relocated path of the Ulster and Delaware Railroad, which ran from Kingston to Oneonta. Surveyed in 1865, the railroad carried 676,000 passengers by 1913 and ceased passenger operations in 1954.

The trail continues west over flat stone and mineral soil past shoulder-high stone corridors, walled in by evergreens, and descends on its way to Cornell Mtn. (3,870 ft.). The terrain flattens and is several feet wide in the saddle between Wittenberg and Cornell at 4.25 mi., in a charming section of trail known as Bruin's Causeway. A few steep pitches follow, one crevice requiring all fours, where backpackers typically remove their packs and hand them up. *It is especially tricky and potentially hazardous, especially when the crack is packed with ice.*

The trail rises onto Cornell's summit (seen on early maps as the "Crown of Cornell") into its thick mantle of virgin red spruce that extends over much of the mountain's western slopes. At 4.7 mi., a short spur to the left of the main trail leads to Cloud Cliff (approximately Cornell's summit). The views here are disappointing in comparison with Wittenberg's, but day hikers are advised that the next view, at 4.8 mi., is spectacular, providing westerly vistas that are unavailable from Wittenberg. Most prominent of the mountains here is Slide itself, looming monstrously ahead, its namesake landslide showing prominently on the north slope. Peekamoose and Table, shaggy with spruce-fir, show up boldly to the left, and to the right (north) are Giant Ledge and Panther. Van Wyck (3,206 ft.) and Woodhull (3,050 ft.) show to the southwest, and trailless Hemlock (3,240 ft.), Spruce (3,390 ft.), and Fir (3,630 ft.) appear to the northwest, over the northern shoulder of Slide.

(NOTE: Most day hikers coming from the Woodland Valley trailhead turn around at this point. Hikers intending to continue across Slide Mtn. should make note of the time and be prepared—this is the "Point of No Return." Water is scarce and in most seasons is entirely absent until hikers approach Slide's summit.)

The descent of Cornell's western slope provides several outcroppings with sustained views. At around 3,300 ft. the trail begins to flatten, and the first of several intermittent streams flows across the trail (varies seasonally) at 6.2 mi. Opportunities for camping in the saddle are excellent, with its six designated (legal) campsites. Water in the saddle becomes very scarce by late summer, and is frequently muddy, so plan on carrying extra water.

The trail continues west, climbing Slide's eastern slopes and passing a spur to an excellent spring at 6.8 mi. (3,900 ft.), which in spite of its elevation has been known to run continuously throughout the season. (Don't depend on it.) Views from this spur are spectacular. Looking back into the northeast as the sun is setting, it is possible to see the sun reflecting off the cab of Tremper Mtn.'s fire tower. The trail soon climbs a series of long, rustic wooden stairways and stone steps, swinging southwest before it arrives at the summit ledge where a bronze plaque commemorates the Catskills' beloved naturalist, John Burroughs. Trail register sign-ins have determined that Slide Mtn. boasts about 35,000 visitor-days every year, equal to those of Giant Ledge. It is not unlikely that on a weekend at the height of the season (August 15 to October 15) hikers may encounter as many as a hundred people on Slide's summit—many of them from various hiking clubs. Many hikers come to Slide because it is a relatively short climb from the Slide Mtn. trailhead and because it is the Catskills' highest peak—but the views are not considered to be as good as Wittenberg's.

The entire Devil's Path is visible from Slide's open rock summit, as well as Kaaterskill High Peak, Black Dome, and Blackhead. Tremper and Plateau mtns. are in the northeast. Cornell and Wittenberg are directly in the east. Friday and Balsam Cap appear to the right, as well as Ashokan High Point (150 degrees). Around 1890, a tower on Slide enabled visitors to see more than 70 named peaks and mountain ranges as far away as Vermont, New Jersey, the Hudson Highlands, and the Berkshires (similar views are available from many Catskill peaks without towers).

Crossing the actual summit, where the fire tower and lean-to once stood, the trail descends gently to the west. (The tower and lean-to were not replaced, in order to limit intensive use here.) Within moments, another vantage point appears to the right (north), again with extensive views, that add to those from the summit to include Giant Ledge, Panther, Halcott, Sherrill, North Dome, West Kill, Windham High Peak, Hunter, and others too numerous and clustered to identify. This view is in many respects better than the summit's. Descending easily, the trail widens (it once served as the fire tower road) and is heavily traveled. At 7.7 mi., Curtis-Ormsbee Trail comes in from the left (southwest) at 3,900 ft. Most hikers prefer to detour onto Curtis-Ormsbee Trail for its scenery, though it is longer.

Wittenberg-Cornell-Slide Trail continues downhill and curves through an unusual section of crumbling white quartz pebbles that early guidebook writers called the Garden Path. This trail soon turns to uneven stone and cobble and descends consistently until reaching the junction with Phoenicia-East Branch Trail at 9.1 mi. Here at the junction with Phoenicia-East Branch Trail, Wittenberg-Cornell-Slide Trail turns right toward the trailhead parking area.

Wittenberg-Cornell-Slide Trail (Burroughs Range Trail, map 1: C7–D6)

Distances from Woodland Valley state campground (1,330 ft.) to
- Terrace Mtn. Trail (2,670 ft.): 2.3 mi., 1,350 ft., 1 hr. 50 min.
- Wittenberg Mtn. summit (3,790 ft.): 3.9 mi., 2,450 ft., 3 hr. 10 min.
- Cornell Mtn. summit (Cloud Cliff) (3,870 ft.): 4.7 mi., 2,750 ft. (rev. 200 ft.), 3 hr. 45 min.
- Slide Mtn. summit (4,190 ft.): 7.0 mi., 3,700 ft. (rev. 650 ft.), 5 hr. 20 min.
- Curtis-Ormsbee Trail (3,970 ft.): 7.7 mi., 3,750 ft. (rev. 250 ft.), 5 hr. 45 min.
- Phoenicia-East Branch Trail (2,810 ft.): 9.1 mi., 3,750 ft. (rev. 1,150 ft.), 6 hr. 25 min.
- Slide Mtn. parking area on CR 47 (2,410 ft.): 9.7 mi., 3,750 ft. (rev. 400 ft.), 6 hr. 45 min.

Terrace Mtn. Trail

Terrace is not a mountain in its own right, but literally a terrace project-ing from the northerly shoulder of Wittenberg. Its main attractions are the lean-to and its surrounding flat ground, which has been used tra-ditionally by large groups. In the off-season, when scouts are not about in numbers, this area can be extremely quiet, especially compared with Wittenberg, where most day hikers are heading. At one time Terrace Mtn. Trail began near the base of Cross Mtn. Hollow and started out across the lovely old suspension footbridge that once spanned the Esopus Creek east of Woodland Valley Campground, about which many older hikers will fondly reminisce. Today, the trail begins in the saddle between Terrace and Wittenberg along Wittenberg-Cornell-Slide Trail at 2,650 ft., an unfortu-nate but necessary compromise that has added substantial distance to this once popular destination.

Terrace Mtn. Trail heads north from the saddle, passing through a short tunnel of hemlock trees. The trail drops out of the evergreens into a hardwood forest, descending to the southeast slightly before turning north again where the trail opens onto a large, tilted rock slab and spruce meadow, with tufts of grass, spruce-fir growth, old fire rings, and rock slab furniture on open bedrock with a northeasterly aspect (Terrace Lookout). This sce-nic area is the place to camp for hikers headed to Wittenberg, rather than taking the extra time to continue down to the lean-to, which lacks any views and will, for lack of exposure, be buggier. From the high (southerly) end of the rocks, near two benchmarks spaced 15 ft. apart, are phenomenal,

close-up views of Panther Mtn. (3,730 ft.) and Giant Ledge (3,200 ft.).
In addition, West Kill, Diamond Notch, Southwest Hunter, Hunter (at
44 degrees), North Dome, Sherrill, Halcott (10 mi. distant), Stony Clove
Notch, and several mountains of the Devil's Path are visible. Samuel's
Point (2,885 ft.) is at 150 degrees. The trail continues to the north, crossing small, open rock meadows (none as scenic as the first) through a hardwood forest over a gullied treadway that flattens as it turns east, where a
few very large hemlock trees appear. On the expansive wooded flats of Terrace Mtn., the lean-to stands in an open, grassy hardwood grove. A bronze
plaque embedded in the logs commemorates Jack Gebel of the Adirondack
Mountain Club's Long Island Chapter.

From the front of the lean-to, to the left 150 ft., the old Wittenberg-
Cornell-Slide Trail to Woodland Valley goes off to the east. It is obscure,
unmarked, and often identified by a tiny rock cairn. Although the trail
has no legal outlet without bushwhacking to state land and fording the
Esopus, it can still be walked and is in excellent condition. Hikers staying
over at the lean-to can explore this old trail, which drops downhill to the
south, switches back at Fiddler's Elbow, and descends through a maturing
sugar maple forest, dropping 1,000 ft. and 1.2 mi. to the Esopus Creek and
the site of the old cable suspension footbridge, which was removed by the
Department of Environmental Conservation several years ago (the concrete
anchors remain). This route is, however, the fastest egress to Woodland Valley
in the event of an emergency and provides a continuous descent to the creek.

Terrace Mtn. Trail (map 1: C7)

Distances from Wittenberg-Cornell-Slide Trail (2,670 ft.) to
- Terrace Lookout (2,556 ft.): 0.3 mi., 0 ft. (rev. 100 ft.), 10 min.
- Terrace Mtn. lean-to (2,350 ft.): 0.8 mi., 0 ft. (rev. 200 ft.), 25 min.

Phoenicia-East Branch Trail

Phoenicia-East Branch Trail (Woodland Valley Denning Trail) begins in
the scenic forest recesses of Woodland Valley, long known for its tumbling
creeks, good trout fishing, and rugged mountain scenery. The trail is used
as an alternate access route to the Giant Ledge-Panther-Fox Hollow Trail,
as well as to Slide Mtn. via Wittenberg-Cornell-Slide Trail (Burroughs

Range Trail.) Beyond the steep topography of Fork Ridge, it follows an old woods road to Denning. Following its junction with Wittenberg-Cornell-Slide Trail, Phoenicia-East Branch Trail is a popular cross-country ski trail among serious backcountry enthusiasts.

From the west end of Phoenicia at the junction of Old NY 28 and NY 28, travel 0.6 mi. west on NY 28, turning left (south) onto Woodland Valley Road. Cross the Esopus Creek at 0.8 mi., and continue right on Woodland Valley Road. At 5.8 mi., park at the Woodland Valley trailhead parking area at the west end of Woodland Valley Road, across from the state campground. (This is the same parking area used to gain entrance to Wittenberg-Cornell-Slide Trail).

From the north side of the parking lot the trail climbs two flights of stone-and-tie steps, ascends, and turns left (west) to traverse Fork Ridge, leveling at 1,900 ft. At 0.5 mi., a steep descent through a boulder-strewn hardwood forest leads to an impressive flight of 50 stone steps, built by an AMC trail crew in 1993. At 1.0 mi., the trail crosses a tributary of Woodland Valley Creek, situated in a rocky ash grove, and ascends through an area of isolated hemlock. At 1.2 mi., the trail turns to the right (west) at the site of a former trail junction. The trail widens and improves as the grade increases over an early roadbed (the old Slide Mtn.-Woodland Valley Road). Crossing another seasonal tributary of the creek, the trail swings south at 1.7 mi. At 2,600 ft., the terrain flattens as it passes a designated campsite on the left (south), within five minutes' walk arriving at the junction with Giant Ledge-Panther-Fox Hollow Trail at 2.5 mi.

Continuing west, the trail soon passes an obvious but unmarked, unsigned path on the left (southwest) at 2,700 ft. This old road is still identified on some maps as the Slide Mtn.-Woodland Valley Road and reaches Slide Mtn. Road in 0.9 mi. It is legally walkable for hikers going over to Slide's trailhead from Giant Ledge or Fork Ridge, and this is the recommended route, rather than descending to Slide Mtn. Road's hairpin turn via Phoenicia-East Branch Trail, losing nearly 600 ft. in elevation in the process. Traditionally, it is most useful to those completing the (usually hiked clockwise) circuit of Wittenberg-Cornell-Slide Trail (Burroughs Range Trail) back to Woodland Valley. (These hikers are at this point sorely in need of a level shortcut.) This section of the old road is unidentified from either direction, and no signed routes indicate its distance or elevation advantage. The only sign, at the east end of Winnisook Lake where the road enters the woods, states: Public Easement Across Private Land.

From the junction with the old road, Phoenicia-East Branch Trail continues straight ahead (west), descending over a very rocky surface and passing through a varied forest of large-in-diameter but low white birch trees and a little hemlock stand at 2,400 ft. Passing a signboard and trail register, continue downhill a few hundred feet to Slide Mtn. Road at the hairpin turn and the Giant Ledge trailhead parking area at 3.4 mi. Phoenicia-East Branch Trail turns left (south-southwest) and follows Slide Mtn. Road (CR 47), passing Winnisook Lake at 4.1 mi., to resume at the Slide Mtn. trailhead parking area on the left (southeast) side of CR 47.

At 5.3 mi., Phoenicia-East Branch Trail continues from the Slide Mtn. trailhead. This trailhead is the traditional, easiest approach to Slide Mtn. (4,190 ft.) from Wittenberg-Cornell-Slide Trail junction (the old truck trail). It is also the less interesting approach, and most hikers with the time will ascend scenic Curtis-Ormsbee Trail (ahead) and descend Wittenberg-Cornell-Slide Trail, making a loop back to the trailhead on the truck trail.

Phoenicia-East Branch Trail crosses the west branch of the Neversink River, continues through a flat sugar maple forest over impacted mineral soil for a few hundred feet, and climbs moderately steeply over large rocks and roots to the old truck trail, bearing right (south) at 5.7 mi., and leveling out. A piped spring is seen on the left. At 6.1 mi., the trail arrives at a T junction where Wittenberg-Cornell-Slide Trail leaves to the left (east).

The trail continues straight ahead (south) over flat terrain. The road shrinks to the width of a footpath for a short distance; old campsites appear in the woods. Crossing a tributary on a wooden bridge, the trail climbs to the south at an easy incline. Within twenty minutes of the bridge, at 6.9 mi., the trail reaches a T and the beginning of Curtis-Ormsbee Trail on the left (east).

Phoenicia-East Branch Trail descends, still assuming the width and character of an old road as it heads south, providing seasonal views of Slide Mtn. to the east. (From this point to Peekamoose-Table Trail, Phoenicia-East Branch Trail is also a section of the Long Path.) The trail crosses a number of seasonal tributaries of Deer Shanty Brook—one of them spanning a deep gully showing the remains of an old timber bridge with stone abutments. At 8.6 mi., the trail passes the junction with Peekamoose-Table Trail on the left (west). (This intersection, or possibly Curtis-Ormsbee Trail, may be the origin of a proposed trail that would connect the Slide Mtn. Wilderness Area to the Biscuit Brook trailhead in the Big Indian wilderness, crossing over Wildcat Mtn. This 4.0-mi. trail would provide the opportunity for extended backpacking trips, joining two wilderness areas, and providing a link for the Finger Lakes Trail.)

The trail soon crosses a footbridge and descends gradually over a stable, road-wide surface, roughly following the east branch of the Neversink River in a deep-forest setting, and arrives at the Denning trailhead at the northeast end of Denning Road near the confluence of Tray Mill Brook and the East Branch of the Neversink River at 9.7 mi. (2,130 ft.). This trailhead is situated in one of the prettiest valleys in the Catskills. Many hikers embark upon day hikes of Peekamoose and Table from here to gain the 1,000-ft. elevation advantage over the route from Peekamoose Road (CR 47), and, less frequently, make round trips to Slide via this trailhead and Curtis-Ormsbee Trail.

Phoenicia-East Branch Trail (map 1: C7–C6)

Distances from Woodland Valley state campground (1,330 ft.) to
- Giant Ledge-Panther-Fox Hollow Trail (2,750 ft.): 2.5 mi., 1,850 ft. (rev. 400 ft.), 2 hr. 15 min.
- Giant Ledge parking area on CR 47 (2,170 ft.): 3.4 mi., 1,850 ft. (rev. 600 ft.), 2 hr. 35 min.
- Slide Mtn. parking area on CR 47 (2,410 ft.): 5.3 mi., 2,350 ft. (rev. 250 ft.), 3 hr. 50 min.
- Wittenberg-Cornell-Slide Trail (2,810 ft.): 6.1 mi., 2,750 ft., 4 hr. 25 min.
- Curtis-Ormsbee Trail (3,070 ft.): 6.9 mi., 3,000 ft., 4 hr. 55 min.
- Peekamoose-Table Trail (2,330 ft.): 8.6 mi., 3,000 ft. (rev. 750 ft.), 5 hr. 50 min.
- trailhead parking area on Denning Road (2,130 ft.): 9.7 mi., 3,000 ft. (rev. 200 ft.), 6 hr. 20 min.

Giant Ledge-Panther-Fox Hollow Trail

Giant Ledge has long been one of hiking's most popular destinations, owing to its easy access, dramatic scenery, and legal ridge-top camping. Overnight camping continues to be a popular activity that imposes upon the pristine nature of the ridge. However, this high-use area is being closely monitored and well kept; at this time, what was once unchecked impact has been regulated and appears to be stabilized.

Gain access to Phoenicia-East Branch Trail junction at the hairpin turn (Giant Ledge parking area), 7.2 miles south of NY 28 on CR 47, locally known as Big Indian Hollow Road, Slide Mtn. Road, or West Branch Road. (From the hairpin turn, hikers must first travel east along Phoenicia-East Branch Trail 0.7 mi. to its junction with Giant Ledge-Panther-Fox Hollow Trail.)

Phoenicia-East Branch Trail heads east into the forest, arriving in few hundred feet at the map kiosk and trail register. The Esopus Creek headwaters run audibly to the left (north) and downhill. The trail climbs, penetrating a northern hardwood forest with large, low-crowned yellow birches. A few natural stone steps are enhanced with contrived steps as elevation is gained. This section of trail is rock strewn but short. At 2,680 ft., the trail flattens into a saddle as a woods road departs to the right (west) toward Winnisook Lake. (This unmarked but legal road can be used as a shortcut to and from the Slide Mtn. trailhead.) The trail junction with Giant Ledge-Panther-Fox Hollow Trail appears at 0.8 mi. on the left (north) amid cherry trees and snarls of blackberry underbrush. It is well identified.

Turning left (north) off Phoenicia-East Branch Trail, Giant Ledge-Panther-Fox Hollow Trail passes over large, flat stones through muddy areas. This brief level stretch gives way to a flight of wide steps built with vertically placed bluestone. After a short ascent, at 0.6 mi. (1,270 ft.) a marked spur leads left (west) to a spring. Climbing from this junction, the trail tops out at 0.8 mi. (3,250 ft.), passing a herd trail to the left (west) of a pair of long, flat rocks. The herd trail leads to two illegal campsites. The main trail continues over rock on a level ridge to another short, unmarked spur on the right (east), the first and perhaps most significant of Giant Ledge's lookouts. *These vertical drops are hundreds of feet high and must be* *considered extremely dangerous.* The views are significant. It was from this interior cirque that a late retreating glacier (perhaps the Catskills' last) scoured the walls of the surrounding slopes into steep, half-bowl profiles. From areas along the cliff, hikers can peer down at trees that have been smashed under breakaway talus and others killed by drought, their skeletonized trunks visible in the forest below.

From left to right the view takes in West Kill and Ox and Stony Cloves to Hunter. Plateau is the longest, flattest summit ridge, to the right of Hunter. Most of the Indian Head Wilderness Area's peaks can be seen from Plateau to Overlook. Wittenberg, Cornell, and Slide (between the latter two peaks is Friday Mtn., 3,694 ft.) are visible. (Don't lean too far out on the ledge to see Slide.)

The trail continues level as it travels straight (north) along the ledge, where several open shelves of rock appear to the right (east), each with its distinct character and expansive views. Blueberries are profuse. Following the first few ledges, at 0.8 mi. a spur trail departs from the main trail to the left (west), leading past two heavily used campsites (legal) to Giant Ledge's only westerly views of the Big Indian Wilderness. (The position of this ledge is 42° 02.318' N, 74° 23.761' W, at an altitude of 3,209 ft.) Across Big Indian Hollow is Fir (3,630 ft.), with Spruce (3,390 ft.) and Hemlock (3,240 ft.) to the left (southeast). Beyond Hemlock is Van Wyck (3,206 ft.). To the right (northwest) of Fir are Big Indian (3,710 ft.), Eagle (3,610 ft.), Haynes (3,420 ft.), and Balsam (3,610 ft.). These peaks are traversed by Pine Hill-West Branch Trail.

As Giant Ledge-Panther-Fox Hollow Trail moves north along the ridge, points looking to the right (east) continue, the ledges too numerous to identify singly. At 1.0 mi., the trail descends, sharply at times, leveling in a densely foliated area of northern hardwood and ferns. This is the saddle between Giant Ledge and Panther, leading to the (720-ft. vertical rise) ascent of Panther. As the trail ascends, at 1.8 mi. a short, unmarked spur to the right (east) at 3,400 ft. opens to views of Slide and Wittenberg. Fork Ridge juts southeast into the cirque, down in the southern foreground.

The trail crosses over to the western side of the ridge, climbing through ledgy terrain to the 3,500-ft. mark. A large rock (false summit) offering only strained views is attained shortly thereafter, at 3,560 ft. For hikers coming up from Fox Hollow, this view is not worth coming across the long flat summit to see (better views exist at the summit).

The trail climbs a bit more, easily, to attain the summit ridge, which is virtually blinded by balsam fir. Panther's true summit is reached at 2.3 mi. (3,730 ft.), offering a view of vast proportions. This little outcropping in the fir faces northeast, and although similar in many respects to the view from Giant Ledge, it offers a look at more northerly territory. West Kill and Hunter remain in sight, but now North Dome (3,610 ft.) and Sherrill (3,550 ft.) appear. The vague bubble-peak sticking up between Plateau and Sugarloaf is Kaaterskill High Peak. The Blackheads appear, but only two of them—Black Dome and Thomas Cole. Up against the northeastern skyline you can see a chip of the Escarpment as it drops toward Dutcher Notch. The Devil's Path mountains, as well as Overlook and Mt. Tobias, are visible. Hunter's fire tower can be seen, as can Tremper Mtn.'s (90 degrees). The Burroughs Range is no longer visible, but low in the valley you can see the piscatorial town of Phoenicia alongside the Esopus Creek.

The trail descends amid white stars of bunchberry and pale-faced oxalis blooms (common wood sorrel), always looking east, and then levels on a flat in boreal Catskill alpine terrain. Little views appear, suspended over Woodland Valley. The trail drops downhill shortly into hardwoods again, crossing over large stones, through ledges and fern glades, and at 3.8 mi. crosses a bald, where discreet upper-elevation camping is possible (there are several such places) without damage to vegetation.

At 4.3 mi. (3,200 ft.), another false summit is reached, with limited views to all but the north. This is a large, open rocky bald, from which many large peaks can be seen to the east and west. Most striking is the profile of Panther itself, close at hand and nearly due south. The trail descends now through open northern hardwood forest, winding in a wide arc from northwest to northeast. The terrain flattens only briefly as it runs cross-slope under a steep hillside covered in rock and yellow birch. Very tall ash and sugar maple are the homogeneous types. Understory sunlight is limited, and with the high canopy providing so much shade, the wet soil enables excruciating stinging nettles to grow in a solid, verdant carpet of ground, covering acres. Thick forest continues as the trail follows a rocky old road, long since abandoned. The trail turns to the east. At 6.4 mi. (1,700 ft.), a spur to the left (north) leads 200 ft. to an open grassy area with a spring and lean-to. The main trail descends through the shady woods of Fox Hollow with its stream and tall hardwoods, following the old settlement road to pass the trail register on the left at 6.7 mi. The trail is heavily eroded now as it crosses a wet spot on a double-stringer bridge, bearing right to the parking lot, where a privy and trail signs are located.

Giant Ledge-Panther-Fox Hollow Trail (map 1: C6)

Distances from Phoenicia-East Branch Trail (2,750 ft.) to
- Giant Ledge (3,210 ft.): 0.8 mi., 450 ft., 40 min.
- Panther Mtn. summit (3,730 ft.): 2.3 mi., 1,150 ft. (rev. 200 ft.), 1 hr. 50 min.
- northernmost false summit (3,390 ft.): 4.3 mi., 1,500 ft. (rev. 700 ft.), 2 hr. 55 min.
- Fox Hollow lean-to spur (1,650 ft.): 6.4 mi., 1,500 ft. (rev. 1,750 ft.), 4 hr. 20 min.
- trailhead at Fox Hollow (1,330 ft.): 6.7 mi., 1,500 ft. (rev. 300 ft.), 4 hr. 30 min.

Curtis-Ormsbee Trail

This trail begins off Phoenicia-East Branch Trail, 1.5 mi. from the Slide Mtn. trailhead on CR 47. It was pioneered in the late 1800s by two avid hikers—"Father Bill" Curtis, an officer of the Fresh Air Club, and his companion, Allen Ormsbee. Unbelievably, both of them died of exposure in a snowstorm on their way to a meeting of the Appalachian Mountain Club on Mt. Washington in August 1900—a grim reminder that the unexpected can happen to even the most experienced hikers. This trail provides the most enjoyable, scenic, and popular approach to Slide Mtn. for hikers "in the know." (The majority uses Wittenberg-Cornell-Slide Trail, which on this side of the range is known informally as Jeep Trail, or Wagon Road.)

Curtis-Ormsbee Trail runs east from Phoenicia-East Branch Trail, remaining flat momentarily until beginning a steady rise from 3,100 ft. After a short steep section at 0.4 mi., the trail opens up on a rock outcropping with good views to the left (north) at 3,400 ft. The vista includes Doubletop (3,870 ft.), Graham (3,868 ft.), Wildcat (3,160 ft.), Big Indian (3,710 ft.), Fir (3,630 ft.), Spruce (3,390 ft.), and Hemlock (3,240 ft.). Balsam Lake Mtn. (3,730 ft.) is behind Graham. The trail continues to climb, passing the 3,500-ft. mark, when at 0.6 mi. a short, marked spur leaves the main trail 200 ft. to the right (south), to an outstanding ledge at 3,550 ft., with views of Table (3,847 ft.), Lone (3,721 ft.), Rocky (3,508 ft.), and Balsam Cap (3,623 ft.). High Point (1,803 ft.) in the township of Sussex, New Jersey, is easily identified (with binoculars) by its monument, a war memorial to the state's soldiers.

The trail eases to a gentle grade as balsam fir begins to take hold, and soon flattens, becoming muddy in spots. Climbing through a forest of pure fir, the path curves to the north and back into the east again before leveling above 3,900 ft. and arriving at the junction with Wittenberg-Cornell-Slide Trail at 1.4 mi. At the junction, the ground is dusted with white quartz pebbles.

Curtis-Ormsbee Trail (map 1: C6–D6)

Distances from Phoenicia-East Branch Trail (3,070 ft.) to
  • Wittenberg-Cornell-Slide Trail (3,970 ft.): 1.4 mi., 900 ft., 1 hr. 10 min.
  • Slide Mtn. summit (4,190 ft.) via Wittenberg-Cornell-Slide Trail: 2.0 mi., 1,100 ft., 1 hr. 35 min.

Peekamoose-Table Trail

From a rugged environment of waterfalls, boulders, and ravines at Rondout Creek's headwaters, Peekamoose-Table Trail rises more than 2,600 ft. in 3.3 mi. Park at the Peekamoose (Peak-of-the-Moose) trailhead, 10 mi. west of West Shokan along CR 42. Watch carefully for the trail signs and parking area on the right. The trail rises immediately from the parking area on the north side of Peekamoose Road. Trail signs are posted here.

The trail ascends to join an old road at 0.7 mi., where the trail register is located in a flat, open area. Beech trees give way to sugar maple and birch as old stone walls appear and a red pine plantation is seen to the east. Skid roads cross the trail, which now climbs, relaxing somewhat through a flat, grassy maple woods, soon crossing an open, east-facing slope exposed to the wind, where hundreds of trees were blown down during Hurricane Floyd in 1999. The downed, large-diameter hardwoods (ash and cherry) will remain visible for years to come. The opened canopy has provided light for mountain ash and wildflowers—asters, nettles, touch-me-nots. Marking and maintenance are good, and tantalizing (but ultimately frustrating) views of Breath Hill (2,536 ft.) and the ridges of Sundown Wild Forest exist to the right (southeast).

The trail rises in pitches, over ledges and flats, ascending steadily to reach a large "balance rock" on a flat slab of fissured, pink sandstone at

1.9 mi. This is Reconnoiter Rock (2,900 ft.), which is viewless during leaf-out season. The trail is mineral soil now, continuing through a lush first-growth forest over rooty, red silt. At 2.3 mi. (3,500 ft.), a ledge is reached, where herd trails have preempted the superior views existing just a bit higher in elevation. Ignore these, instead continuing on the main trail to the lookout above the 3,500-ft. sign, where at 2.4 mi. a large ledge appears to the right. The view is excellent, including Big Indian (3,710 ft.), Doubletop (3,870 ft.), and Balsam Lake Mtn. (3,730 ft.) and its fire tower (319 degrees). High Point in Sussex, New Jersey, can be seen at 212 degrees. Van Wyck, Wildcat, and Woodhull lie among the southwestern hills.

The following terrain has several ledges worthy of exploration and has the feel of a summit, but there remains a good distance to the true summit of Peekamoose. The trail continues flat through white birch and red spruce thickets, with black cherry over ferns. Leaving the fern glades, the trail rises over red silt again as a spring appears to the left of the trail—nearly in the trail—draining into a cloudy puddle. The trail climbs into balsam and passes briefly over duff, rising onto the thickly boreal summit at 3.5 mi.

Encased in dense balsam fir cripplebrush, Peekamoose summit (3,843 ft.) is punctuated by a solitary conglomerate boulder in the corner of a small clearing. Even climbing the rock won't provide views over the canopy of low fir. The trail descends beyond the summit on a treadway of sandy glacial till and flattens in a brief saddle before rising gradually, then more steeply through a boreal corridor to the summit of Table Mtn. at 4.3 mi. (3,847 ft.). While it is possible to discover views from Table, it is difficult to do so without damaging the sensitive upper-elevation vegetation through the encouragement of herd paths, of which there are several. Try to avoid these, as just past the summit there is a view ledge to the left of the trail. As the trail descends the north side of Table, marginal summertime views of Slide Mtn. appear to the north. Just below the 3,500-ft. mark at 4.7 mi., a spur to the left (southwest) leads to the Boughton Memorial lean-to, with some views of Van Wyck. A lower spur trail to the right at 3,430 ft. leads ⚠ 100 ft. to a piped spring. *The trail descends into the west and travels easily across slope, passing a lookout ledge to the left (southwest), with a dangerous drop overlooking Van Wyck Mtn. (3,206 ft.).* Increasingly large cherry trees follow and the trail drops down to 2,700 ft., passing another southwest-facing, treed-in spur trail to the left with no summer views. Ascending to a knoll, the trail drops steadily thereafter through a ledgy hemlock woods, where designated campsite disks identify a spur trail on the right (north). The spur trail follows the spine of a hemlock bluff above the Neversink River for 100 yd. to a large and attractive campsite with room for a dozen tents. The main trail continues, descending slightly to pass another designated site on the left.

Keep a close watch on the trail markers as you come west through the various stream channels at the confluence of Deer Shanty Brook and the Neversink's east branch. This is beautiful country, and forest management has taken several steps to ensure that it remains pristine. One was the removal of a lean-to so that the site complies with the 150-ft. rule (and because the proximity of the river discourages the building of a privy) and to minimize user impact in an area so close to a trailhead. (Several designated sites remain in the area.) The trail continues across the confluence of creeks here, where log bridges have been placed. The spring runoff is so boisterous it has defied efforts to place permanent footbridges. *Be careful crossing these stringer bridges, which are slippery when* *wet and high enough to result in injury in the event of a fall.* From the west side of Deer Shanty Brook, the trail climbs gently to meet Phoenicia-East Branch Trail at 6.7 mi.

Peekamoose-Table Trail (map 1: D6)

Distances from trailhead on CR 42 (Peekamoose Road) (1,230 ft.) to
- view ledge (3,510 ft.): 2.4 mi., 2,300 ft., 2 hr. 20 min.
- Peekamoose Mountain summit (3,843 ft.): 3.5 mi., 2,600 ft., 2 hr. 55 min.
- Table Mtn. summit (3,847 ft.): 4.3 mi., 2,800 ft. (rev. 200 ft.), 3 hr. 35 min.
- Boughton Memorial lean-to spur (3,480 ft.): 4.7 mi., 2,800 ft. (rev. 350 ft.), 3 hr. 45 min.
- Phoenicia-East Branch Trail (2,330 ft.): 6.7 mi., 2,850 ft. (rev. 1,200 ft.), 5 hr.

SUGGESTED HIKES

Easy Hike

Deer Shanty Brook campsite via Phoenicia-East Branch Trail and Peekamoose-Table Trail [rt: 2.8 mi., 1:30]. This mostly flat, easy hike leads to the enchanting Deer Shanty Brook, the southerly watershed of the Burroughs Range (Slide, Wittenberg, and Cornell Mtns.). This crystal-clear mountain stream is easily explored, and has designated camping nearby.

Strenuous Hikes

Wittenberg Mtn., via Wittenberg-Cornell-Slide Trail, from Woodland Valley trailhead [rt: 7.8 mi., 6:20]. Wittenberg is the darling of many devoted Catskill hikers, with its attractive, boreal ascent and its far-reaching, lofty, southerly viewshed. It is among the most rewarding day hikes in the range.

The Burroughs Range, via Wittenberg-Cornell-Slide Trail, from Woodland Valley to the Slide Mtn. parking area or as a loop returning to the Woodland Valley state campsite [ow: 8.5 mi., 8:00; loop: 14 mi., 12:00]. This challenging and highly scenic weekend backpack can be undertaken as a loop from Woodland Valley state campground, or as a shortened overnight with a vehicle spotted at the Slide Mountain parking area on Slide Mtn. Road in Oliverea.

Take Slide-Wittenberg-Cornell Trail (Burroughs Range Trail) to summit Wittenberg (side trip to Terrace Mtn. lean-to for a two-night option), Cornell, and Slide Mtn. Spectacular views and upper-elevation camping in the col between Cornell and Slide are the highlights of this hike. Stage from Woodland Valley state campsite and shuttle back from the Slide Mtn. parking area (4,000 ft. cumulative elevation gain), or close the loop by following Slide Mtn. Road past Winnisook Lake, taking the first right after the lake on a legal, maintained, nameless woods road to the junction with the Phoenicia-East Branch Trail and across Fork Ridge to the Woodland Valley campsite (5,000-ft. elevation gain).

SECTION 13
SHANDAKEN WILD FOREST

The Shandaken Wild Forest is located on the borders of Greene and Ulster counties in the towns of Lexington and Shandaken, respectively. The four-parcel, 5,400-acre aggregate of forest lands lies west of the West Kill Mountain Wilderness, and north of the Slide Mountain Wilderness, in proximity to the high-peaks region. The area of interest to recreational users is the Rochester Hollow parcel, largest of the four at 2,475 acres. Within it are three hiking trails—two of them loops—two primitive campsites, and a lean-to. The area is popular with scout groups, backcountry skiers, hikers, and hunters. Trails (with the exception of Rochester Hollow Trail) were created with skiers and mountain bikers in mind. The three hiking trails, however, are less than ideal for winter sports enthusiasts. Fit and experienced skiers will stride or herringbone here and there on steep, steady inclines. Even the upper loop trails are difficult ski trails, owing to their layout over rough terrain and, with the exception of Rochester Hollow Trail, void of any real diagonal striding terrain. Because of the number of hikers using the trails, post holes will logically prevent the formation of a tracked surface. The payoff, of course, is in the glide back down to the parking area, for which a good snow cover is preferable. Snowshoers finding unpacked snow will find the climb more rewarding, but still a substantial workout. This area receives such high use that new snowfalls will quickly become packed down.

Signs of early settlement here, such as stone walls and foundations, and a few scattered fruit trees suggest that this area was extensively farmed. Tanneries, sawmills, and bluestone quarries existed throughout the surrounding wild forest area. The Raymond C. Riordan School, formerly located in Highland, New York, once maintained a demonstration fruit farm in the upper realms of the hollow. The school's namesake, Raymond Riordan, was a philanthropist who catered to troubled adolescents in the early part of the twentieth century. The school was responsible for the Burroughs Memorial, which stands at the head of the hollow, and for the extensive stone walls and spruce plantations that appear along Yellow Loop Trail. Today there are few other signs of habitation.

Rochester Hollow Trail is an uphill-and-back-down trip, with the two additional trails and the lean-to situated at the height of elevation. Two primitive campsites near Rochester Hollow trailhead are close enough to the road to serve as staging camps for those headed into the nearby high-peaks trailheads.

Rochester Hollow Trail

Marked with blue state-trail disks, Rochester Hollow Trail enters the woods at the site of a trail register.

From the trail register, Rochester Hollow Trail climbs easily alongside a brook in a second-growth northern hardwood forest. The trail follows a dirt road. Within a short distance are two nicely situated primitive campsites on the left, with the brook nearby. The trail steepens and continues on a steady grade. (This incline will frustrate cross-country skiers, who should come equipped to carry their skis to a point where they can be used efficiently.)

At a point where two old bluestone pillars once formed a gate at 1.4 mi., the trail steepens again. It soon passes Yellow Loop Trail on the right, just prior to the top of the hollow. Immediately across a small stream as the trail levels, the Riordan School's monument to John Burroughs is on the right at 1.8 mi. The naturalist was from Roxbury, a town not far to the northwest. Rochester Hollow Trail continues on a flat section of the old road until reaching the lean-to (3.0 mi), which is situated 100 yd. off trail to the right (north). This spot marks the end of the blue-marked Rochester Hollow Trail. Red Loop Trail, the loop of which uses this last end of the blue trail, begins a few hundred yards ahead on the left.

Rochester Hollow Trail (map 2: C6-B6)

Distances from trailhead (1,350 ft.) to
- Yellow Loop Trail, lower junction (2,150 ft.): 1.8 mi., 800 ft., 1 hr. 20 min.
- Red Loop Trail, lower junction (2,200 ft.): 2.0 mi., 850 ft., 1 hr. 25 min.
- lean-to (2,250 ft.): 3 mi., 900 ft., 1 hr. 50 min.

Yellow Loop Trail

Yellow Trail is a short and interesting recreational trail, which forms a loop using a 0.4-mi. road section of Rochester Hollow Trail. The trail is not graded for skiing. Though advanced skiers would have no problem with it and beginners could manage in deep snow conditions, it is best skied from the western end.

The trail heads northeast and then nearly due west, passing through the spruce plantations of the old Riordan School's demonstration fruit farm. Aside from the beautifully constructed and unusually high bluestone walls, no other signs of habitation exist. The trail crosses a small plank bridge and drops south to join Rochester Hollow Trail at 0.7 mi.

Yellow Loop Trail (map 2: B6)

Distances from trailhead, lower junction (2,150 ft.), to
- Rochester Hollow Trail (2,200 ft.), 0.7 mi., 120 ft., 25 min.

Red Loop Trail

With its many elevation changes and a narrow footway (in many ways similar to Yellow Loop Trail), Red Loop Trail is most suited to foot and snowshoe travel. The trail begins a few hundred feet west of the bend at the top of the hollow, where the Burroughs Memorial is located, and turns left (southwest) into the woods, descending. The trail climbs up- and downhill for its entirety, rarely settling on level terrain. Midway through the trail an old settlement foundation is seen, and scattered apple trees appear here and there.

As the trail gains distance into the west it ascends very easily, meeting the blue-marked Rochester Hollow Trail again at 1.2 mi. The unmarked dirt road that departs to the left here enters private property, and is gated farther to the west. (It is a continuation of the road the blue-marked

Rochester Hollow Trail uses.) Bear right, following the blue markers, leaving the lean-to on the left, to return to the parking area.

Red Loop Trail (map 2: B6)

Distances from trailhead, lower junction, (2,150 ft.) to
- Rochester Hollow Trail (2,200 ft.), 1.2 mi., 250 ft., 40 min.
- lean-to (2,200 ft.), 1.3 mi., 300 ft., 50 min.
- lower junction, Red Loop Trail (2,150 ft.), 2.0 mi, 140 ft., 1 hr. 20 min.

SUGGESTED HIKE

Moderate Hike

Rochester Hollow Trail [rt: 6.0 mi., 3:30] The centerpiece trail in the Shandaken Wild Forest, Rochester Hollow Trail has a beautifully situated lean-to at its end. The trail's steepness accounts for its rating as moderate, and it may be considered strenuous by some. For variation, take either the Red or Yellow Loop Trail on the descent.

SECTION 14
WILLOWEMOC WILD FOREST

Hikers with young families and those seeking relatively easy backpacking and shakedown trips—or simply moderate hiking—will find this 15,900-acre region of gentle hills and waterways ideal for their purposes. Several of the trails can be reached directly from the Mongaup Pond Public Campground, which lies within the Willowemoc Wild Forest; this is an ideal place to stay while using this forest. The maximum elevation is 3,100 ft. (streams and ponds are numerous) and the topography is not as mountainous as parcels to the east and north. The area offers unusually good opportunities for mountain biking and backcountry skiing and has the largest snowmobile-trail system in the Catskills. Horseback riding is permitted here, except on marked foot trails or on ski and snowmobile trails that are covered with snow or ice. There are 26 mi. of hiking and cross-country ski trails, 15 mi. of hiking-only trails, and 29 mi. of marked snowmobile trails, as well as a great number of primitive camping areas in twelve designated sites adjacent to excellent fishing streams. (Some of the best of these sites are located at the north end of Flugertown Road in the southeast of the area, along the Willowemoc Creek's headwaters.) Other designated camping areas, free and open to the public, are at nearby Waneta Lake on CR 151, and along the northern perimeter of the forest, off Shin Creek Road. (There is one designated site on Beaver Kill Road east of Turnwood as well.)

The Frick Pond-Quick Lake trail system just west of the Mongaup Pond Campground and intensive-use area is a matrix of old roads and settlement areas, once the homesteads of farmers and loggers.

This area is known for its trout fishing. The state fish hatchery at DeBruce, just outside the Mongaup Pond Public Campground, is a good place to see the spawning stock and to learn about the Catskills' trout populations. The Department of Environmental Conservation releases more than half a million fish into Catskill public waterways each year. Fir Brook, along Pole Road, also offers good trout fishing and excellent public access.

This area is habitat to deer and bear, and many early accounts document the capture and killing of large panthers in the area around Willowemoc. The Willowemoc band of the Lenni-Lenape established a popular trade and travel route known as the Sun Trail here. The Lenni-Lenape sold this land to Johannes Hardenburgh in 1706, a transaction resulting in its protection and later its annexation as a state forest preserve.

Big Rock Trail

This trail unevenly bisects both the Frick Pond-Quick Lake trail system from the northeast to the southwest. The southern 0.5-mi. section of Big Rock Trail west of Frick Pond (flat) is among the most attractive trails in the area and can be fashioned into a loop using Logger's Loop Trail, avoiding Big Rock's steep section completely. The northern 1.1-mi. section, however, claims the steepest vertical rise over any equivalent distance in the Frick Pond-Quick Lake trail system. As a rejoinder to the Flynn trailhead in a loop hike, it is preferable to travel south (downhill) on Big Rock Trail as conditions allow, whether on horseback, skis, snowshoes, or foot, rather than ascending it to return on Flynn Trail.

From the Flynn Trail junction east of Hodge Pond, yellow-marked Big Rock Trail drops sharply downhill (south), losing 500 ft. in elevation in the process.

The trail drops downhill from Flynn Trail, arriving in 1.1 mi. at Times Square Junction, a four-way trail intersection. Big Rock Trail continues straight across the junction (southwest), following along the west shore of Frick Pond. Logger's Loop Trail, also yellow, goes left and right. At first the hardwood surroundings and sometimes muddy trail will seem dull, but soon hemlock takes over, emanating from a lush inlet marsh to the right (west), and two short bridges are crossed in idyllic surroundings. It then crosses an enchanting 275-foot-long boardwalk—unusual for the Catskills—offering forest and lake views. The trail ends at its conjunction with Quick Lake Trail, in view of Frick Pond to the left (northeast).

Big Rock Trail (map 2: D4)

Distances from Flynn Trail (2,750 ft.) to
- Logger's Loop Trail at Times Square junction (2,150 ft.): 1.1 mi., 0 ft. (rev. 600 ft.), 35 min.
- Quick Lake Trail and Frick Pond (2,120 ft.): 1.7 mi., 0 ft. (rev. 50 ft.), 50 min.

Flynn Trail

Beginning at the north end of Beech Mtn. Road, across the road from the Frick Pond trailhead parking area, this foot trail provides the shortest access to the Beech Mountain Nature Preserve. As you face the signboard and map kiosk, the trailhead and signage is at your back (east). The trail descends slightly into the woods, heading northeast at 2,100 ft. elevation, passing the trail register within 50 ft. After skirting a private inholding (this is the Beech Mountain Nature Preserve's gatehouse parcel), the trail regains Beech Mtn. Road (dirt) and turns right (north), ascending steadily. Sparse views appear to the left (west). At 2,700 ft., arrive at the junction with Big Rock Trail, a four-way intersection. Mongaup Pond Snowmobile Trail comes in from the right (northeast), and continues across the junction onto Big Rock Trail, on the left (southwest).

The trail goes straight (north) crossing the state-land boundary and entering the public easement into Beech Mountain Nature Preserve at a barrier gate at 1.8 mi. At 1.9 mi., at a wide, grassy T, the trail goes left (west). Marking is obscured by trees on the right (north) side of the trail as it turns west. No destination signage is present and marking is obscure or absent. The trail is up to 80 ft. wide here and in the rest of the preserve.

The trail descends and arrives at a junction near the south shore of Hodge Pond. This very appealing mountain pond contains brook trout and can be legally fished with artificial flies only. No bait of any kind—alive or dead—is permitted. Permission to camp is available by permit only. No boats, rafts, or canoes are allowed.

At 2.1 mi., the trail crosses the outlet, leaves the pond, and ascends gently through the preserve lands. Preserve rules require that hikers stay on the state-marked trail unless fishing in Hodge Pond. At an unsigned Y, the trail bears left and climbs to a barrier gate, returning to state lands in the Willowemoc Wild Forest, and is still an established woods road. The grass-covered trail flattens over scarce patches of flat rock in a dense hardwood forest, until reaching Junkyard Junction and Quick Lake Trail at 3.2 mi. This is the end of Flynn Trail. From this point Quick Lake Trail departs both to the right (west, for Quick Lake) and to the left (south, to Frick Pond and the trailhead parking area on Beech Mtn. Road).

Flynn Trail (map 2: D4)

Distances from trailhead on Beech Mtn. Road (2,150 ft.) to
- Big Rock Trail (2,750 ft.): 1.7 mi., 600 ft., 1 hr. 10 min.
- Hodge Pond (2,590 ft.): 2.1 mi., 600 ft. (rev. 150 ft.), 1 hr. 20 min.
- Quick Lake Trail at Junkyard Junction (2,750 ft.): 3.2 mi., 750 ft., 2 hr.

Quick Lake Trail

This long trail is popular among mountain bikers and cross-country skiers. Trails in the area are generally wide and grassy, but provide little in the way of scenery. Perhaps the biggest attraction Quick Lake Trail has to offer is its isolation. Few if any other hikers will be encountered west of Logger's Loop Trail and Frick Pond.

Enter this trail from the north end of Beech Mtn. Road, 1.0 mi. outside (southwest) of the main entrance to the Mongaup Pond State Campground (see Mongaup-Hardenburgh Trail for directions). The trail leaves from the northwest corner of the Frick Pond trailhead parking lot. A signboard with maps and information concerning the adjoining parcel of the Beech Mountain Nature Preserve (accessible with restrictions) is posted here.

The trail follows the established, rocky treadway slightly downhill and north, shortly reaching the footprint of an old road, now a worn path invaded by vegetation. The trail turns left (west) here, passing the trail register and continuing west until reaching a junction in an open field just east of Frick Pond (not yet visible), at Graveyard Junction. A headstone commemorating Marjorie and Lyle Lobdell, residents of an early farm that stood here, rests to the southeast.

To the right is the yellow-marked Logger's Loop Trail. Continue left (west) to arrive at Frick Pond, where there are limited views north to Mongaup Ridge. This 6-acre, seasonally low, beaver-impounded pond is contained by receding, grassy banks and has no recorded fish-collection inventory. It is believed to contain bullheads, shiners, and pickerel. After crossing the outlet on a wooden footbridge, the trail crosses two small plank bridges as it approaches a junction, still in view of the pond. At 0.7 mi., Big Rock Trail leaves to the (right) north.

Quick Lake Trail continues straight, following red markers. A nearly pure understory of fern growth characterizes this section of trail, which is seldom used as of this writing. Ascending easily through an open forest of black cherry, the trail heads gradually north, crossing a washout. A hardwood stand takes over as Iron Wheel Junction (2,350 ft.) is approached. At this T (1.5 mi.) lies a small but heavy set of iron wheels, possibly those of a horse-drawn log transport. Logger's Loop Trail goes to the right here. Quick Lake Trail turns left (south).

Shared briefly by the snowmobile trail, the trail goes left, uphill, over a grassy treadway, and arrives at a Y at 1.7 mi. (The snowmobile trail leaves to the left and rises steeply to meet the red foot trail ahead, at Coyote Junction.) The trail bears right here, following the red trail toward Junkyard Junction. There is no destination or distance signage. As the trail climbs, red markers are sparse. The trail is road-width and self-guiding, washed out in places and grassy in others, the eroded, thin soils leaving a sandy surface. The trail ascends gradually through a quiet, densely forested woodland to reach Junkyard Junction at 3.2 mi. (2,700 ft.), where Flynn Trail (blue markers) turns right (east) toward Hodge Pond. Quick Lake Trail turns left (west).

Immediately to the left is an open, flat, rocky clearing, the site of the former Beech Mountain Boy Scout camp's junkyard—the junction's namesake. It has been recovered to its natural state, and only small bits of trash are evident. The trail traverses a thickly wooded ridge. Following the north slope of a nameless ridge averaging 2,700 ft., the trail soon turns into the south, providing thin, seasonal views to the west at 4.1 mi. This is the Westerly Vista—the foot trail provides no other views. The trail descends to Coyote Junction at 4.3 mi. (To the left, the snowmobile trail descends to Quick Lake Trail and Iron Wheel Junction.)

Quick Lake Trail turns right (west) at this grassy junction onto a flat section of trail shared by the snowmobile trail, and at 4.9 mi. it arrives at Bobcat Junction. Signage is poor and deteriorating. This section of the foot trail begins level and quickly loses elevation. (The snowmobile trail goes right, descends steeply, and offers open but narrow views of the northern lowlands.) The wide, grassy thoroughfare has no distinct treadway. There are vague summertime views westward, with little definition. Patches of exposed flat rock appear as the trail levels and again descends to Flatrock Junction at 5.9 mi., a four-way intersection of exposed, broken rock. Although from this vantage the foot trail looks less inviting than the snowmobile trail, it is the more interesting choice. The snowmobile trail leaves to the left.

Quick Lake Trail goes right (west), and descends, passing a low, crumbling ledge to the right. Marking is poor or absent. At an unnamed junction at 6.8 mi. (2,200 ft.), the snowmobile trail joins the foot trail from the left (east) and descends to end at Quick Lake at 7.2 mi., arriving on the north shore near a crude campsite. The foot trail is the extension of an old estate road that descends a few hundred feet to the west, following Gee Brook into the Beaver Kill Valley, crossing private lands. This is the fastest egress from this isolated outpost in the western Willowemoc Wild Forest in the event of an emergency. The adjacent private parcels are heavily hunted and several clubs post lands here. Quick Lake is a low, sluggish pond, 6 acres in area and impounded by beavers. There are no plans to repair the ruined, human-made dam. The only break in the homogeneous hardwood forest is the few hemlock trees at the campsite (2,000 ft.).

Quick Lake Trail (map 2: D4)

Distances from trailhead on Beech Mtn. Road (2,150 ft.) to
- Logger's Loop Trail at Graveyard Junction (2,128 ft.): 0.4 mi., 0 ft., 10 min.
- Big Rock Trail (2,120 ft.): 0.7 mi., 0 ft. (rev. 50 ft.), 20 min.
- Logger's Loop Trail at Iron Wheel Junction (2,300 ft.): 1.5 mi., 200 ft., 50 min.
- Flynn Trail at Junkyard Junction (2,750 ft.): 3.2 mi., 650 ft., 1 hr. 55 min.
- Coyote Junction (2,650 ft.): 4.3 mi., 800 ft. (rev. 250 ft.), 2 hr. 35 min.
- Bobcat Junction (2,680 ft.): 4.9 mi., 850 ft., 2 hr. 55 min.
- Flatrock Junction (2,450 ft.): 5.9 mi., 900 ft. (rev. 300 ft.), 3 hr. 25 min.
- Quick Lake (2,000 ft.): 7.2 mi., 900 ft. (rev. 450 ft.), 4 hr. 5 min.

Logger's Loop Trail

The trail begins at Graveyard Junction (junction with Quick Lake Trail), 0.4 mi. west of the Frick Pond trailhead parking lot. At this open, grassy trail junction, Logger's Loop Trail heads north, following cross-country ski trail disks (yellow) and yellow foot-trail markers.

Following the easterly margin of an open field, the path enters the woods where a privy stands to the left. There is a designated campsite area here, although it appears overgrown and little used. Frick Pond can be seen through the trees to the left (west). The trail ascends very slightly, levels, and descends gently again to Times Square Junction at 0.6 mi., a four-way intersection with Big Rock Trail. Identify Logger's Loop Trail across this intersection. This section of the trail, to Iron Wheel Junction, is open to snowmobiles. The trail continues through the intersection.

Following a brief rise, the trail levels through a sugar maple forest, crossing the Hodge Pond outlet (0.5 mi. south of Hodge Pond) and several seasonal runoff gullies, each tending to wash out and erode the trail in spots. The trail makes a sweeping turn into the south, providing skiers with more outstanding diagonal striding terrain. A pair of black plastic culverts, often plundered and unearthed by a boisterous inlet tributary of Frick Pond, is crossed shortly before Iron Wheel Junction and the end of the trail is reached at 1.8 mi. To complete the loop, turn left (southeast). Quick Lake Trail arrives at Logger's Loop Trail at 2.7 mi. Straight ahead at 3.2 mi. Quick Lake Trail ends at the Frick Pond trailhead parking area on Beech Mtn. Road.

Logger's Loop Trail (map 2: D4)

Distances from Quick Lake Trail at Graveyard Junction (2,128 ft.) to
- Big Rock Trail at Times Square junction (2,150 ft.): 0.6 mi., 50 ft. (rev. 50 ft.), 20 min.
- Quick Lake Trail at Iron Wheel Junction (2,300 ft.): 1.8 mi., 300 ft. (rev. 100 ft.), 1 hr. 5 min.
- Distance for complete loop from trailhead on Beech Mtn. Road (2,150 ft.) via Quick Lake Trail and Logger's Loop Trail: 3.7 mi., 350 ft., 2 hr.

Campground Loop Trail

This fun family walk combines the Mongaup Pond Public Campground road with a section of the multiuse trail on the pond's eastern shore. The loop is popular with hikers and cyclists and appropriate for children. Bring bug dope and snacks. It is easily entered from anywhere in the campsite on foot. (Consult Mongaup-Hardenburgh Trail for directions to the campground.)

Find the trailhead between campsites 144 and 147 in Loop G. Trailhead parking is available just beyond site 151 on the right (north) side of the road. Follow blue foot-trail markers (this is the beginning of Mongaup-Hardenburgh Trail) and red snowmobile markers through the campsite area. The lake appears on your right. Blueberries grow along the shore. The trail is flat and, at 0.3 miles, arrives at a trail junction where Campground Loop Trail turns right (southeast). Follow it; don't make the mistake of continuing on Mongaup-Hardenburgh Trail. There is no destination or distance signage at this junction. The trail crosses a long footbridge over the pond's northernmost inlet. At 0.4 mi., cross another bridge, as the trail follows the lake and climbs easily, then another bridge in a maple woods, and still another, until at 0.8 mi. a trail junction with signage is reached (Mongaup-Willowemoc Trail, 2,225 ft.). Continue straight ahead (south). The lake is no longer visible to the north (right). The trail flattens and soon descends to another junction in a hemlock woods.

A sign here indicates Mongaup Pond Campground, straight ahead. No distance is given. Continue straight ahead, crossing a slightly muddy outlet marsh near the headwaters of Mongaup Creek. Soon the trail exits the woods at campsite 38. To complete the loop, turn left. The campsite road does not circle the lake. Passing the bathhouses and beach area through the campground's most scenic area, the road heads north and back to the point of departure at the trailhead.

Campground Loop Trail (map 2: D4)

Distance from Loop G (2,150 ft.)
- around Campground Loop: 2.4 mi., 100 ft. (rev. 100 ft.), 1 hr. 15 min.

Mongaup Pond Snowmobile Trail

This short section of multiuse trail represents the northwesternmost section of Mongaup-Willowemoc Trail. Its intended purpose—to provide an alternative route to Flynn Trail Junction from the interior campsite area of the Mongaup Pond Public Campground—is seldom taken advantage of. The trail is lightly used by hikers and shows a slight impact from mountain bikes. Gain access to the trail just beyond campsite 158 in Loop G, where small signs are posted. Trailhead parking can be found adjacent to campsite 151, ahead on the campground road (for directions to the Mongaup Pond Public Campground see Mongaup-Hardenburgh Trail).

The trail follows the snowmobile trail disks north, immediately crossing a small stone bridge over Sucker Brook. The trail is level for a short distance as it travels to the left (west) of a small wetland, until rising steeply over a good surface. As elevation is gained, short sections of the trail are washed out and rocky. Above 2,700 ft., the trail levels and undulates. In a northern hardwood forest, the snowmobile trail descends over a wide, grassy surface until reaching Flynn Trail junction.

Mongaup Pond Snowmobile Trail (map 2: D4)

Distance from Loop G (2,150 ft.) to
• Flynn Trail (2,750 ft.): 2.1 mi., 750 ft. (rev. 150 ft.), 1 hr. 25 min.

Quick Lake Snowmobile Trail

This section of the snowmobile trail that comes west from Times Square to Iron Wheel Junction is a continuation of Mongaup Pond Snowmobile Trail. Like most of the trails in this wild forest area, it follows old settlement roads woven together by newly created sections of trail.

Mongaup Pond Snowmobile Trail follows Big Rock Trail to Logger's Loop Trail, joins Quick Lake Trail for a short distance at Iron Wheel Junction, and heads northwest, crossing Quick Lake Trail several times before terminating at Quick Lake. Quick Lake Snowmobile Trail is not as attractive to hikers as Quick Lake foot trail. It is not maintained as a hiking trail and can become obstructed by vegetation during the summer months.

Quick Lake Snowmobile Trail (map 2: D4–D3)

Distances from Quick Lake Trail at Iron Wheel Junction (2,350 ft.) to
- Coyote Junction (2,650 ft.): 2.4 mi., 300 ft., 1 hr. 30 min.
- Bobcat Junction (2,700 ft.): 3.0 mi., 50 ft., 2 hr.
- Flatrock Junction (2,390 ft.): 4.0 mi., 128 ft., rev. 410 ft., 2 hr. 30 min.
- Quick Lake (2,000 ft.): 5.4 mi., 100 ft., rev. 500 ft., 3 hr. 30 min.

Wild Azalea Trail

From Butternut Junction, east of Mongaup Pond Public Campground off Mongaup-Willowemoc multiuse trail, Wild Azalea Trail heads south-southwest. It can be used to provide a link in a very large loop around the campground and is ideal for all-terrain cyclists and skiers as well as for hikers. There are no views. At Butternut Junction, the trail leaves the yellow-marked Mongaup-Willowemoc Trail and follows snowmobile markers.

The trail ascends easily through thick, second-growth hardwood. Leaf litter covers the trail, and a few blowdowns may be encountered. Crossing a wooden bridge over a tributary of Butternut Brook and leveling out on a knoll at 2,540 ft., the trail passes through a stand of thin beech trees. At 1.0 mi., it turns northwest briefly, moving through a maturing hardwood forest, ascending slightly and leveling, passing through a lush clearing, thick with fern, blueberry, strawberry, and scattered cherry trees. Entering the woods again, the trail crosses a bridge at 2,280 ft., ascends into open forest, crosses another open, grassy clearing, and arrives at the junction with Hunter Road at 2.8 mi. It then turns right (northwest), toward Mongaup Pond. This established gravel road borders private property to the south. Descending, the trail passes a power line right of way and then a tiny tributary of Mongaup Creek at the site of an early settlement. A few stone ruins remain in the dense underbrush. Domestic ornamentals appear: barberry, apple, Norway and blue spruce, day lily, and lupine. A short distance uphill and beyond the brook, the trail levels at an intersection, bending right. To the left, the trail follows what remains of Hunter Road as it heads toward Mongaup Pond Road, terminating just south of its intersection with Beech Mtn. Road. To the right at 3.5 mi. are direction signs for Karst Trail.

Karst Trail

Karst Trail begins at the intersection with Hunter Road, south of Mongaup Pond Public Campground. Bearing right at the Hunter Road and Karst Trail junction (see Wild Azalea Trail), the trail leads to an open field. Marking is poor, leaving no indication as to the correct direction of travel. Straight across the field on a vague treadway in the grass and a short distance into the woods are a fire ring and undesignated (legal) campsite. Instead, walk diagonally to the left (northwest) a short distance (where little or no evidence of a path is visible) and find the trail again at the edge of the woods, well-marked and moving northwest between a Scotch-pine plantation on the left and a stand of large red oak to the right.

The trail soon ascends slightly into deep forest then levels, following to the right (east) of a wetland. Ascending again, easily, the trail pulls away from the wetland and back again as it descends into hardwoods, the treadway hemmed in stinging nettles. The type shifts to hemlock, many ghostly skeletons of which may still be seen in the marsh to the left (west). At 2,170 ft., arrive at the cutoff to Mongaup Pond State Campground. To reach it, follow left to cross a muddy clearing, leaving the woods at campsite 38.

Mongaup-Willowemoc Trail

Enter the trail from a point 0.4 mi. west of Flugertown Road at its junction with Long Pond-Beaver Kill Ridge Trail. Heading southwest, the trail is somewhat rocky, but flat, and soon crosses Sand Lake Road, a well-used dirt right of way leading to private lands in both directions. Cross the road and, very soon, a small brook. Through shady hardwood stands the trail is grassy and only lightly impacted, the rocks showing scratches from snowmobile use. The trail follows an embankment above lively Butternut Brook in a picturesque setting and draws closer to the creek as it moves northwest, soon crossing the brook on a wooden bridge. The trail ascends slightly, passing an abandoned trail on the left, shortly thereafter arriving at Butternut Junction and Wild Azalea Trail at 1.4 mi. Each direction is identified with red foot-trail and snowmobile-trail markers.

The trail becomes grassier, crossing the gravelly washout of a small creek, then a small footbridge. Heading west and soon ascending, eroding, and finally topping out beneath a tall hardwood canopy, the route descends until reaching a T intersection with the Mongaup Pond campsite loop at 3.1 mi. Turn left to enter the campsite at site 38, from there bearing left again on the campground road to reach the main entrance. Hikers completing the loop hike using Mongaup-Hardenburgh Trail and Long Pond-Beaver Kill Ridge Trail should turn right (north) to return to their point of departure in Loop G.

Mongaup-Willowemoc Trail (map 2: D4)

Distances from trailhead on Flugertown Road (1,970 ft.) to
- junction with Long Pond-Beaver Kill Ridge Trail (2,220 ft.): 0.4 mi., 250 ft., 25 min.
- Wild Azalea Trail at Butternut Junction (2,200 ft.): 1.8 mi., 350 ft. (rev. 100 ft.), 1 hr. 5 min.
- Mongaup Pond Campground Loop (2,230 ft.): 3.1 mi., 650 ft. (rev. 250 ft.), 1 hr. 55 min.

SUGGESTED HIKES

Easy Hike

Campground Loop Trail [lp: 2.4 mi., 1:15]. An easy family hike on nearly flat terrain, circling Mongaup Pond and returning to the campsite.

Moderate Hike

Logger's Loop Trail, from Quick Lake Trail, Graveyard Junction [lp: 3.7 mi., 2:00]. These woodland hikes are easy, are sheltered by woods, and, though they provide no substantial views, are excellent foot trails. The lack of many rocks or blowdowns makes for easy, unimpeded hiking through old settlement areas.

Strenuous Hike

Quick Lake Trail [rt: 14.4 mi., 8:10]. Recommended as an overnighter, this is the ideal backpacking hike, featuring easy ascents and descents through low, rolling woodlands with sparse views to the west.

PART 3
CENTRAL CATSKILLS

For the purposes of this guide, the Central Catskills include the Big Indian Wilderness, the Dry Brook Ridge Wild Forest, and the Balsam Lake Mountain Wild Forest. Sections of north-lying detached parcels of the Shandaken Wild Forest, Halcott Mountain Wild Forest, and the western section of the Hunter-West Kill Wilderness Area (all trailless) lie within the region. The Belleayre Mountain Ski Center management unit is attached to the Big Indian Wilderness in the north.

The Central Catskills include several long ridge trails: Dry Brook Ridge Trail, Mill Brook Ridge Trail, and Pine Hill-West Branch Trail. Opportunities for hikes of several days' duration are possible in each forest area. This is the lonely, reclusive heart of the Catskills, with forests that attract few visitors in comparison with the neighboring hills to the east. Steep slopes and rolling ridge tops provide for rugged and often challenging hiking. Several long ridges and eight mountains above 3,200 ft. characterize the setting—primarily forested by northern hardwood groups (some in virgin tracts), along with isolated conifer stands and extensive plantations.

Much of the Catskills were preserved for one major reason: the Hardenbergh Patent. Beginning with a petition to Queen Anne for a small tract of vacant land, Major Johannes Hardenbergh and company managed through a combination of exploitation (of the native people), political power, and Hardenbergh's personal influence (he fought at Blenheim and was knighted by the queen) to procure 2 million acres of Catskill lands. The reasons for this land grant are many, suspect, and complex, but the result was the preservation of the Catskills for a long period of time, long enough to protect it from resale, subdivision, and diffuse ownership. The patent was divided up into Great Lots, and shared among its "investors," which included the Livingstons. (The deeds purchased from Nisinos, a sachem of the Lenni-Lenape, cost less than 100 pounds sterling.) The patent was a determining factor in the sparse settlement in the Catskills, which resulted in a great deal of taxable, open space, much of which was eventually purchased or appropriated by the state and annexed to the forest preserve.

Roads opened the way for settlers, many of whom left their names on mountains and hollows in the region: Haynes, Rider, Seager, McKenley. The region developed an active tourist following. Many small hotels and boarding houses appeared, among them Jim Dutcher's Panther Mountain House, the Slide Mountain House, and the Grand Hotel along the Ulster and Delaware railroad line. During this time, large tracts of land were purchased by the wealthy, among them Jay Gould, a robber baron who purchased land in the Dry Brook Valley and fought with the Vanderbilts for control of the Erie Railroad in 1869. Most of the lands in this area were purchased by tax sale from the county prior to 1930.

Section 15
Big Indian Wilderness

A ruggedly mountainous and remote hiking area, the Big Indian Wilderness includes more than 33,500 acres of steep valleys and hollows, long ridges, and the high peaks of Big Indian, Balsam, Eagle, and Haynes, as well as the trailless summits of Spruce, Fir, Hemlock, and Doubletop. There are six lean-tos and roughly 30 mi. of trail in the area (views are limited). The wilderness is nearly completely forested by dense northern hardwoods (beech, birch, maple, and often cherry), except for the higher summits, which are typically clad in fir. The minimum elevation is 1,500 ft., with a maximum of 3,840 ft.

The headwaters of the Esopus Creek, Beaver Kill, Willowemoc Creek, and the west branch of the Neversink River add considerably to the wilderness appeal of this area. They are important, scenic trout streams with public access areas convenient to most of the local trailheads and state campsites. The Esopus is noted for its spring runs of rainbow trout, and there is perhaps no other trout stream in the East as renowned or productive as the Beaver Kill.

The Beaver Kill-Big Indian Range forms the watershed divide between the Hudson River to the east and the Delaware River to the west. A number of the hikes in the area are characterized by long, relaxed approaches to the high ridge, where the hiker will pass through early settlement areas, old orchards, and stone ruins, followed by steep and direct ascents to the summit ridgeline. This wilderness area is not heavily used by hikers, possibly because it does not offer scenic vistas of the kind found in the neighboring wilderness areas. Instead, those in search of solitude and privacy will seek out this region. Many designated campsites exist along the trails, in addition to seven lean-tos, some of which are located near streams and wetlands.

The single most popular trail is Pine Hill-West Branch Trail, which runs north–south from Pine Hill to the west branch of the Neversink River. This 14.9-mi. trail is most often walked from south to north, a strategy that employs only a slight elevation advantage, but which culminates in the ascent of Belle Ayr Mtn. and provides access to the scenic rewards that are available from Belle Ayr Ridge Trail at the northern extreme of the area (technically, both Belle Ayr Ridge and Pine Hill-West Branch trails end in the adjoining Belleayre Mountain Ski Center Intensive Use Area). Other trails in this wilderness area are treated as access to the singular peaks in the range.

Pine Hill-West Branch Trail

Seasoned hikers seeking the remote surroundings and isolated feel of a large wilderness area will find this trail a welcome respite from the much busier trails of the Eastern Catskills, while newcomers may be discouraged by the relatively scant views. In any case, this is a remote area, where few people will be encountered. At nearly 15 mi., the trail is also longer than many. (Additional proposed mileage would connect this trail to the neighboring Slide Mountain Wilderness Area.) Logistics can be simplified by spotting cars at either end of the trail or by hiking the individual peaks via the side trails from either Big Indian Hollow (Oliverea-Mapledale Trail extending to Rider Hollow and Lost Clove Trail) or from the Dry Brook Valley (Seager-Big Indian Trail, Mine Hollow Trail). The northern trailheads can be reached conveniently by bus from Pine Hill, but those traveling independently may prefer to begin from the more traditional starting point on West Branch Road (CR 47), which allows for a trailhead elevation advantage of 600 ft.

From Big Indian, travel 12.5 mi. south from NY 28 on CR 47, or Slide Mtn. Road, and park at the Biscuit Brook trailhead parking area. (At this point CR 47 is called West Branch Road.) The trail begins 200 ft. to the right (east) of the parking area on the north side of the road.

The trail heads north and turns rooty in a shady hardwood forest, immediately passing the trail register to the right. Blue markers are frequent and the trail is self-guiding as it begins to turn left (northwest), crossing a small seasonal brook at 2,185 ft. and beginning to ascend moderately steeply to the northwest. Large trees keep the area heavily shaded even on very bright days. The terrain levels as the path rises into the north-northeast at 2,400 ft., passing a vague old woods road, which descends to the southwest, toward Frost Valley. Remaining level for a stretch, then descending amid witch hobble, fern, and wood sorrel on a mile-long, westerly slope of Spruce Mtn. (3,390 ft.), the trail passes a nameless tributary at 2,350 ft. Crossing several seasonal runnels off the same slope, the route passes a small wet area to the left. At 2,360 ft., the trail splits, with the main branch continuing right (north). Off a short spur to the left (west) at 1.9 mi. is the Biscuit Brook lean-to, situated above the brook itself, facing west among a few large hemlock trees. The spur continues to a flat, impacted tent space. This lean-to is an older structure with a hand-hewn floor, oakum chinking, and an uncharacteristic 4-ft.-by-4-ft. timber roof.

The main trail continues north, following next to a small tributary of Biscuit Brook (lively in July), until crossing it on stepping-stones above a large pool at 2,370 ft., a few hundred feet after leaving the lean-to. The trail ascends slightly and the main branch is crossed as the stream widens into a flood channel. Walking next to the brook now, ascending, alert hikers will observe a few maple trees with extremely large dab (diameter breast height)—nearly 5 ft. At 3,150 ft., the trail rises above and away from the creek, although it remains in audible distance. Ravens croak in this otherwise nearly silent, peaceful woods, where the trail turns west to begin its ascent of Big Indian Mtn. with a series of switchbacks and levels at 3,400 ft. in a subalpine community of oxalis, red cherry, beech, and small balsam fir. The walking is easy on the feet now along this viewless but effortless flat, which reaches 3,470 ft. and the site of an old junction where an unmarked, disused trail goes off to the left (northwest) and drops away toward Seager. Yellow-paint blazes denote the boundary of state and private lands here, a large parcel of the latter containing both Doubletop (3,870 ft.) and Graham Mtn. (3,868 ft.) to the west. These mountains are seasonally visible to the west as the trail moves north along the western ridge of Big Indian Mtn. (3,710 ft.). Pass the 3,500-ft. mark at 4.5 mi., where a well-established, cairned herd trail leads to the right for Big Indian's summit and a canister maintained by the Catskill 3500 Club. Climbing to 3,600 ft., the terrain remains flat until at 4.9 mi. the trail descends north off the shoulder of Big Indian Mtn. None but winter views to the west greet hikers as the trail drops steadily and easily downhill. Hemlock reappears as an ascent leads to the junction with Seager-Big Indian Trail at 5.4 mi. (3,100 ft.).

The trail continues straight ahead (north), and turning northwest climbs through deciduous woods to a shallow ledge on the approach to Eagle Mtn. (3,610 ft.), reaching the 3,500-ft. mark at 6.8 mi. A few scattered balsam appear as the trail rises to a point east of the true summit of Eagle Mtn. at 6.9 mi., where an unmarked trail leads west over flat terrain 0.1 mi. (approximately) to the viewless summit (the Catskill 3500 Club does not maintain a canister on this summit). Balsam fir grows profusely beneath a hardwood canopy through the remaining upper elevations of the mountain, where limited seasonal views are possible but never expansive. Dropping into the saddle at 3,300 ft., the trail is easy and relatively flat as it follows along the Delaware-Hudson watershed until the ascent to Haynes Mtn. begins. The elevation change is barely noticeable—less than 150 ft. from the ridge's average elevation. Crossing a small, flat rock distinguished by a shallow crack, the trail rises gently over a grass surface. This lush but viewless expanse at 8.4 mi. is Haynes's summit (3,420 ft.). The trail remains level only momentarily until beginning the northerly descent. Balsam Mtn. appears to the northeast, looming large and appearing to be farther off than it is, only 1.5 mi. distant. The trail drops steeply to the junction with Oliverea-Mapledale Trail at 9.1 mi. (3,100 ft.).

To the southeast, Oliverea-Mapledale Trail drops very steeply into McKinley Hollow. To the northwest, a more relaxed descent penetrates Rider Hollow. Continuing northeast on Pine Hill-West Branch Trail, hikers will see red-berried elder—a favored bird food appearing in rich woods—and flowering, tall meadow rue, which appears alongside partridgeberry and Canada mayflower, the latter going to seed by late July.

Climbing uphill consistently now, this section of the trail to Balsam Mtn. is the steepest ascent along Pine Hill-West Branch Trail since the southerly slopes of Big Indian. At the 3,500-ft. mark, ascend through rocky balsam-covered ledges into a forest of cherry, over glades of thick fern, where the trail turns lazy curves through lush woods. At 9.9 mi., Balsam's summit (3,610 ft.) is a primordial-looking wreckage of blowdowns, stumps, rotting snags, and rock piles—the most ravaged peak, appearance-wise, in the range. Again, there are no views. Vague herd paths, created by zealous hikers, head to the right (east), revealing little or nothing. Private postings have frustrated attempts to identify vistas elsewhere.

Balsam Mtn. is not entirely without its rewards, however. The trail continues north to the site of a small, flat boulder on the right at 10.1 mi. (3,550 ft.), where a cut vista provides a limited but unexpected view east of West Kill, Hunter (its fire tower can be seen), Blackhead, Black Dome, Thomas Cole, Windham High Peak, Rusk, Evergreen, Sugarloaf, Twin, and a piece of Indian Head. Overlook and its fire tower (107 degrees) are visible. The upper Esopus Valley and McKinley Hollow lie below, with the long, north-projecting ridge of Panther Mtn. above.

The trail proceeds north-northwest, soon reaching another viewpoint around an elevation of 3,100 ft., where the terrain is steepest and the treadway is most heavily eroded. A short, unmarked spur leads right (east), to a flat, mossy rock above a ledge, looking north. This natural vista looks to the right of Belle Ayr Mtn., which occupies the northwest skyline, at Halcott Mtn., Vly, and Bearpen. The trail descends and flattens at 2,800 ft. beneath a few very large specimens of beech and maple. At 11.1 mi. (2,890 ft.), the trail arrives at the junction with Mine Hollow Trail, which drops moderately steeply but also very quickly to the Rider Hollow trailhead, offering the shortest, easiest route onto and off the Big Indian Range. The main trail continues straight ahead, turning slightly to the north.

Pine Hill-West Branch Trail rises following a short, flat section after the junction, ascending to 3,000 ft., through a forest of large, cankered black cherry. Turning northeast, winter views of Panther Mtn. are seen to the right. The trail climbs very steeply through ledges as it turns north again toward Belle Ayr's final approach. A relaxing grade yields to the open summit (viewless) at 12.3 mi. (3,430 ft.). Two benchmarks (1942) are seen in the stone here, where a fire tower and lean-to once stood. A fire ring off a short spur to the north is all that remains of a once popular campsite. To the left (northwest), Belle Ayr Ridge Trail goes to the Hirschland lean-to and Belleayre Mtn. Ski Center's Sunset Lodge (3,325 ft.), which is open during the summer months (fast food, phone). The Hirschland lean-to is newer and in a more scenic location (at the top of the Roaring Brook ski trail) than the Belle Ayr Mtn. lean-to, ahead and downhill on Pine Hill-West Branch Trail. The trail turns right (east), following the road-width, graded trail (once a fire road and still negotiable via ATV) that soon descends, providing winter views of open country and ridges to the north (Halcott Mountain Wild Forest, Shandaken Wild Forest), passing the lean-to on the left at 12.7 mi. Pine Hill-West Branch Trail continues to descend, flattening at the junction with Lost Clove Trail at 13.0 mi. and turning to the north.

Carolinian hardwood forest follows, featuring large red oak. The trail continues straight ahead on blue markers (there is no destination signage) as an old woods road. Handmade trail signs for Giggle Hollow Trail (originally Guigou), depart to the right (east) for Belleayre Beach and the Pine Hill public recreation area. Pine Hill-West Branch Trail curves gently around to the left (west), descending easily. The trail moves across slope toward Woodchuck Hollow and joins a private road (legal easement), turning left (west) at the appearance of a yellow trail arrow. Descending, the trail goes around a locked gate, joining Woodchuck Hollow Road. Still descending, arrive at the corner of Depot Road and the trailhead at 14.9 mi. (to the west are blue markers, following the rail bed to Cathedral Glen Trail). It is possible—and legal—to park at the top of Woodchuck Hollow Road (pullover parking), but this area is not as secure or convenient as the Depot Road access. There is no trailhead signage for either Cathedral Glen Trail or Pine Hill-West Branch Trail, but marking is adequate.

Pine Hill-West Branch Trail (map 2: D6–B6)

Distances from Biscuit Brook trailhead on CR 47 (2,190 ft.) to
- Biscuit Brook lean-to (2,350 ft.): 1.9 mi., 300 ft. (rev. 150 ft.), 1 hr. 5 min.
- side path to Big Indian Mtn. summit (3,550 ft.): 4.5 mi., 1,500 ft., 3 hr.
- Seager-Big Indian Trail (3,130 ft.): 5.9 mi., 1,600 ft. (rev. 500 ft.), 3 hr. 45 min.
- side path to Eagle Mtn. summit (3,590 ft.): 7.0 mi., 2,050 ft., 4 hr. 30 min.
- Haynes Mtn. summit (3,430 ft.): 8.4 mi., 2,250 ft. (rev. 350 ft.), 5 hr. 20 min.
- Oliverea-Mapledale Trail (3,030 ft.): 9.1 mi., 2,250 ft. (rev. 400 ft.), 5 hr. 40 min.

- Balsam Mtn. summit (3,610 ft.): 9.9 mi., 2,850 ft., 6 hr. 25 min.
- Mine Hollow Trail (2,870 ft.): 11.1 mi., 2,900 ft. (rev. 800 ft.), 7 hr.
- Belle Ayr Mtn., east summit and Belle Ayr Ridge Trail (3,430 ft.): 12.3 mi., 3,400 ft., 7 hr. 50 min.
- Lost Clove Trail (2,830 ft.): 13.0 mi., 3,400 ft. (rev. 550 ft.), 8 hr. 10 min.
- Pine Hill trailhead on Depot Road (1,650 ft.): 14.9 mi., 3,400 ft. (rev. 1,200 ft.), 9 hr. 10 min.

Mine Hollow Trail

This trail provides the shortest access to Balsam Mtn. (3,610 ft.). It begins at the 0.3-mi. point off the junction with Oliverea-Mapledale Trail in Rider Hollow. There are several designated campsites in the hollow and a good lean-to on Oliverea-Mapledale Trail. Mine Hollow Trail bears left (northeast) at the trail junction, where a small angle-iron suspension bridge spans the brook to the right (south) on Oliverea-Mapledale Trail. Follow next to a creek on the level for a short distance, beneath a few very large hemlocks. The trail climbs away from the creek and into hardwoods (beech) at 2,500 ft., swinging north at 0.4 mi. through a large hemlock stand. Continue uphill to the junction with Pine Hill-West Branch Trail at 0.9 mi.

Mine Hollow Trail (map 2: C5)

Distance from Oliverea-Mapledale Trail (2,050 ft.) to
- Pine Hill-West Branch Trail (2,870 ft.): 0.9 mi., 800 ft., 50 min.

Seager-Big Indian Trail

Seager, situated at the head of the Dry Brook Valley below Drury Hollow, is in one of the Catskills' wildest, most scenic valleys and provides the most expeditious approach to both Eagle (3,610 ft.) and Big Indian Mtn. (3,710 ft.) for both short day hikes and extended backpacking along Pine Hill-West Branch Trail. Seager-Big Indian Trail joins Pine Hill-West Branch Trail equidistant from the two peaks at 3,150 ft. The walk to the lean-to is easy—thereafter the trail climbs radically. Find the trailhead 9.7 mi. north of Arkville at the end of Dry Brook Valley Road (CR 49). Bear right at the covered bridge just before reaching the trailhead parking area.

The trail heads southeast, following Dry Brook through a hemlock forest. The brook and off-trail area are contained within a private easement.

The trail rises above the creek slightly, crossing Flatiron Brook adjacent to a small waterfall and natural rock pool (private). At the intersection of a dirt road at 0.9 mi., Camp Flatiron (private) is posted to the southwest. On the left (northeast), a small bridge crosses Dry Brook (private). Trail signs are posted here. The trail, following a dirt road, goes straight ahead as the road becomes wide and rocky while following the edge of the creek. The road soon crosses the creek, while the trail fords just upstream at 1.2 mi. This ford is difficult in moderately high water.

Watch the markers carefully after fording. The trail turns right (southeast) on the same road that crossed Dry Brook a moment ago, goes 100 ft., and turns left (east, uphill), following markers to a grassy roadway, which the trail follows to the right (southeast), rising above the creek. The trail climbs easily into the east, now following Shandaken Brook, soon crossing it at 2,400 ft. and ascending into the Big Indian-Beaver Kill Wilderness Area.

Even in dry months, a spring runs across the trail from the hill opposite the lean-to. At 1.9 mi., the trail crosses Shandaken Brook (dry in late summer) to the lean-to. This older structure is enclosed by a half wall in front. There is a privy to the north as well as a very small designated campsite suitable for a single tent, in a pinch. The trail continues along the north side of the creek, heading east. It rises moderately, relaxes, descends, and then climbs relentlessly until nearing the ridge. It rises again minimally as the junction is reached at 2.8 mi. Remarkably, reinforcing stones appear on the downhill side of the trail at this elevation (3,130 ft.), indicating that this steep trail was once a road used to drive cattle to Oliverea.

Seager-Big Indian Trail (map 2: C5–C6)

Distances from end of Dry Brook Valley Road (CR 49) (1,970 ft.) to
- Shandaken Creek lean-to (2,450 ft.): 1.9 mi., 500 ft., 1 hr. 10 min.
- Pine Hill-West Branch Trail (3,130 ft.): 2.8 mi., 1,150 ft., 2 hr.

Lost Clove Trail

This trail rises steeply from scenic Big Indian Valley into the Shandaken Wild Forest, which lies at the northern extreme of the Big Indian Wilderness Area.

At the corner of CR 47 (Big Indian Hollow Road) and Lost Clove Road, 0.5 mi. south from NY 28, the trail is identified with signage. Turn right (northwest) to cross the Esopus Creek and at 1.0 mi. find the designated parking area on the right (north) side of Lost Clove Road. Initially the trail ascends gradually on a dirt skid road from the site of a log decking area at 1,600 ft. (public easement). The ascent steepens, sidehilling its way up a southeasterly slope of Belle Ayr Mtn. The trail is road width and in good condition, although recent, extensive logging operations on private property have made some impact both on the road itself and in surrounding woods. Watch markers carefully as the trail passes straight through a diagonal intersection at 2,200 ft. and climbs more gradually as it approaches the junction with Pine Hill-West Branch Trail in a red oak woods at 1.2 mi. (2,830 ft.). Belle Ayr Mtn.'s summit is 0.6 mi. to the left (west).

Lost Clove Trail (map 1: C6)

Distance from trailhead on Lost Clove Road (1,530 ft.) to
  • Pine Hill-West Branch Trail (2,830 ft.): 1.2 mi., 1,300 ft., 1 hr. 15 min.

Giggle Hollow Trail

A relatively recent addition to the trail system of the northern Big Indian Wilderness Area, Giggle Hollow Trail came into being as a designation of logging skid trails and informal old roads, some of them originally created by the charcoal and tanbark industries. The hollow is named for Augustus A. Guigou, builder of the Empire Tannery (1831). The trail provides an alternative means of access to the northern wilderness area where few other convenient trailheads exist. Hikers will find the trail useful as a northern access point mostly for day-hiking, owing to the fact that parking is available only during daylight hours from the trailhead, which lies within the confines of the Belleayre Beach (Pine Hill Lake) recreation area (parking fee required). Roadside parking is available although limited outside of the park's confines (walk-in fee required). The main attraction for day hikers in this area is Belle Ayr Mtn., which is more directly approached from Cathedral Glen trail lying farther to the west—a more attractive and direct route to the summit.

Because the northeastern parcel of this wilderness area was acquired by the state following intensive logging, the floristic appeal of the trail has been compromised. Evidence of logging is everywhere in the form of both selective and clear-cutting, and is especially evident in the harvest of a climax black cherry forest above 2,450 ft. as Pine Hill-West Branch Trail is approached. The trail itself, having been created primarily by all-terrain log skidders, is often steep and eroded, with many intervening, unmarked skid trails.

The trailhead (blue markers) begins east of the lake past the entrance kiosk and across the covered bridge and straight ahead, at a point beyond two picnic pavilions. A trail register appears to the left of the railroad trestle. The trail follows underneath the trestle, immediately passing the red-marked "Belle Ayr Mtn. hiking trail," a recently marked and maintained loop with unofficial trail markers. (The section of the red trail that follows the railroad tracks is useful for the closing of a loop from the westerly Woodchuck Hollow Road.) Giggle Trail rises to the southeast easily through a matrix of logging roads, soon steepening and widening. As elevation is gained, ridges and hills in the Slide Mountain Wilderness Area are seen to the east. The trail switches back at 2,200 ft., avoiding steep Giggle Hollow, and turns west as it approaches Pine Hill-West Branch Trail, rising in pitches through grassy, sparse woods with views of Balsam Mtn. to the south.

Giggle Hollow Trail (map 2: B6–C6)

Distances from trailhead (1450 ft.) to
- Pine Hill–West Branch Trail (2,700 ft.): 2.1 mi., 1,250 ft., 1.5 hr.

Oliverea-Mapledale Trail

From the east end of Rider Hollow Road (2.5 mi. off CR 49A), at the trailhead parking area, the trail leaves to the east adjacent to Rider Hollow Brook. A signboard is located here.

The trail passes a designated campsite on the right and turns left to cross the brook, soon entering a small clearing of burdock, bee balm, milkweed, and berry bushes. Reentering the woods, within 100 ft. the trail reaches the Mine Hollow Trail junction at 0.4 mi. Bearing right over a small, angle-iron suspension bridge and left across a stringer bridge, proceed alongside the creek in a mixed red pine, hemlock, and hardwood forest. Designated campsites to the right (southwest) offer camping on flat ground. At 0.5 mi., the Rider Hollow lean-to appears on the left (northeast) in an attractive streamside setting. (The area is busy on most weekends during good weather.) The trail crosses the creek at 2,150 ft. and makes a long, low-angle climb on a dirt roadbed to the south among red pine and maple, amid stone walls and rock piles—evidence of early settlement and cultivation. Drawing closer to the creek again and descending to cross it at 1.1 mi. (2,350 ft.), the trail turns south near a stand of tall tamaracks. Again crossing a streambed, the trail begins to climb, becoming steeper to the southeast as it leaves a sparse stand of large hemlock, at 1.6 mi. arriving at the four-way intersection with Pine Hill-West Branch Trail at 3,100 ft.

Continuing through the junction, the trail passes a designated campsite to the left (north) and descends, immediately steepening. The terrain is at its steepest where a seasonal creek crosses the trail from the south side, and a landslide scrape is seen directly left (northeast) of the trail. *Mineral* *soil and loose rock makes this section (2,500 ft.) potentially hazardous, particularly for those hiking in wet or icy periods, when this trail should be approached with calculated caution and preparation or else avoided.*

Relenting to an easy grade at 2,200 ft., the trail eases but still drops through open hardwood forest, making a long, sweeping turn through the hollow at 1,900 ft. and crossing the brook on two short sets of stone steps. This area is very attractive if not serene—a good staging location for hikers planning an ascent from the east side of the ridge. At 3.0 mi., the lean-to is set in an open hardwood forest of large sugar maple near the brook; past this along the trail is a fine stand of Norway spruce on flat ground, deep enough to provide legal camping between the trail and the creek. Now following the footprint of a dirt road, the walking is easy and nearly flat. The trail crosses a washout and then the creek at 1,800 ft., where cottages appear to the left (northeast) as the trailhead is approached. From a large washout that was once the original roadway into the hollow, the trail turns north, crossing a footbridge, and joins McKinley Hollow Road at 3.9 mi. A yellow trail arrow identifies the trail (it is not obvious to those coming up into the hollow—watch carefully). The McKinley Hollow trailhead parking area is 500 ft. to the right at 3.6 mi. and 1,700 ft.

Big Indian Hollow Road is 0.5 mi. to the east.

Oliverea-Mapledale Trail (map 2: C5–C6)

Distances from end of Rider Hollow Road (1,970 ft.) to
- Mine Hollow Trail (2,050 ft.): 0.4 mi., 100 ft., 15 min.
- Rider Hollow lean-to (2,100 ft.): 0.5 mi., 150 ft., 20 min.
- Pine Hill-West Branch Trail (3,030 ft.): 1.6 mi., 1,050 ft., 1 hr. 20 min.
- McKenley Hollow lean-to (1,790 ft.): 2.7 mi., 1,050 ft. (rev. 1,250 ft.),
  1 hr. 55 min.
- McKenley Hollow Road (1,630 ft.): 3.3 mi., 1,050 ft. (rev. 150 ft.),
  2 hr. 10 min.

Belle Ayr Ridge Trail

Running from the summit lodge and ski lifts of the Belleayre Mtn. Ski Center, east to the summit of Belle Ayr Mtn. (3,430 ft.), this pleasant dirt road ridge trail provides access to the Big Indian Wilderness Area via Pine Hill-West Branch Trail and provides access to Cathedral Glen and Lost Clove trails. It is often used by hikers who climb the service road from the ski center to its summit lodge, and more recently by backcountry skiers and mountain bikers creating loops back to Belle Ayr's base lodge. Views from the open slopes and from the deck of the summit lodge are extensive. From the lodge's deck to the south are Balsam Lake Mtn. (fire tower), Millbrook Ridge, and Dry Brook Ridge across Chimney Hollow. Graham, Double-top, and Eagle Mtns. are visible, as well as Hiram's Knob in the low foreground. To the north from the ski slopes themselves are Vly and Bearpen, Monka Hill, Halcott, North Dome, Sherrill, West Kill, and Hunter. These are the only scenic vistas available from the matrix of Belle Ayr's summit trails, besides views from the ski trails themselves.

The Belleayre Mtn. Ski Center is located off NY 28 in Highmount. From the summit's Sunset Lodge (3,300 ft.), which can be reached during winter and summer months from the ski lift or on foot, red state-trail markers appear on the south margins of a clearing. Unofficial, square orange markers also appear. The trail heads east over deep-red silty soil on a service road and climbs gently into increasingly remote woods. At the top of a ski trail on the north side of the trail, ski area signs point the way to Highmount Rail Station and Belleayre Beach. At 0.5 mi., pass the Hirschland lean-to on the left (north), which is easy to miss for hikers coming west, perched above the Roaring Brook ski trail and facing north (it is in a far better location and in better shape than the nearby Belle Ayr Mtn. lean-to on Pine Hill-West Branch trail). The trail continues straight ahead (east), passing Cathedral Glen Trail to Pine Hill at 0.7 mi., and at 1.0 mi. arrives at the (viewless) summit of Belle Ayr Mtn. (3,430 ft.) in an open, grass-and-bedrock clearing. This was once the location of a fire tower and lean-to. Pine Hill-West Branch Trail departs to the south. Ahead, downhill, are the Belle Ayr Mtn. lean-to and Lost Clove Trail into Big Indian Hollow.

Belle Ayr Ridge Trail (map 2: C5)

Distances from Sunset Lodge (3,320 ft.) to
- Cathedral Glen Trail (3,250 ft.): 0.7 mi., 50 ft. (rev. 150 ft.), 25 min.
- Belle Ayr Mtn., east summit and Pine Hill-West Branch Trail (3,375 ft.): 1.0 mi., 200 ft., 35 min.

Cathedral Glen Trail

From the village of Pine Hill, take Bonnie View Avenue to Mill Street, turning south to cross the historical stone arch bridge. Continue, passing under the railroad bridge of the old Rondout and Oswego line. (The rail-road changed hands to become the Ulster and Delaware line in 1875.) Turn right immediately after the bridge (trail arrows are posted on a tree at the southwest street corner) and park on the left-hand side of the road (Depot Road, pullover parking). The trail follows the rail bed northwest. Blue markers appear without destination signage.

Follow the right of way west for 0.5 mi., over intact ties and rails that soon become tunneled over in saplings. Cathedral Glen Trail begins on the left (south) just before the small snowmaking reservoir (for Belleayre Mtn. Ski Center) is reached. Locate the markers and No Motorized Vehicles signs. There is still no destination signage. The trail rises through an extensive and beautiful hemlock stand with the deep Cathedral Glen on the right. As hardwoods begin to take over, the trail enters the north side of an open clearing at 1.1 mi. The trail follows left (east) along the tree line, continuing straight uphill. Ski area signs to the right identify Roaring Brook and Discovery Lodge trails. Marking is sparse.

The trail (now a grassy ski trail) becomes extremely steep for the next 0.5 mi. until reaching a second large clearing at 1.6 mi., where Super Chief and Cathedral Brook ski trails converge. Watch carefully for blue markers as the trail turns left (east) into the woods, away from the ski area's trail system.

Climbing, the trail is sometimes indistinct and is too seldom used to be fully self-guiding. Marking is sufficient. Continuing uphill, the trail curves back into the south and joins Belle Ayr Ridge Trail (a dirt road) at 1.6 mi., just east of the Hirschland lean-to (the Belle Ayr Mtn. lean-to is below the summit at 3,000 ft. along Pine Hill-West Branch Trail). To reach the Hirschland lean-to turn right (west). Services are available at the ski area's summit lodge, 0.7 mi. to the right (west) at the end of the ridge trail. The summit of Belle Ayr Mtn. itself (viewless) is to the left (east) 0.3 mi. on Belle Ayr Ridge Trail.

Cathedral Glen Trail (Map2: C5–B6)

Distance from trailhead on Depot Road (1,650 ft.) to
  • start of trail (1,740 ft.) via railroad grade: 0.5 mi., 100 ft., 20 min.
  • Belle Ayr Ridge Trail (3,250 ft.): 2.1 mi., 1,600 ft., 1 hr. 55 min.

Mongaup-Hardenburgh Trail

Access to this trail is from the Mongaup Pond Public Campground in DeBruce. To find the campground, take Exit 96 off NY 17 at Livingston Manor, turn left, following CR 81 and CR 82, and go 6.0 mi. to DeBruce. Turn left (north) on Mongaup Road, and go 3.0 mi. to the campsite.

Many hikers begin here to hike Mongaup-Hardenburgh Trail to Beaver Kill Road and Dry Brook Ridge Trail to Balsam Lake Mtn., but more people use this trailhead to hike the Mongaup Pond Loop, an 8.5-mi. outing from the Mongaup Pond Public Campground that uses Long Pond-Beaverkill Ridge Trail and Mongaup-West Branch Trail to bring them back to the campground. Mongaup-Hardenburgh Trail begins between campsites 144 and 147 in Loop G. Trailhead parking is located just beyond site 151. Follow blue foot-trail markers and snowmobile-trail disks along the edge of the lake. At 0.3 mi., a junction is reached, with signs to the left.

The foot trail goes left (north), beginning level and rocky but soon climbing, leveling at 2,170 ft. A stand of hemlock trees is encountered at 2,235 ft., as the trail ascends steadily but easily and remains self-guiding and well marked until a blowdown area is reached around 0.8 mi. (2,300 ft.). Vegetation resulting from open sunlight has obscured the trail slightly for a short distance. Blackberry and mountain ash crowd the way where the loss of standing trees has deterred marking somewhat. Red-paint blazes appear. Obscured views to the south reveal parts of Mongaup Pond.

Blowdowns disappear as the trail rises steeply, topping out at 2.0 mi. (2,989 ft.) where, to the trail's left, the words "The Top" are crudely etched on a conspicuous rock. This is the summit of Mongaup Mtn.'s middle peak. There are no views. The trail turns east, downhill, over a sparsely used treadway, following a saddle at 2,550 ft. before climbing out of it to reach the east summit of Mongaup Mtn. at 2.7 mi. (2,928 ft.). It then descends Mongaup Mtn. onto the Beaver Kill Ridge in a forest of dense hard-woods, moss-topped boulders, wood sorrel, and ferns. At 3.4 mi. (3,000 ft.), the trail reaches the junction with Long Pond-Beaver Kill Ridge Trail. Mongaup-Hardenburgh Trail bears left (northeast) here.

Ascending slightly to 3,150 ft., the trail follows a flat ridge top briefly, descending again through beech and cherry woods. There's plenty of flat ground nearby for tenting. A short distance off the trail here it is possible to find views (even in summer) to the east of Table (3,847 ft.) and Peeka-moose Mtns. (3,843 ft.). Of all places in the forest preserve, this one—gen-erally lacking any unimpeded views—would seem to merit a cut vista. The trail descends again to a small fern-clad clearing where a rock to the right provides the only view of Denman Mtn. (3,053 ft.). Descending off this knoll to 2,985 ft. the trail becomes level. At 2,950 ft., it rises steeply, and after a short distance levels again, thereafter rising gently. The spine of the ridge is reached at 5.2 mi. (3,228 ft.), where the terrain flattens, offering winter views to the left (west) of the low-lying Delaware Ridge. Descend-ing to 3,200 ft. the trail remains level until it drops down off the northerly slopes of the ridge, descending moderately and switching back until reach-ing the suspension bridge spanning the Beaver Kill. It then rises on a long flight of stone steps to the trailhead parking area at 6.8 mi. This prime trout water is heavily posted. In fact, the entire Beaver Kill is posted in this area all the way up to Vly Pond, and postings are taken very seriously. Hik-ers can fish in the upper headwaters early in the spring when the water is high, or from public access areas farther downstream.

Thru-hikers (this trail is popular with backpackers) to Balsam Lake Mtn. will turn east here, following yellow markers 1.8 mi. and rising 300 ft. in elevation to the Balsam Lake Mtn. trailhead parking area (see Dry Brook Ridge Trail for connections to Balsam Lake Mtn. Trail). Neversink-Hardenburgh Trail (aka Claryville Trail) departs from the southeast corner of the Balsam Lake Mtn. trailhead parking area, while Dry Brook Ridge Trail departs from the northeast corner.

> **Mongaup-Hardenburgh Trail (map 2: D4–C5)**
>
> Distances from Mongaup Public Campground and Day Use Area (2,150 ft.) to
> - Mongaup Mtn., middle summit (2,989 ft.): 2.0 mi., 850 ft., 1 hr. 15 min.
> - Mongaup Mtn., east summit (2,928 ft.): 2.7 mi., 1,250 ft. (rev. 450 ft.), 2 hr.
> - Long Pond-Beaver Kill Ridge Trail (3,000 ft.): 3.4 mi., 1,400 ft. (rev. 100 ft.), 2 hr. 10 min.
> - summit of Beaver Kill Ridge (3,224 ft.): 5.2 mi., 1,850 ft. (rev. 250 ft.), 3 hr. 20 min.
> - trailhead on Beaver Kill Road (2,190 ft.): 6.8 mi., 1,900 ft. (rev. 1,050 ft.), 4 hr. 5 min.

Neversink-Hardenburgh Trail (Claryville Trail)

From Livingston Manor, the northern trailhead is reached by traveling east on CR 151 (Johnston Hill Road), passing Waneta (Juanita) Lake and the Beaver Kill State Campground, onto CR 152 in Lew Beach, passing Barkaboom Road to Little Pond State Campground, and arriving at the dead end of Beaver Kill Road and the Balsam Lake Mtn. trailhead parking lot. The total distance is about 22 mi.—much of it follows next to the heavily posted world-famous Beaver Kill trout stream. (Hikers will have passed Mongaup-Hardenburgh trailhead to Mongaup Pond, 1.8 mi. west of the Neversink-Hardenburgh trailhead.)

From the parking area, two trails depart in opposite directions. Neither is adequately identified. Dry Brook Ridge Trail leaves from the northeast corner of the lot, offering the shortest route to Balsam Lake Mtn. summit and fire tower. Neversink-Hardenburgh Trail (aka Claryville Trail) leaves from the southwestern corner and is not identified as such. Only a Finger Lakes Trail disk exists at the trailhead at this time. A signboard located in the parking lot will aid in orientation. This is a remote trailhead and a rather long walk into an area nearly as remote, and although there are roads at the trail's end there are no villages or services—or even telephones—anywhere nearby. Be prepared for all conditions.

Neversink-Hardenburgh Trail follows southeast along the western edge of a field, revealing two large peaks to the left: Doubletop (3,870 ft.) and Graham (3,868 ft.). The trail enters the woods near the trail register, descends, and crosses several stone water bars, at 0.5 mi. crossing Black Brook on a footbridge. The trail is narrow, rocky, and sometimes leaf-littered, the overstory changing type from hemlock and birch to dense sugar maple, cherry, and beech. At 1.3 mi. (2,400 ft.), the trail crosses Gulf of Mexico Brook on a 40-ft. bridge, soon thereafter reaching a dirt road, and continuing slightly to the right across the road. The trail descends to cross Vly Pond outlet, a lively brook with no bridge, downstream of a beaver meadow, and then rises into a hemlock grove, its surface strewn with cones and needles. The trail crosses the outlet of Tunis Pond, named for one of the last Delaware to live in the Catskills; he lived on this pond's shore.

At 2.8 mi., the trail reaches a dirt road and follows it to the left (southeast) along the Beaver Kill. Hikers traveling north must pay close attention to this turn, as it is marked with only a yellow trail arrow and disk. Careful investigation will turn up the trail signs. The junction lies at the following coordinates: (42° 01.170' N, 74° 34.329' W)

The trail heads upstream (southeast) on the dirt road and soon crosses a small bridge where a feeder creek comes in from the left (northeast). The road is sandy, wide, and well trafficked by the owners of a private hunting camp on an inholding at 3,000 ft. Pass a designated campsite on the left. This site is little used and is normally a patch of ferns. The trail continues straight ahead at a junction where a bridge supported by railroad rails turns right (southwest), following the Beaver Kill straight onto a footpath identified with two yellow trail markers. (More-obvious signage is needed here.)

The trail passes adjacent to the creek for a short distance, and small sections of trail have washed into the creek. Fording on stones, the trail leads to a more severely eroded section of the kill, where hikers momentarily walk in the streambed itself. Just as the trail seems to vanish altogether it takes shape again, continuing as a small path above a union of two tributaries. At 3.1 mi., 200 ft. to the left (east) on a thin spur, situated high and dry in a hemlock stand above the confluence, is an ideal designated campsite. The trail continues over an improved surface now, leading to an active beaver pond on the left at 3.5 mi. Doubletop is visible to the northeast.

This section of trail is muddy, but soon hardens into the vestiges of a nineteenth-century road, marked as a hiking trail since 1935. The trail passes through a wet area shortly before reaching the Fall Brook lean-to at 4.3 mi. Porcupines have chewed the floor, but the shelter is sound. A privy is nearby.

The trail becomes wide and rocky now, serving as a seasonal stream-bed before the runoff finds its way into Fall Brook, leaving a comfortable treadway of duffy soil. Trending south, the route crosses a ravine carved by a tributary of Fall Brook, originating on a steep southwest-facing slope of the Beaver Kill Range.

As it approaches the northern end of Black Bear Road, the trail passes directly in front of a seasonal residence, crossing the front lawn and continuing on the lot's south side over an established dirt road. Once out of the forest onto Black Bear Road at 6.0 mi., striking views of the southeastern mountains appear to the left. Peekamoose (3,843 ft.) and Table (3,847 ft.) are easily identified by Table's long, flat summit. Passing through a detached parcel of the Willowemoc Wild Forest and (legally) back through private lands, the trail walks past several hunting camps, descending. Red Hill (2,990 ft.) and its fire tower can be identified easily. (Seeing the fire tower may require binoculars.) Slightly southwest is Denman Mtn. (3,053 ft.). Wildcat Mtn. (3,100 ft.) stands in the middle ground, with Wood-hull (3,050 ft.) just beyond the Neversink's East Branch. Farther along the road, hikers will enjoy a complete view of Slide Mtn.'s (4,190 ft.) ridgeline contour and summit.

The trail descends Black Bear Road to the trailhead parking lot. Those hiking the Neversink-Hardenburgh from the south will most likely be using this lot, as it is no longer practical to park pullover style up above, as it once was. As in the north, hikers will be discouraged not to discover any signage for Neversink-Hardenburgh Trail. Rely on the map.

Neversink-Hardenburgh Trail (Claryville Trail, map 2: D5–C5)

Distances from trailhead at end of Beaver Kill Road (2,530 ft.) to
- bridge over Gulf of Mexico Brook (2,430 ft.): 1.3 mi., 200 ft. (rev. 300 ft.), 45 min.
- crossing of Beaver Kill (2,560 ft.): 3.1 mi., 450 ft. (rev. 100 ft.), 1 hr. 45 min.
- Fall Brook lean-to (2,610 ft.): 4.3 mi., 550 ft. (rev. 50 ft.), 2 hr. 25 min.
- north end of Black Bear Road (2,575 ft.): 6.0 mi., 550 ft. (rev. 50 ft.), 3 hr. 15 min.
- Black Bear Road trailhead parking lot (2,030 ft.): 8.6 mi., 550 ft. (rev. 550 ft.), 4 hr. 35 min.

Long Pond-Beaver Kill Ridge Trail

As well as connecting the Big Indian Wilderness to the Willowemoc Wild Forest, this northerly section of the trail forms the second leg in the Mongaup Mtn.-Mongaup Pond loop. From its junction with Mongaup-Hardenburgh Trail at 3,000 ft., the trail leaves to the south, heading in the direction of Flugertown Road, following red markers along a high, wooded narrow ridge. A black cherry woods opens up slightly to reveal views of Graham Mtn. (3,868 ft.), Doubletop Mtn. (3,870 ft.), and the Beaver Kill Range. Oak appears as the route descends southward to an easterly shoulder at 2,754 ft. The trail has recently been remarked but is little used. Obscure summer views exist to the right (south). Descending and turning gradually to the southwest, the trail enters the Willowemoc Wild Forest and flattens at 2.0 mi. (2,200 ft.), meandering through a thick hardwood forest with stands of pure sugar maple where meadow rue and wild leek (ramps) are common. Many large cherry trees have blown across the trail in this area and have been cut away by trail maintenance crews. Assuming the footprint of an old road now, the trail is nearly flat as it descends to the junction with Mongaup-Willowemoc Trail at 2.4 mi. (2,200 ft.).

The trail turns left (east) on a section shared by both Long Pond-Beaver Kill Ridge Trail and Mongaup-Willowemoc Snowmobile Trail, at 2.8 mi. arriving at Flugertown Road. In this area are several primitive, designated campsites along the Willowemoc Creek, a popular trout stream during high spring water levels. There are trail signs on the southeast side of Flugertown Road across from this fairly obscure trailhead at 2,000 ft.

The trail turns right (south) on Flugertown Road, and in a very short distance (250 ft.) Long Pond-Beaver Kill Ridge Trail enters the woods on the (unsigned) red-marked multiuse trail, proceeding left (south). A trail sign appears within 100 ft. at a footbridge crossing the Willowemoc. The trail crosses another bridge and ascends steeply for a few hundred feet. The incline relaxes and flattens into the south. On the right (southwest) side of the trail an unmarked, discontinued snowmobile trail heads back to the Willowemoc Creek. Continue straight, southeast, over flat and sometimes muddy ground to a junction in a hemlock forest at 4.1 mi. The trail is identified with red foot-trail and snowmobile-trail markers in every direction. To the right (south) is the Long Pond lean-to at 0.1 mi.

The trail continues east toward Black Bear Road as the forest type changes from hemlock to hardwoods. Following is a flat and grassy section that passes an unmarked spur trail leading right (west) toward the east shore of Long Pond. The trail continues flat, and often muddy, to a junction.

To the right (south) is a (visible) barrier gate leading onto a private inholding. Go left (north), soon reaching an intersection with Basily Road at 5.1 mi. (2,240 ft., dirt). Bearing right (east), Basily Road climbs, the treadway becoming rocky but passable by four-wheel-drive vehicles (this section is a town road). The trail passes a designated campsite to the right and climbs to 2,300 ft., where the road crests in front of a hunting camp. A road (private) leads north at this point. The trail continues north on the maintained road now, descending to Black Bear Road trailhead parking area, where signs are posted at 6.9 mi.

Long Pond–Beaver Kill Ridge Trail (map 2: D4–D5)

Distances from junction with Mongaup-Hardenburgh Trail (3,000 ft.) to
- junction with Mongaup-Willowemoc Trail (2,220 ft.): 2.4 mi., 50 ft. (rev. 850 ft.), 1 hr. 15 min.
- trailhead on Flugertown Road (1,970 ft.): 2.8 mi., 50 ft. (rev. 250 ft.), 1 hr. 25 min.
- side trail to Long Pond lean-to (2,170 ft.): 4.1 mi., 250 ft., 2 hr. 10 min.
- junction with Basily Road (2,150 ft.): 5.1 mi., 300 ft. (rev. 50 ft.), 2 hr. 40 min.
- Black Bear Road trailhead parking lot (2,030 ft.): 7.4 mi., 500 ft. (rev. 300 ft.), 3 hr. 55 min.

SUGGESTED HIKES

Moderate Hike

Long Pond-Beaverkill Ridge Trail [rt: 6.6 mi., 3:40]. Perfect for an overnight backpack, this gentle trail leads to the quiet and isolated Long Pond and its lean-to. Gain access from Black Bear Road trailhead parking lot.

Strenuous Hikes

Balsam Mtn. via Oliverea-Mapledale Trail [rt: 5.0 mi., 3:10]. This hike provides one of the only substantial viewsheds available from the Big Indian Wilderness, at elevation of 3,100 ft. Gain access from McKenley Hollow Road.

Belle Ayr Mtn. via Cathedral Glen Trail [rt: 5.4 mi., 3:20]. The most interesting approach to Belle Ayr summit and Sunset Lodge, following ski slopes with open northerly vistas to the flat ridge top. Gain access from Depot Road.

Mongaup Pond Loop, via Mongaup-Hardenburgh Trail, Long Pond-Beaverkill Ridge Trail, and Mongaup Willowemoc Trail [loop: 8.5 mi., 4:20]. A long and varied hike with some steep ascents. Combine the hike with an overnight at the Mongaup Pond State Campsite.

SECTION 16
DRY BROOK RIDGE WILD FOREST

The main topographical feature of interest to hikers in the Dry Brook Ridge Wild Forest is its central ridge (3,460 ft.), and the scenic vistas scattered along its length. Many hikers enjoy the quiet and solitude of this area. Many use the ridge trail as a thru-hike from north to south that culminates in the ascent of Balsam Lake Mtn. (3,730 ft.), and they usually arrange for a shuttle from Mill Brook Road or the logistically more involved Beaver Kill Road in Hardenburgh. It is simpler to backtrack north from Balsam Lake Mtn. back out to Mill Brook Road. The forest's eastern access at German Hollow is also its steepest. The northerly ascent to Pakatakan Mtn. (viewless) is the conventional trailhead for thru-hikes of the ridge, although more popular is Huckleberry Loop Trail, which provides access to the views of Dry Brook Ridge while omitting the miles of approach from north and south. The northerly leg of Huckleberry Loop Trail (that portion of the trail north of Huckleberry Brook Road) is the single most popular approach to the ridge and views from the Penguin Rocks. Opportunities for camping throughout the unit are unlimited. Northern hardwood forest occupies most of the area (beech, birch, maple), with a smattering of ash, cherry, basswood, and oak. Hemlocks are present in small, isolated stands. Large plantations of Norway spruce and red pine exist. Deer are present in large numbers, but bear are not abundant. *The Second Atlas of Breeding Birds in New York State* (Ithaca, NY: Cornell

University Press, 2008) indicates 47 confirmed species of breeding birds in the area, among them the red-shouldered hawk, hairy woodpecker (blue list), Louisiana waterthrush, and eastern bluebird.

There are three lean-tos in the Dry Brook Ridge Wild Forest. One is in German Hollow and another is north of Mill Brook Road on the ridge trail itself. The third lean-to—and the best choice for latecomers or trailhead bivouacking—is the Mill Brook lean-to, located within walking distance west of southerly Mill Brook Road trailhead.

Dry Brook Ridge Trail

This long ridge provides seclusion and privacy for hikers in search of scenic isolation. In general, the terrain is lower and easier than the mountain trails of the neighboring Southern Catskills. Trail additions (Huckleberry Loop Trail) have made this trail more accessible to hikers seeking moderate day outings to the top of the Dry Brook Ridge.

Turn left (southeast) onto Fair Street, 0.4 mi. west of Margaretville off NY 28/30. Turn left again (north) at 0.6 mi. onto South Side Spur (Road), and at 0.7 mi. locate the trailhead on the right (east) side of the road. Pullover parking is on the left (west).

The trail ascends, leading 200 ft. to an old road, bearing left (northeast) past a shallow rock overhang, and ascending through hemlocks and mixed hardwood forest. As the terrain flattens out, wild forest signage appears. Long switchbacks follow, the first turning through a westerly curve at the site of a small hut (private) to the right (southwest) of the trail (this turn, which shortcuts back onto the woods road, is not as obvious to those coming from the south). Hardwoods dominate as the trail turns south-southwest and the road is covered in pieces of broken bluestone, fragments from a quarry (which can be seen to the right of the trail) that was apparently mined to reinforce the road farther downhill. A sugar maple forest follows as the trail flattens at 1,900 ft., turning grassy and rising moderately steeply as the forest type changes to oak, and heads east. The trail then levels as it crosses the ridge, moving around a rocky knoll on the right approaching 2,400 ft., and climbs again, easily now. A few very large cherry trees appear as the trail climbs through a section of dense forest, where it flattens briefly before two steeper pitches that relax on the treed-in summit elevation of

Pakatakan Mtn., at 2,700 ft., and the junction with German Hollow Trail at 2.4 mi.

The trail continues straight (south) from the trail junction and ascends, leveling before rising again in brief pitches through ledgy terrain and open hardwood. The trail travels along an easterly slope, descending, and is both poorly routed and in marginal condition along this section, in need of minor improvements. At 2,970 ft., it turns right and uphill to the south-southwest and crests a rise in the ridge, arriving at the junction with Huckleberry Loop Trail at 3.3 mi. (3,100 ft.).

There is no destination signage here for southerly points along Dry Brook Ridge Trail. Continue south, through a fern glade. The trail is level initially but rises gently just beyond the junction, circling a dry bog (which is sometimes full of rainwater) populated with sedges at 3,150 ft. The trail adheres to the ridgeline elevation now, and the atmosphere of the ridge becomes light and airy—a welcome change from the heavy, dark, lower-elevation woods—and is self-guiding, although in a few locations it is invaded by low vegetation. At 4.4 mi. (3,200 ft.), following a brief ascent, limited views appear to the right (west) from an isolated rock. Better views lie ahead a very short distance, off a very short spur (easy to miss, and initially looking less spectacular than it actually is) to the right (west). These are the Penguin Rocks, representing the best year-round views from the ridge. What's unusual about this outcropping is the appearance here of the three-toothed cinquefoil, which botanist Dr. Michael Kudish notes is "a largely arctic tundra plant . . . it occurs in only eight other places in the Catskills; the presence of this plant on the exposed ledges suggests that forest never invaded this site since the ice age." The cinquefoil blooms in early to midsummer. The views westward from this rock ledge are good and include the easternmost arm of the Pepacton Reservoir (where the east branch of the Delaware enters it—in reality, the Pepacton's waters are the dammed waters of the Delaware), and hills from Pakatakan in the north through the west-lying Cross Mtn., Barkaboom Mtn., and Touch-Me-Not Mtn. Across Cold Spring Hollow and the Huckleberry Brook Valley is Mill Brook Ridge, running west to east. Open pasturelands dot the valley below, and to the northwest are subtle glimpses into the hills beyond Dunraven, in the town of Andes. South, above Clark Hollow, is Woodpecker Ridge.

A nonconforming campsite exists just east of this spur, illegal due to its proximity to the trail (within 150 ft.). There is flat ground available all over the ridge for tenting beyond this site, irresistible for its proximity to the Penguin Rocks. The trail continues southeast along this westerly side of the ridge where another spur leads right (west) to a large boulder at the top of a precipitous drop above a talus slope. After hiking through a viewless section of woods, at 3,420 ft. the trail tops out at the edge of another ledge, achieving its maximum elevation beneath the ridge's summit knoll at 5.0 mi. (3,460 ft.). The trail continues through cherry-and-beech woods until reaching the southerly junction of Huckleberry Loop Trail at 5.6 mi., which descends westward to Ploutz Road.

Straight ahead (south), Dry Brook Ridge Trail descends and ascends before leveling, remaining at ridge-top elevation until decisively (and sometimes steeply) descending at 7.2 mi. through broken, low ledges, crossing an old but distinct woods road at the edge of private lands just under 2,900 ft. This extensive elevation drop (800 ft.) brings you off the upper ridge and down to the lean-to at 8.2 mi., which faces west into the hardwoods at 2,700 ft. Just 150 ft. north of the lean-to is a tributary of Mill Brook that dries up in late summer.

Following the lean-to the trail continues southeast, gaining elevation to 3,085 ft., and descending thereafter over a few stone water bars, where conifers appear. Winter views are limited to the south here, restricted by heavy hardwood growth. The trail again descends gently across slope, passing a small Norway spruce stand to the left of the trail. Switching back in front of a crumbling ledge, the terrain levels and turns easterly in a transitional zone between a Norway spruce forest on the right and hardwoods (sugar maple) on the left. This is perhaps the trail's most attractive forest, with a nearly pure fern ground cover. The trail switches back again, heading south and down a few small stone steps where small ledges appear to the right and broken-off boulders lie scattered across the forest, heaped with detritus and moss. Millbrook Road is soon visible. Signing out at the trail register on the left, arrive at Dry Brook Ridge parking area at 8.8 mi.

This trailhead is the most popular access to Balsam Lake Mtn. summit. (The shortest approach, however, is from the south, coming north on Dry Brook Ridge Trail and taking the red-marked Balsam Lake Mtn. Trail, but the access from Beaver Kill Road is remote.)

Dry Brook Trail continues on the south side of Mill Brook Road, following a dirt road to the west, on the left side of Mill Brook Road (within view of the trailhead parking area). This wide fire tower access road goes uphill (south) easily but steadily, passing the trail register on the left (east). The trail switches back to the 3,000-ft. point, soon passing a spring on the right (west) about 50 ft. off the trail down a set of stone steps. The grade eases as the trail follows the westerly shoulder of a high ridge, with seasonal views to the west. At 2,700 ft., an unmarked trail to the left (east) enters a private parcel (with no legal public easement) to ascend Graham Mtn. (3,868 ft.). At 11.9 mi. (3,270 ft.), arrive at the northern junction of Balsam Lake Mtn. Trail.

The trail continues straight ahead (southwest) at this wide, flat junction into an area that receives little use (most hikers using the area ascend Balsam Lake Mtn. by either the north or south Balsam Lake Mtn. trailheads, avoiding this section entirely). This old road descends along the side of a slope, varying in surface quality from rocks to grass. Uphill to the right (west), a talus slope appears, covered in yellow birch. Views to the east (left) are limited to the Black Brook Valley and the ridge above Young's Hollow. Uphill the talus is decorated with mountain ash, their scarlet berries showing by late July. Descending easily to 2,900 ft., the trail reaches the junction with Balsam Lake Mtn. Trail at 11.8 mi. in a hardwood forest.

The trail descends easily through hardwoods, soon approaching its terminus beside a scenic, open, fern-covered pasture, passing an old tree farm on the right where Scotch pine and European larch are escaping cultivation. To the left (east) is a deep, alluring forest of tall maple. At 12.7 mi., the trail ends in the Balsam Lake Mtn. parking area at the location of the Neversink-Hardenburgh trailhead (which begins from the southwest corner of the parking lot). A signboard is posted here. Mongaup-Hardenburgh Trail begins from Beaver Kill Road, 1.8 mi. to the right (southwest) of the Balsam Lake Mtn. trailhead parking area. Alder Lake is 8.0 mi. southwest on Beaver Kill Road and 2.6 mi. north on Alder Lake Road.

Dry Brook Ridge Trail (map 2: B4–C5)

Distances from trailhead on South Side Spur (1,390 ft.) to
- German Hollow Trail (2,790 ft.): 2.4 mi., 1,400 ft., 1 hr. 55 min.
- Huckleberry Loop Trail, north junction (3,110 ft.): 3.3 mi., 1,800 ft. (rev. 100 ft.), 2 hr. 35 min.

- Penguin Rocks viewpoints (3,360 ft.): 4.4 mi., 2,100 ft. (rev. 50 ft.),
  3 hr. 15 min.
- Huckleberry Loop Trail, south junction (3,430 ft.): 5.7 mi., 2,250 ft.
  (rev. 100 ft.), 3 hr. 55 min.
- Dry Brook lean-to (2,730 ft.): 8.2 mi., 2,400 ft. (rev. 850 ft.), 5 hr. 20 min.
- trailhead on Mill Brook Road (2,580 ft.): 8.9 mi., 2,700 ft. (rev. 450 ft.),
  5 hr. 55 min.
- Balsam Lake Mtn. Trail, north junction (3,330 ft.): 11.0 mi., 3,450 ft.,
  7 hr. 40 min.
- Balsam Lake Mtn. Trail, south junction (2,900 ft.): 11.9 mi., 3,450 ft.
  (rev. 450 ft.), 8 hr. 5 min.
- trailhead on Beaver Kill Road (2,530 ft.): 12.8 mi., 3,450 ft. (rev. 350 ft.),
  8 hr. 30 min.

German Hollow Trail

Alternate access to Dry Brook Ridge Trail from the north is available from Arkville via this steep trail through an old settlement area. It is a more direct but considerably steeper path to the ridge than from the Dry Brook Ridge trailhead itself, beginning in Margaretville. Its advantages lie in the lean-to and water source above the trailhead at Chris Long Road, and in the convenient, walkable distance to and from Arkville. There is pull-over but no designated parking at the trailhead and parking here is not recommended.

On the west side of Arkville, follow Dry Brook Road south, 0.3 mi. to Chris Long Road (dead end). Go right and at 0.2 mi. park on the left side of the road's end by a low stone wall just before reaching a private garage. The trailhead is visible across the parking area (on the west side) of this private parcel. The landowners have generously allowed day parking on their property but prefer that overnight visitors use the adjacent road.

Follow markers 150 ft. to the trail register. The trail climbs over a rocky, washed-out road and into the reclaimed pastures (1,680 ft.) of a farm dating from 1869 that belonged to J. H. Dean. (Forest historian and botanist Dr. Michael Kudish points out the existence of Tartarian honeysuckle, lilac, European Saint-John's-wort, and bigtooth aspen here.) The trail climbs through a logged-over private parcel into second-growth hardwoods. Rising steadily, the grade eases as the lean-to is reached. A piped spring is located 500 ft. to the south at the end of an unmarked path on the north slope of Reservoir Hollow. The trail swings hard right nearly 180 degrees around the front of the lean-to and switches back into German Hollow, climbing steeply. After a stiff climb through oak woods, the trail eases at 2,700 ft. This brief reprieve is followed by easier ascents and flats. The trail finally levels out in a maple stand, trending southwest to the junction with Dry Brook Ridge Trail.

German Hollow Trail (map 2: B5–B4)

Distances from trailhead on Chris Long Road (1,490 ft.) to
  • German Hollow lean-to (2,030 ft.): 0.7 mi., 550 ft., 40 min.
  • Dry Brook Ridge Trail (2,790 ft.): 1.5 mi., 1,300 ft., 1 hr. 25 min.

Huckleberry Loop Trail

Loop trails are uncommon in the Catskills, and Huckleberry Loop Trail was created in light of this fact. The trail also represents the only westerly access to the Dry Brook Ridge, an otherwise long and logistically impractical day hike. Signage and destination identification may be confusing, inconsistent, or absent. The trail is noteworthy for its easy access to the Dry Brook Ridge summit views (Penguin Rocks) and its plantations of Norway spruce.

Find the trailhead west of Margaretville from South Side Road, which runs adjacent to (and south of) NY 28/30. Two miles west of the village, South Side Road leads to Huckleberry Brook Road, which leads to Hill Road. Bearing left on Hill Road, find the trailhead 1.3 mi. on the left (north), with trailhead parking directly across the road. For hikers intending to walk the entire loop—a long outing in itself—the Huckleberry Brook Road trailhead may optionally be used and has a larger parking area (it is 0.6 mi. southeast beyond the intersection of Huckleberry Brook Road and Hill Road, on Huckleberry Brook Road, and 0.3 mi. south on Huckleberry Brook Trail from the Hill Road trailhead parking area). Day hikers planning on visiting only the Penguin Rocks along Dry Brook Trail (rather than walking the entire loop), may prefer to start on the recommended shorter leg from the Hill Road trailhead in order to optimize time spent on the ledges. In comparison, the southern leg of the loop (the section crossing Ploutz Road from the Huckleberry Brook Road trailhead) is longer and less appealing. Hiking the loop from the north will also save 500 ft. in elevation.

The trail leaves from Hill Road at 1,900 ft., at the sign kiosk and register, and heads uphill (north) into an extensive stand of Norway spruce. Red pine follows. This changes to hardwoods as the terrain flattens and the route trends east, switching back and following the edge of the red pine plantation. Oak woods follow. The trail is wide and roadlike. A fine stand of spruce again appears, followed by more red pine with a striking understory belt of striped maple. Soon crossing an old disused woods road and continuing to the east the trail relaxes, still ascending at 2,500 ft. and climbing more steeply as it moves along the southerly side of the ridge. It then flattens out to allow seasonal views to the south across Cold Spring Hollow. Stunted northern hardwoods characterize the upper ridge as the junction with Dry Brook Ridge Trail is reached at 2.5 mi.

The trail turns right (southeast). At 3.2 mi., ledges begin to appear on the right and continue for the next 0.5 mi. (see Dry Brook Ridge Trail for details). At 4.8 mi., Huckleberry Brook Trail junction (south leg) is reached at 3,400 ft. The trail turns right (south) and descends through fern glades and sugar maple. The trail shows little use but is well marked. The grade eases below 3,000 ft. as an early, reclaimed (by vegetation) settlement is reached, where evergreens and stone walls provide a welcome respite from the deciduous forest. Passing through walls that once defined a pasture, the trail continues to descend easily through red pine and at 6.0 mi. arrives at (seasonally maintained) Ploutz Road where apple trees, stone foundations, a trail register, a signboard, and a trailhead parking area are located above a tributary of Mill Brook. Mill Brook Road is 1.5 mi. to the left (south), the nearest egress from this point.

From Ploutz Road the trail heads downhill into the southwest, turning right (west) within 100 ft. of the trailhead parking area. A stand of large European larch (a deciduous conifer) thrives here in the wet headwaters of Mill Brook. The trail follows next to a crumbling stone wall through a Norway spruce-and-pine plantation and rises up a long slope on an old road, turning right (northeast) next to a stone wall and steepening. Oak yields to maple as the trail enters a dense plantation of Norway spruce. Blue-paint blazes, remaining from the trail's construction in 1995, accompany red markers. Walk between two boulders into hardwoods, ascending to pass southwest of and below a wooded knoll at 2,832 ft. The trail swings west at 5.6 mi. (2,600 ft.) to cross over a knoll at 6.6 mi. (2,800 ft.).

Continuing west, the trail descends easily into a saddle at 2,400 ft., enters another Norway spruce forest, turns to the right (north) following a tilted block of sedimentary sandstone, and travels along the easterly margins of a hemlock woods. At 8.0 mi., at the edge of a large, open field, the trail is no longer self-guiding, whereupon it follows sparse markers along the northeasterly (right) forest edge and crosses the field following cairns (piled rocks) that have been erected in the open field itself (nearly hidden by tall vegetation at the height of summer), taking a generally northerly course to the woods, where red markers are posted.

From the field's northern edge the trail ascends into hardwoods, passing another isolated sedimentary boulder among scattered hemlocks, sidehilling as it begins to descend and switching back east-northeast, dropping more steeply. The trail crosses several seasonal creeks and levels somewhat, bearing right (east). Although this section of the trail is little used, it has been worn to mineral soil in places and is nearing its carrying capacity. Additional pressure will require improvement or rerouting, made difficult by the extreme slope. Turning left (north), the trail directly descends the slope, joins a woods road, and swings northwest. The surface widens and improves as a wet, minor confluence is crossed amid hemlock and mixed hardwood, and finally becomes washed out, nearly disappearing as the trail turns sharply to the right, heading north (this turn is not adequately marked and is barely self-evident). The trail descends steadily and gently into red pine, turning to hemlock as Huckleberry Brook Road appears to the north (left) and crosses the bridge spanning Huckleberry Brook at 9.6 mi.

The trail turns right (east), following Huckleberry Brook Road, soon passing the trailhead parking area on the left. The Department of Environmental Conservation's Huckleberry Brook storage area appears on the left (north) at 11.2 mi. The trail crosses a small bridge onto the storage area lot. Trail signs appear on the side of the storage building itself.

The trail turns right (east) across the front lawn of the storage area and enters the woods at the east edge of the lot, thereafter turning left (north) and ascending through an evergreen forest, arriving at Hill Road at 11.5 mi. The parking area is 150 ft. to the left (west).

Huckleberry Loop Trail (map 2: B4)

Distances from trailhead on Hill Road (1,920 ft.) to
- north junction with Dry Brook Ridge Trail (3,110 ft.): 2.2 mi., 1,200 ft., 1 hr. 40 min.
- Penguin Rocks viewpoints (3,360 ft.): 3.3 mi., 1,500 ft. (rev. 50 ft.), 2 hr. 25 min.
- south junction with Dry Brook Ridge Trail (3,430 ft.): 4.5 mi., 1,650 ft. (rev. 100 ft.), 3 hr. 5 min.
- Ploutz Road (2,400 ft.): 5.7 mi., 1,650 ft. (rev. 1,050 ft.), 3 hr. 40 min.
- first knob on Huckleberry Ridge (2,810 ft.): 6.7 mi., 2,150 ft., 4 hr. 25 min.
- west trailhead on Huckleberry Brook Road (1,450 ft.): 10.7 mi., 2,450 ft. (rev. 1,700 ft.), 6 hr. 35 min.
- east trailhead on Huckleberry Brook Road (1,610 ft.): 11.4 mi., 2,600 ft., 7 hr.
- trailhead on Hill Road (1,920 ft.): 11.7 mi., 2,900 ft., 7 hr. 20 min.

SUGGESTED HIKE

Strenuous Hike

Huckleberry Loop Trail [loop: 11.7 mi., 7:00]. A showcase of the Dry Brook Valley, where hikers can go as far as the scenic Penguin Rocks (for a round trip of 8.8 mi.) or complete the loop. One of the few loop hikes in the Catskills.

SECTION 17
BALSAM LAKE MOUNTAIN WILD FOREST

Positioned at the head of the scenic Beaver Kill Valley, most of this wild forest area lies within the Ulster County town of Hardenburgh, bounded by Mill Brook Road in the north, across which lies the Dry Brook Ridge Wild Forest. High mountain ridges, deep hollows, steep-sided valleys, a lake, and a number of streams and beaver dams characterize this 14,000-acre area with its 16.8 mi. of foot trails and 5.5 mi. of cross-country ski trails. The highest elevation is the summit of Balsam Lake Mtn. (3,730 ft.), while the lowest is at Kelly Hollow (1,800 ft.), a designated cross-country ski trail system.

Hikers visiting the area will find primitive camping opportunities (and a lean-to) at Kelly Hollow along Mill Brook Road and at the Little Pond and Beaverkill public campgrounds to the west off Beaver Kill Road. Additional primitive camping is available at several scenic sites along Alder Lake Loop Trail, and at a limited number of designated campsites along Beaver Kill Road east of Turnwood, and Shin Creek Road south of Turnwood. There are five lean-tos within this area as well. The most attractive is the Beaver Meadow lean-to, located along Mill Brook Ridge Trail, east of Alder Lake. Northern hardwood slope forest covers most of this area.

There are several important fisheries in the area, most notably the Beaver Kill itself, which has earned the area the reputation as the "cradle of American fly fishing." This river is a part of the system of rivers lying within the most productive eastern trout waters, known by fly fishers the world over as "The Charmed Circle." This stream is heavily posted where it abuts the forest preserve and elsewhere, although hikers can find public access along Neversink-Hardenburgh Trail and in the villages east of Beaver Kill Road.

Scenic resources in this wild forest area are significant and have a great deal to do with the placement of the first fire tower in the state, on Balsam Lake Mtn.'s summit as early as 1887. Because it is a fairly isolated, high, western summit, the mountain provides far-reaching views in every direction.

The Department of Environmental Conservation estimates that nearly 4,000 recreationists use this forest area annually, which is far below the large quotas of the eastern wilderness areas. Approximately 1,500 of these hikers climb the summit of Balsam Lake Mtn. The next-largest user group comprises fishers, campers, and day hikers who use the Alder Lake area. Hikers will accordingly enjoy considerable privacy, access to shelters, good scenery, and excellent fishing while visiting this wild forest.

Mill Brook Ridge Trail

From the trail junction at the eastern shore of Alder Lake, Mill Brook Ridge Trail follows yellow markers east. The trail ascends, evening out through hardwoods over a good surface next to Alder Creek, penetrating a notch between Mill Brook and Cradle Rock Ridges. At 2,300 ft., the trail begins to level, passing close along the northerly margin of a beaver meadow. Coneflowers crowd the heads of little feeder creeks where aster and meadow rue appear. There are a few huge specimens of beech and maple in the area. The trail ascends again, with the creek still to the right (south). At 1.4 mi., a short, unmarked spur leads right to the edge of another beaver meadow that is presently drained. A small brook (the headwaters of Alder Creek) runs through the center. The trail skirts the north edge of the meadow, arriving at the junction of the spring and lean-to spur trails at 1.5 mi.

A slow-running piped spring is 100 yd. to the left (northwest) on a spur. To the right (southeast), toward the meadow and looking out across it, is an excellent lean-to, one of the most attractively situated shelters in the Catskills. The trail passes the lean-to's privy 100 ft. beyond the junction. Ascending, the trail passes another beaver meadow to the south. Rising and leveling moderately and in stages, the trail ascends as it heads southeast, passing a treed-in lookout to the northwest at 3,400 ft. as it turns into hardwoods to reach the crest of a viewless knoll at 2.8 mi. (3,480 ft.). The trail descends to the east, dropping several hundred feet into a saddle above Beecher Lake, which is sometimes visible through the forest to the south. The treadway becomes rocky and uneven, tunneled over by birch and cherry trees. Climbing out of the saddle to 3,300 ft., and offering no summer views to the south, the trail rises to a peat-covered lookout punctuated by one large south-facing rock at 3.9 mi. Mongaup Mtn., Beaver Kill Ridge, Woodpecker Ridge, and Cradle Rock Ridge are visible.

The trail continues flat until dropping off the easternmost section of Mill Brook Ridge at the location of a ledgy lookout point with obscured views of the Balsam Lake Mtn. fire tower. A minimal descent settles onto level terrain as the route traverses hardwood forest around the top of a steep ravine above Balsam Lake, passing close to a number of steep and— at least in one instance, vertical—ledges. Woodpecker Ridge comes into view to the right as the trail climbs into the northeast briefly and negotiates a flight of makeshift steps, switching back southeast on a longer ascent. At the 3,500-ft. mark, balsam fir appears. Shortly beyond the 3,500-ft. sign the trail switches north again, arriving at a bare ledge at 5.7 mi. with westerly views. Turn east at right angles to the lookout, entering an upper-elevation forest of mountain ash and balsam fir. The trail arrives at the junction with Balsam Lake Mtn. Trail at 5.9 mi. (3,650 ft.). Balsam Lake Mtn. (3,730 ft.) and the fire tower are to the left (north) 0.1 mi., on Balsam Lake Mtn. Trail.

Mill Brook Ridge Trail (map 2: C4–C5)

Distances from Alder Lake Loop Trail (2,210 ft.) to
- Beaver Meadow lean-to (2,710 ft.): 1.5 mi., 500 ft., 1 hr.
- high point on Mill Brook Ridge (3,480 ft.): 2.9 mi., 1,250 ft., 2 hr. 5 min.
- south viewpoint (3,370 ft.): 3.9 mi., 1,500 ft. (rev. 350 ft.), 2 hr. 40 min.
- Balsam Lake Mtn. Trail (3,650 ft.): 5.9 mi., 2,050 ft. (rev. 300 ft.), 4 hr.

Alder Lake Loop Trail

Alder Lake is an out-of-the-way trout pond and camping destination in the western Balsam Lake Mtn. Wild Forest region. The trail is used by family campers, day hikers, and backpackers who wish to approach Balsam Lake Mtn. "the long way"—from the west (see Mill Brook Ridge Trail). Alder Lake can be reached from the north by following Mill Brook Road 10.6 mi. west from Stewart's Turn in Seager (Dry Brook Road, CR 49) and coming south on (rough) Cross Mtn. Road 4.3 mi. to the Alder Lake trailhead parking area. It is easily accessible from the west, from Exit 96 off NY 17, by following CR 151 and CR 152 east (Johnson Hill Road) to Lew Beach and continuing east on CR 54 (Beaver Kill Road) to Turnwood (about 18 mi.). Alder Lake is just north of Turnwood off Alder Lake Road.

From the Alder Lake trailhead parking area and map kiosk, proceed past the foundation and cobble walls of Coykendall Lodge, once a derelict mansion built by Samuel D. Coykendall, railroad and canal builder, in 1899. Several attempts to renovate the building failed, and its recent placement on the state register of historic places in 2002 did not lead to its preservation. This is the parcel formerly known as Alder Lake Scout Camp.

The lake and dam are visible from the lodge to the right (south). The trail bears right and crosses the dam. (Tent campers will wish to use the designated sites on the north shore.) The trail does not initially follow directly along the lakeshore, where a herd path leads to several highly impacted campsites, but heads to the right (west) where a solitary signpost indicates the trail's location. From the signpost the trail goes south and uphill gently, within a few hundred feet turning left (east), passing under power lines at a brushy intersection of goldenrod and bushy aster. Red trail markers are consistent, and the trail is in good shape, soon becoming a woods road and crossing a footbridge. The lake is to the left (north) after several hundred feet. Yellow birch is abundant as the trail crosses another footbridge. Herd trails, perhaps leading to primitive tent sites, are numerous. At 0.8 mi., the trail reaches the junction with Mill Brook Ridge Trail on the right (east) and continues on the dirt road treadway. A piped spring appears on the trail's left-hand side, in view of the junction. After crossing a pair of small wooden footbridges where hummingbirds sip at bee balm, the trail swings into the west, passing several designated campsites, most of them heavily used but well maintained and attractive. A few have stone chairs and tables, often with supplies of firewood left behind by other campers. The area becomes busy on most weekends, attracting perennial visitors who are avoiding the crowds at the nearby public campsites. Common to the area are the waterloving hawthorn (with a pear-shaped leaf and fruit that looks like a rose hip) and arrowhead alder in thickets, which are planted for wildlife cover and crowd the trail near the west end.

The trail continues west along the lake's north shore to the grassy lake-front of Coykendall Lodge at 1.4 mi.

Alder Lake Loop Trail (map 2: C4)

Distances from Alder Lake trailhead parking area (2,210 ft.) to
- Mill Brook Ridge Trail (2,210 ft.) via south loop: 0.8 mi., 0 ft., 25 min.
- return to Alder Lake trailhead parking area via north loop: 1.4 mi., 50 ft. (rev. 50 ft.), 45 min.

Balsam Lake Mtn. Trail

The shortest route to Balsam Lake Mtn. Trail is from Dry Brook Ridge Trail's southerly terminus (Balsam Lake Mtn. trailhead parking area). This is the fastest (and steepest) way to the summit of this large westerly Catskill peak. By virtue of its fire tower, the views from Balsam Lake Mtn. are extraordinary. The trails in this area are popular, but remote.

The trailhead parking area is at the eastern extreme of Beaver Kill Road, which can be reached most easily from Exit 94 off NY 17, by traveling east on CR 151 and CR 152 (Johnson Hill Road) to Lew Beach, and continuing on CR 54 (Beaver Kill Road) to its end (about 22 mi.). Beaver Kill Road can also be reached from the north by turning left (east) off Alder Lake Road onto Beaver Kill Road (see Alder Lake Loop Trail for details). Access to Balsam Lake Mtn. Trail can also be gained from the north off Dry Brook Ridge Trail, using the Dry Brook Ridge trailhead on Mill Brook Road, 2.2 mi. west of Dry Brook Road (CR 49) at Stewart's Turn.

Dry Brook Ridge Trail (blue markers) leaves from the northeast corner of the Balsam Lake Mtn. trailhead parking area and leads 0.9 mi. to the Balsam Lake Mtn. trailhead (red markers). Signage is poor at the Dry Brook Ridge trailhead. There is good signage at the junction. Trail mileage begins here.

At the junction of Balsam Lake Mtn. Trail and Dry Brook Ridge Trail, Balsam Lake Mtn. Trail goes left (north) following red markers and climbs steeply to the lean-to spur at 0.3 mi. on the left (west) side of the trail. The spur is 0.2 mi. long, and leads through a patch of cow parsnips across a seasonal creek emanating from an uphill spring. To the west there are only obscure, seasonal views of Woodpecker Ridge. This is the Elinore Leavitt memorial lean-to (in excellent condition), built in recognition of Mrs. Leavitt's involvement in conservation issues.

The main trail continues and rises steeply, ascending a few stone steps past a spring. The trail flattens above this point, where an older campsite (illegal) appears on the right (east) near the 3,500-ft. elevation mark. The trail eases now, in scrubby beech-and-cherry woods as summit elevation is approached and the junction with Mill Brook Ridge Trail is reached at 0.5 mi.

Continuing straight ahead (north) and nearing the summit, the trail ascends slightly into a nearly pure fir forest. The tower stands in the corner of the small summit clearing at 0.8 mi., with an observer's cabin and privy nearby. Views from the tower are excellent. On weekends an observer may be present. To the east and slightly south are Peekamoose, Table, and Lone Mtns. In the foreground is Doubletop. Moving north, Slide dominates the far horizon. Graham, Giant Ledge and Panther, Indian Head, Twin, Sugarloaf, and Plateau can be seen. Hunter, West Kill, Blackhead, Black Dome, and Thomas Cole are visible to the northeast. In the foreground is Red Hill, its fire tower visible. On the right of Red Hill is Denman Mtn. The peaks of the Big Indian Range can be identified.

The trail continues northeast from the summit, descending through boreal forest on a steep truck trail. The descent continues easterly, dropping below the 3,500-ft. level, and the trail ends at its junction with Dry Brook Ridge Trail at 1.4 mi.

Balsam Lake Mtn. Trail (map 2: C5)

Distances from south junction with Dry Brook Ridge Trail (2,900 ft.) to
- Elinore Leavitt memorial lean-to spur (3,450 ft.): 0.3 mi., 550 ft., 25 min.
- Mill Brook Ridge Trail (3,650 ft.): 0.5 mi., 750 ft., 40 min.
- Balsam Lake Mtn. summit (3,730 ft.): 0.8 mi., 850 ft., 50 min.
- north junction with Dry Brook Ridge Trail (3,330 ft.): 1.4 mi., 850 ft. (rev. 400 ft.), 1 hr. 10 min.

Kelly Hollow Trail

Beautifully situated within a trio of nameless tributaries above Mill Brook, this designated cross-country ski trail makes a fine year-round day outing or overnight destination. It is convenient to both the Dry Brook Ridge and Alder Lake Loop trailheads. Car and tent camping in designated sites at the western trailhead, in addition to the (access by foot only) lean-to at Beaver Pond, make this a popular destination for hikers and, especially in late summer, long-term campers. (A permit is required for stays longer than three days.) Unlimited opportunities for tent camping exist in the serene pine-and-Norway spruce forests throughout the hollow. Larger parties should restrict themselves to the impacted, designated sites inside the west entrance.

The trail leaves from the eastern trailhead and designated parking area on Mill Brook Road, 6.6 mi. west of Dry Brook Road (CR 49). (The western trailhead and designated camping area is 0.3 mi. farther to the west.) A privy is situated near the parking area. Locate the yellow cross-country ski trail markers, which the trail follows south into a mature red pine stand, turning left (east) over a creek to join an old road. The trail then turns right (south) and heads uphill through a barrier gate. A stone wall appears on the right (west) as the trail ascends next to a brook, where hemlock becomes dominant. At 0.5 mi., the trail continues straight ahead (south) at the Short Loop junction, where signs are posted. (Short Loop departs downhill to the right, crossing a footbridge above a scenic glen, rises to Halfway Point, spans the brook's west branch, and joins the main trail again. Short Loop receives little use and is often blocked with blowdowns. The west branch plank bridge is in poor condition at this writing. Those wishing to shorten the hike can follow the Short Loop west to rejoin the Long Loop, then turn right to the west-end trailhead.)

Avoid the Short Loop (a visit to the footbridge, visible from this junction, is worthwhile) and proceed straight ahead toward Beaver Pond. To the left (east) a large Norway spruce plantation begins. The trail crosses the head of a sluggish creek in a strip of hardwoods before reentering the plantation, the latter so heavily shaded that there is little to no plant growth. At the top of the east branch, the trail turns west and north in a long, flat arc above the hollow. Hardwood yields to spotted spruce and hemlock, turning to nearly pure hemlock as the trail rises slightly to the well-situated lean-to at Beaver Pond, which sits in a north-facing depression of Mill Brook Ridge among tall spruce trees at 2.0 mi. The pond is frequently dry, depending upon beaver populations. The trail continues along the east edge of the pond, heading south. Marking is poor and the trail is crowded with brush and brambles, yielding large batches of black raspberries in late summer. Circling the lake to the northwest, the trail improves as it joins an old dirt road through a farmed area of which only stone walls remain, turns right (north), and descends easily.

Descending more steeply now, at 2.4 mi. the trail passes Short Loop on the right (east) and crosses a footbridge as it flattens out. Soon a grave-yard appears to the left, and the trail joins the main camping-area road on the west end of the hollow. Go around the barrier gate, keeping the designated campsites to the right, at 3.1 mi. reaching Millbrook Road. At 150 ft. to the right (east) of the west entrance along Mill Brook Road, the cross-country ski trail signs lead back into the woods, heading east. This connector trail will save hikers from walking the (short) road distance back to the east branch parking area. (The road is also pleasant, and never busy.) The trail is not consistently self-guiding and marking on this section is poor. Keeping Mill Brook Road visible to the left (north), arrive at the parking area at 3.2 mi.

Kelly Hollow Trail (map 2: C4)

Distances from east trailhead on Mill Brook Road (1,770 ft.) to
- east junction with Short Loop (1,950 ft.): 0.5 mi., 200 ft., 20 min.
- beaver pond and lean-to (2,250 ft.): 2.0 mi., 500 ft., 1 hr. 15 min.
- west junction with Short Loop (1,930 ft.): 2.4 mi., 500 ft. (rev. 300 ft.), 1 hr. 25 min.
- west trailhead on Mill Brook Road (1,750 ft.): 3.1 mi., 500 ft. (rev. 200 ft.), 1 hr. 50 min.
- Distance for complete loop: 3.2 mi., 500 ft., 1 hr. 50 min.
- Distance for Short Loop: 1.4 mi., 200 ft., 50 min.

Mill Brook Lean-to Spur Trail

The Mill Brook lean-to is a convenient camping spot, located a very short distance off Mill Brook Road, less than a mile west of the Dry Brook Ridge trailhead parking area. Come west from Stewart's Turn at the corner of Mill Brook Road and Dry Brook Road (CR 49), passing the Dry Brook

Ridge trailhead parking area at 2.2 mi. Continue another 0.9 mi., and park on the right side of the road by the lean-to spur.

The lean-to spur trail crosses a tributary of Mill Brook and climbs easily though a hemlock woods 0.2 mi. to the lean-to. The forest setting and proximity to water make this a popular shelter, yet it remains clean and well maintained by the Adirondack Mountain Club.

Mill Brook Lean-to Spur Trail (map 2: C5)

Distance from Mill Brook Road (2,250 ft.) to
  • Mill Brook lean-to (2,350 ft.): 0.2 mi., 100 ft., 10 min.

SUGGESTED HIKES

Easy Hike

Alder Lake Loop Trail [loop: 1.4 mi., 0:45]. A short, easy, pretty hike around the lake, suitable for young children. Primitive camping is available.

Moderate Hike

Kelly Hollow Trail [loop: 2.0 mi., 1:50]. An attractive hemlock woods trail to a beaver pond (Beaver Pond) with a lean-to. Taking the shorter loop cuts an hour off the hike.

Strenuous Hike

Balsam Lake Mtn. Trail via Dry Brook Ridge Trail with access gained from Mill Brook Road trailhead [rt: 6.0 mi., 3:10]. A very scenic hike to Balsam Lake Mtn. summit and its fire tower, featuring dense balsam forests and a 360-degree viewshed.

PART 4
WESTERN CATSKILLS

The Western Catskills are largely contained in the Delaware Wild Forest, where the landscape is characterized by open fields, mature hardwood forests, and hills with steep slopes leading to long, flat ridges. The main trail in the area is a ridge-and-valley route joining several other trails, collectively known as Delaware Ridge Trail, leading from Russell Brook Road in the west to Alder Lake for a distance of 27 mi. with seven road crossings. These trails are among the quietest and least used in the Catskills. Vistas, although present, are infrequent, but several natural lakes in the area are open to camping and fishing.

The Western Catskills shared many of the industries common to the rest of the range, with the addition of acid manufacturing, another extractive and ravaging forest product industry. Because the acid-manufacturing process depends on hardwood, the post-tanning-period Catskills were well suited to the task. Early postcards of the Western Catskills, particularly around the villages of Roscoe and Rockland, show the clear-cut landscapes resulting from the acid-production industry in the late nineteenth century.

True to form in the succession of regional development, the railroads were followed by a brisk recreational and tourist industry, most of it focusing on hunting and fishing. It is a reputation the area maintains today. Perhaps no other spot in the East is as renowned for its trout fishing—in the 1980s, the Fly Fishing Federation of America labeled Roscoe "Trout Town, USA." Lying at the confluence (Junction Pool) of the Beaver Kill and Willowemoc—easily ranking among the country's most historical and legendary trout streams—the town sustains its status as an angler's mecca. Nearby Livingston Manor is host to the Catskill Fly Fishing Center and Museum. It was along the banks of the Beaver Kill that Theodore Gordon, the father of American fly fishing, developed his artificial dry fly patterns (such as the Quill Gordon) that so effectively imitate the mayflies that trout feed on.

The Western Catskills are accessible from Mongaup Pond, Beaverkill, and Little Pond public campgrounds.

SECTION 18
DELAWARE WILD FOREST

Located in the towns of Colchester and Andes in Delaware County, Herdenberg in Ulster County, and Rockland in Sullivan County, this 27,800-acre wild forest is mountainous, with trails ranging from moderate to steep. The forest is characterized by its several wetlands, more than 22 mi. of snowmobile trails, ten tributary stream systems, and 33 mi. of foot trails. Little Pond Campground lies in the eastern portion of the forest. The dominant ridge trail is part of a continuous trail system spanning the Delaware Ridge. Elevations in this wild forest run from 2,200 ft. to 2,800 ft. and the area is almost entirely covered in forest of the Allegheny hardwood group, including cherry, red and sugar maple, American beech, yellow birch, and hemlock.

This wild forest contains three lean-tos and is ideal for day and overnight hikers seeking solitude and quiet in a little-used area. Several of the wild forest's most westerly trails are used by mountain bikers, in particular Trout Pond-Mud Pond Loop. North of Trout Pond, however, the terrain is difficult and self-limiting to multiuse recreationists.

Russell Brook trailhead is the one most commonly used by hikers, and the main attractions of the area around the trailhead are the falls and hemlock forests close to the road itself. No threatened or endangered species officially exist in this area, although there are believed to be timber rattlesnakes—a threatened species. Hikers should avoid exploring quarries or ruins during the warm, early months of spring when rattlers are active. Many of the area's wetlands (two of which are large enough to enjoy federal protection under the Freshwater Wetlands Act) are host to beaver populations and help to create a greater diversity of wildlife. Trout Pond has been a popular fishing destination in the past and maintains a population of the Catskill strain of brook trout.

Trout Pond Trail

From Exit 93 off NY 17 (Butternut Grove, Cooks Falls), Trout Pond Trail begins 3.7 mi. east on Russell Brook Road. At 1.2 mi. from NY 17, Russell Brook Road is seasonally unmaintained. Both the Trout Pond and Mud Pond trail segments west of Trout Pond are used by mountain bikers and cross-country skiers.

Signs are posted next to the gated road adjacent to the trailhead parking area on the northwest side of Russell Brook Road. The trail follows this access road and descends a short distance to Russell Brook, crossing a pair of wooden bridges. The ruins of an early bluestone dam and bridge can be seen 200 ft. to the right (northeast, upstream). A heavily used, designated campsite is situated to the right (east) of the trail, within view of the trail register. Ahead 200 ft. is Trout Pond Trail's junction with Russell Brook Trail.

A stone foundation—the first of many to be seen in this early farming area—appears in the woods to the left. The trail bears right (north) toward Trout Pond over a wide, rocky road through hardwoods at 2,045 ft., ascending easily and passing an unmarked spur to the left that leads 400 ft. to a designated campsite. Trout Pond comes into view at 1.0 mi., where an unmarked spur leads to a shingle beach on the south end of the pond. Beyond the concrete spillway, a rough (unmarked) path continues around the lake to the west. On the trail's right (east), amid tall hardwoods and a patch of striking, scarlet bee balm, an arrow indicates the direction to the lean-to. A privy stands to the east of the trail here. The trail follows beside Trout Pond's northeastern shore and passes a legal, undesignated campsite on the right, after which a spring appears to the right of a footbridge where the Department of Environmental Conservation maintains a trout-spawning box. This piped spring provides a steady supply of cold water to a contrived spawning bed on the pond's east shore. Fishing in Trout Pond (brook trout) has proven productive in the past. Ahead a very short distance is a trail junction, in view of the lean-to. To the left, the unsigned snowmobile trail leaves around the north end of Trout Pond, heading southwest to Mud Pond.

Rebuilt in the late summer of 2001, the Trout Pond lean-to is constructed of flat-sawn timbers, an unusual contrast to the old-style shelters made of peeled logs and hand-hewn planks. Trout Pond Trail turns right (north) at the junction at 1.2 mi., climbing steadily into the northeast, at 2,500 ft. arriving at a height-of-land where Trout Pond Trail continues left and a snowmobile trail leaves to the right (southeast) for Morton Hill Road.

Descending, the trail switches back before leveling into the east, thereafter descending steeply to a footbridge spanning the headwaters of Campbell Brook (dry in late summer) at 2,100 ft. The trail flattens as hemlock appears in a pure stand before a second footbridge is crossed and the trail rises through hardwoods, deteriorating underfoot but remaining self-guiding and adequately marked. Stone walls denote the bounds of early settlements where late, second-growth hardwoods are taking hold. Passing around a barrier gate, Trout Pond Trail crosses Campbell Brook Road at 3.0 mi.

Continue to the left (north) on Campbell Brook Road, within 400 ft. turning right (east), regaining Trout Pond Trail. Climbing gently uphill into hardwoods, the quiet trail is fringed with blackberries and beech trees. At 3.7 mi. (2,500 ft.), the trail levels through a flat summit knoll with no views. A downhill stretch to the southeast follows amid very tall hardwoods and a small quarry-talus heap, partly concealed by vegetation and detritus, appears to the right. The trail crosses a footbridge on the northerly headwater branch of Campbell Brook, after which an interesting house or barn foundation is seen on the left as the trail enters a stand of maturing Norway spruce trees. The trail (almost continuously an old dirt roadway) rises through this early farmstead area, where pioneer species (those taking hold after a fire or other disturbance) have taken hold in the open, grassy terrain and asters, Scotch pine, apple, and escaped cultivated plants are growing. Ascending to 2,175 ft., and passing around a barrier gate at 4.7 mi. where a signboard stands at the shoulder of Campbell Mtn. Road, Trout Pond Trail ends. Campbell Mtn. Trail begins directly across the road. Finger Lakes Trail disks may be posted here, where there is a small parking lot designated as a snowmobile parking and off-loading area. This spot is isolated.

Trout Pond Trail (map 2: D2–C2)

Distances from trailhead on Russell Brook Road (1,770 ft.) to
- Mud Pond Trail and Trout Pond lean-to (2,130 ft.): 1.2 mi., 350 ft., 45 min.
- Campbell Brook Road (2,190 ft.): 3.0 mi., 700 ft. (rev. 300 ft.), 1 hr. 50 min.
- Campbell Mtn. Road (2,170 ft.): 4.7 mi., 1,150 ft. (rev. 450 ft.), 2 hr. 55 min.

Mud Pond Trail

This quiet trail leads to a mountain pond through deep woods and is the westernmost trailhead on state land in the Catskills. The forests in this area have reclaimed a number of old farms and orchards, of which hikers will see some remains.

From Exit 93 off NY 17 (Butternut Grove, Cooks Falls), Mud Pond Trail begins 2.3 mi. east on Russell Brook Road (1.2 mi. from NY 17, Russell Brook Road is seasonally unmaintained). Both the Trout Pond Trail and Mud Pond Trail segments west of Trout Pond are used by mountain bikers and cross-country skiers. The trail leaves to the north from the trailhead pullover parking area.

The trail enters the wood, passes the trail register on the right and climbs, passing beneath a transmission line over the West Delaware Aqueduct right of way (1,673 ft.). At 0.2 mi., a beaver pond appears to the west as the trail levels, draining through a small hemlock grove and into wet meadow to the east. The trail traverses one of the many old roads that penetrate the surrounding wild forest area, passing through a shallow, picturesque hollow, carved by the outlet stream of Mud Pond. The trail ascends and levels, and at 1.0 mi., Mud Pond is visible to the right. Turning right (east) 90 degrees at a trail arrow where a snowmobile spur departs west to the head of Dry Brook Road (private), Mud Pond Trail continues east, crosses Mud Pond's seasonal inlet creek, and passes several hand-laid bluestone foundations on the Mud Pond (right) side of the trail. At 2.0 mi., watch carefully for the easily missed, unmarked spur trail to the right, leading 400 ft. to the pond. Just beyond the spur along the main trail, an undesignated campsite and fire ring exist to the right (south). At 1.5 mi., arrive at a junction where Mud Pond Trail turns left (north), and Russell Brook Trail (blue, snowmobile corridor 20A) continues straight ahead (southeast) to the Russell Brook Road parking area. Bear left.

Rising through sugar maple, the trail crosses the site of an early pasture, in the process of natural reclamation by a forest of vigorous maple saplings. Ascending with Russell Brook to the left (west), the trail rises to a point east off of Cherry Ridge at 2.5 mi. (2,500 ft.). Now the trail descends to the east, crossing the Trout Pond inlet and approaching the north shore of the pond, where a designated campsite lies just to the right (west). A new, well-built lean-to stands within sight of Trout Pond Trail junction at 3.9 mi.

Mud Pond Trail (map 2: D2–C2)

Distances from trailhead on Russell Brook Road (1,530 ft.) to
- spur trail to Mud Pond (2,090 ft.): 1.5 mi., 600 ft. (rev. 50 ft.), 1 hr. 5 min.
- Russell Brook Trail (2,100 ft.): 2.0 mi., 600 ft., 1 hr. 20 min.
- Trout Pond Trail and Trout Pond lean-to (2,130 ft.): 3.9 mi., 1,000 ft. (rev. 350 ft.), 2 hr. 30 min.

Russell Brook Trail

This trail follows an early woods road to join Mud Pond Trail and offers several attractive camping possibilities. Beginning at the junction with Trout Pond Trail a few hundred feet north of the Russell Brook Road parking area, this trail provides the shortest access route to Mud Pond and enables a loop connection for walks around both Trout and Mud Ponds (assuming that Russell Brook Road is used to complete the Mud Pond loop). Ascend over rolling terrain as Russell Brook appears to the left (south), becoming a deep, dry gully by late summer. Campsites are designated at both sides of a footbridge spanning the brook. The trail soon descends, arriving at the T junction with Mud Pond Trail at 0.9 mi.

Russell Brook Trail (map 2: D2)

Distance from Trout Pond Trail (1,750 ft.) to
- Mud Pond Trail (2,100 ft.): 0.9 mi., 350 ft., 40 min.

Campbell Mtn. Trail

This trail crosses isolated Campbell Mtn. before descending to cross NY 206 and climbs across Brock Mtn. before connecting to Pelnor Hollow Trail and points east and south. It forms a major link in Delaware Ridge Trail.

The trail begins on Campbell Mtn. Road, a continuation of Trout Pond Trail to the west. A parking area is located here, 0.8 mi. north of Jug Tavern Road on Campbell Mtn. Road.

The trail begins past a barrier gate, and climbs gently through a mixed forest of white pine and hardwoods. Turning south and north again around a knoll (2,461 ft.), the trail flattens momentarily as it heads southeast, with red oaks increasing. Passing a small but obvious footpath to the right (south) at 0.4 mi. (which heads off in the direction of Wedemeyer Road), hikers may hear highway noise filtering up through Cat Hollow from CR 7 (NY 206). The trail descends through an oak-and-maple wood, and passes an old, discontinued trail to the right across a seasonal rill, arriving at the lean-to spur at 1.1 mi. (2,100 ft.). A sign indicates the shelter to the right, across the same (former) kill, which is dry in late summer.

Continuing downhill, the trail switches back at a large quarry site to the left (north), where the hiker is guided by trail arrows. Through 1,800 ft. of elevation, a microburst has felled a substantial section of forest on the hollow's western slope. Continuing south the trail flattens, entering hemlock woods and crossing a tributary that flows 2.0 mi. north into the Pepacton Reservoir. A gratifying, dense Norway spruce plantation follows—one of the few such stands encountered this far west in the Catskills—and thick yellow blooms of coneflower appear in this neighborhood of reclaimed farmlands. The trail curves left (north) and rises out of the woods along the side of a slope, reaching CR 7 (NY 206) at 2.2 mi. This is a fairly busy highway. Signs and a register are present. Pullover parking is available.

Carefully cross the road and regain the trail on the east side, beginning the ascent of Brock Mtn. (2,512 ft.) as the trail climbs an embankment into the woods, heading northeast. Old stone walls stand to the right (south). Climbing through hardwoods followed by an extensive red pine woods, the trail deteriorates into a rough path, at first ascending steeply, then relaxing in a mixed hardwood area before climbing again, leveling off at roughly 2,400 ft. Extensive tailing piles from a large quarry appear immediately to the trail's left (north), extending northeast. The talus field and strip mines are accessible from a small (vague) access path on the left (north) of the main trail. The quarry itself is overgrown and unspectacular—far inferior to those of the Eastern Catskills—but it's worth a small detour a few hundred feet along this path to see the intriguing remains of an early-1900s dump truck—a solemn memorial of another era. Continuing east, the roadlike trail improves over the route of the original quarry road, which joined present-day CR 7. Ahead, be careful to watch for the trail's 90-degree left-hand turn (north) as the quarry road continues straight ahead, passing through a now-private inholding. Although the road is sometimes "blocked" with sticks to alert hikers, it's easy to continue on this more established but incorrect route.

Follow the trail to the southeast as it ascends, passing north of Brock's southeastern summit at 3.8 mi. (2,760 ft.). The trail is level for a short distance, soon passing through a high (2,700 ft.), grassy area punctuated by a small, flat clearing on exposed bedrock. The trail immediately descends through a forest of tall maple and scattered large, flat boulders, dropping nearly 500 ft. in elevation over the next 0.5 mi. At 4.6 mi., the trail reaches a woods road (dirt) that runs north–south. Signage is absent, and marking is poor. A stone wall stands directly across the road. To the right (south), red snowmobile markers lead to School House Road (private). Campbell Mtn. Trail continues to the left (north), where snowmobile markers and (scant) blue markers head in the direction of the Miller Hollow Road spur. Watch carefully as Campbell Mtn. Trail follows the snowmobile trail a distance of approximately 200 yd. before turning hard right (east) and sidehilling along a north-facing slope. As you travel east, within a few moments an unmarked woods road leaves to the right (south) onto private property toward School House Road. The main trail turns into the north, descending slightly, and turns southeast, leveling and again descending, passing through an extensive, well-made stone wall and into a maturing Norway spruce forest.

At 5.6 mi., the trail arrives at a junction where a red-marked snowmobile trail leaves to the left (north) on a dirt road, ultimately joining (private) Berg Brook Road. The trail to the right, toward Little Spring Brook Road (still Campbell Mtn. Trail), leads to Pelnor Hollow Trail. This intersection is marked only with blue and red markers, with a trail arrow pointing right (south). Avoid the red snowmobile trail to the left, and turn right (south) following the grassy trail, within minutes reaching a T junction, where as of this writing, signage appears on a post beneath an apple tree at 5.9 mi. This is the end of Campbell Mtn. Trail. Little Spring Brook Trail leaves to the south, and Pelnor Hollow Trail goes left (east) to join Mary Smith Trail.

Campbell Mtn. Trail (map 2: C2–C3)

Distances from Campbell Mtn. Road (2,170 ft.) to
- Campbell Mtn. lean-to (2,000 ft.): 1.1 mi., 250 ft. (rev. 400 ft.), 40 min.
- NY 206 (1,830 ft.): 2.2 mi., 400 ft. (rev. 300 ft.), 1 hr. 20 min.
- high point near summit of Brock Mtn. (2,730 ft.): 3.8 mi., 1,350 ft. (rev. 50 ft.), 2 hr. 35 min.
- Pelnor Hollow Trail and Little Spring Brook Trail (2,090 ft.): 5.9 mi., 1,650 ft. (rev. 950 ft.), 3 hr. 45 min.

Pelnor Hollow Trail

Pelnor Hollow Trail begins at the intersection of Campbell Mtn. and Little Spring Brook trails and rises to the east before turning south to meet Mary Smith Trail. Heavily forested, the trail provides an egress/ingress route from Delaware Ridge Trail to the south, via Berry Brook Road and Pelnor Hollow Road, just west of the Beaver Kill Public Campground. The area (especially the Pelnor Hollow lean-to) is popular with hunters.

Pelnor Hollow Trail heads east following blue markers, crossing a seasonal creek into an extensive forest of red pine and Norway spruce, providing decent camping potential for thru-hikers en route to the Pelnor Hollow lean-to. Climbing steeply and switching back through hardwoods, at 2,500 ft. the trail turns south, flattening along a west-facing ridge with low ledges on the left. A break in the forest looking west is the location of Split Rock Lookout, a prominent vista. This area is also an attractive rest stop because the open ledge provides some visual relief as well as summer exposure to prevailing breezes. *Approach cautiously, especially during snow cover or low light, watching for a shallow but potentially hazardous (20-ft.) crack where the ledge has fissured away from the ridge.* To reach the ledge (not necessary in order to get the full view), go around to the left of a large boulder, avoiding the temptation to jump across the mossy crevice. Views to the west across the Little Spring Brook valley provide a welcomed contrast to the enclosed woodlands, exposing Brock Mtn. (2,512 ft.), Cherry Ridge (avg. 2,600 ft.), and the hills of Hamden in the northwest. Climbing steeply but briefly, the trail arrives at the junction with Mary Smith Trail at 0.8 mi.

Heading south, the trail becomes obscured by ground vegetation but soon provides an open and clear track, which is well marked and self-guiding. Descending slightly before climbing to the enclosed crest of a nameless ridge at 2,672 ft., and turning briefly into the northwest and leveling, the trail soon descends south again as it approaches Pelnor Hollow. Amid the ash, red oak, and gray birch, hikers may see an occasional shagbark hickory tree and old snowmobile trail markers. At 3.4 mi. the lean-to—well situated in an open forest of tall maple—is reached, where a beaver pond is visible a short distance downhill to the southeast.

Continue south through a flat area of thin beech trees, turning through the west and descending to the (dirt) Pelnor Hollow Road at 4.4 mi. The lack of trailhead parking here is problematic for hikers heading north to the lean-to, and the road is both rough and heavily posted.

Pelnor Hollow Trail (map 2: C3–D3)

Distances from Campbell Mtn. Trail and Little Spring Brook Trail (2,090 ft.) to
- Mary Smith Trail (2,660 ft.): 1.2 mi., 550 ft., 55 min.
- Pelnor Hollow lean-to (2,230 ft.): 3.4 mi., 850 ft. (rev. 750 ft.), 2 hr. 10 min.
- Pelnor Hollow Road (1,910 ft.): 4.4 mi., 850 ft. (rev. 300 ft.), 2 hr. 40 min.

Little Spring Brook Trail

This short spur descends from its intersection with Pelnor Hollow Trail and Campbell Mtn. Trail, passing a small pond on the left (east), crossing its outlet (Little Spring Brook), and ending at the northern terminus of Little Spring Brook Road (off NY 206/CR 7, aka Cat Hollow Road). Trailhead parking on Little Spring Brook Road is limited to room for a car or two (pull-over) near the driveway of a private residence, where a hand-painted sign identifies the parking pull-off. There is destination signage along the trail. Marking exists. This trail represents one of the few (legal) trails leaving/entering Delaware Ridge Trail from the south, between the much longer Pelnor Hollow Trail and the trailheads along area roads running north–south.

Little Spring Brook Trail (map 2: C3)

Distance from Pelnor Hollow Trail and Campbell Mtn. Trail (2,090 ft.) to
- Little Spring Brook Road (1,910 ft.): 0.7 mi., 0 ft. (rev. 200 ft.), 20 min.

Mary Smith Trail

Starting at 2,650 ft., 1.2 miles southeast from the beginning of Pelnor Hollow Trail, Mary Smith Trail descends to the northeast. The trail quickly descends, becoming steeper before leveling in a mixed hardwood forest of basswood, birch, and large ash trees. Ferns and viburnum crowd the well-marked trail, which gets little use. Nearing Holliday and Berry Brook Road, the path first passes under power lines, beneath which is buried the East Delaware Aqueduct (not visible). This system carries water from the Cannonsville, Pepacton, Neversink, and Rondout reservoirs east to the Croton watershed and its dozen reservoirs to supply New York City's drinking water.

Relocating the trail on the other side of the power-line right of way will demand a bit more attention from hikers coming west. (Because of the recessed tree line on the west side, there is nowhere to post a trail marker.) The trail crosses the right of way diagonally, but is not self-guiding across the clearing. Watch carefully for markers. The trail picks up again slightly to the left after passing under the power lines. Blackberries are abundant. The state has posted signs here prohibiting target practice (hunters prefer to sight their rifles where they can place a target several hundred feet distant—the power line is an ideal place for this).

The following flat section of trail crosses a private easement. Hikers planning to camp near the trailhead should do so only after entering the wild forest boundary. A grassy area leads to the road, where signs are posted. There is a large parking area on the east side of Holliday and Berry Brook Road, where Mary Smith Trail continues from the north end of the lot. Finger Lakes Trail signs and markers are posted here. Roughly 5.0 miles to the south on Berry Brook Road is the Beaver Kill Public Campground. The trail continues, following red markers as it leaves the parking lot, crosses a private easement, and quickly climbs into the northeast amid oak and maple trees, turning south and switching back at the site of a shallow overhanging rock. Here the path relaxes, penetrates a broken ledge, and begins to level at 2,600 ft. on a westerly knoll approaching the summit of Mary Smith Hill (2,760 ft.). Watch for a yellow arrow, where the route turns sharply to the right (southeast). The treadway is crowded with brush by late summer, but this vegetation—primarily viburnum and berry bushes—thins as the trail moves east. Marginal, seasonal views exist to the right (south). Following along the flat ridge for a mile beyond the summit, the trail arrives at a boulder and the site of a narrow (30 degrees) cut vista looking south across Huggins Hollow. The off-trail area is flat, legal, and suitable for tenting. The trail continues downhill into a maple forest, switching back steeply to the northeast, ending at Mary Smith Hill Road at 3.9 mi. (2,230 ft.). Across the road on the left (north) is a designated campsite. Trailhead parking is a short distance south.

Mary Smith Trail (map 2: C3)

Distances from Pelnor Hollow Trail (2,660 ft.) to
- Holliday and Berry Brook Road (2,130 ft.): 1.0 mi., 0 ft. (rev. 550 ft.), 30 min.
- high point on Mary Smith Hill (2,760 ft.): 2.0 mi., 650 ft., 1 hr. 20 min.
- Mary Smith Hill Road (2,230 ft.): 3.9 mi., 900 ft. (rev. 800 ft.), 2 hr. 25 min.

Middle Mtn. Trail

On Mary Smith Hill Road, 3.1 mi. north of the Lew Beach four corners on Beaver Kill Road, Middle Mtn. Trail heads east, forming another link in the Delaware Ridge Trail system. At the edge of the road's right (east) side, next to the trail register and a designated campsite, locate the trail signage.

Follow the established pathway east into the woods. The trail for a moment remains flat. Stone walls appear to the right as the track rises into hardwoods. Altitude is gained quickly and steeply. Views to the west of Mary Smith Hill are seasonal, improving as the trail relaxes and switches into the southeast, rising gently. Turning east, the bulk of the remaining ridge-top elevation is achieved at 2,975 ft. on the summit of Middle Mtn. (viewless) at 0.9 mi. The trail continues on the level to Middle Mtn. Vista at 1.1 mi., a narrow but welcome cut view (30 degrees) looking south across Whitcomb Hollow and Lew Beach toward Mongaup Mtn. The trail descends hereafter, where jack-in-the-pulpit gone to red berries (in season) appear. After descending, a shallow saddle is crossed at 2,650 ft.; the corresponding ascent follows to Beech Hill at 1.5 mi. (2,844 ft.), where the path is level amid ferns and cherry trees. (You will see copious bear scat while the red cherry is in fruit in July and August.) Seasonal views exist to the northeast toward Cabot Mtn. (2,970 ft.). The trail descends steadily off the northeast face of Beech Hill until reaching a dirt road. One hundred ft. to the left (west) is private, posted property. Turn right (east), following the road (it is not well marked) to Beech Hill Road at 2.1 mi. A Finger Lakes Trail sign identifies the trailhead. To the right (southeast) 0.2 mi. is the trailhead parking area and the Touch-Me-Not Mtn. trailhead.

Middle Mtn. Trail (map 2: C3)

Distances from Mary Smith Hill Road (2,230 ft.) to
- Middle Mtn. summit (2,975 ft.): 0.9 mi., 750 ft., 50 min.
- Middle Mtn. vista (2,900 ft.): 1.1 mi., 750 ft. (rev. 100 ft.), 55 min.
- Beech Hill summit (2,844 ft.): 1.5 mi., 900 ft. (rev. 200 ft.), 1 hr. 10 min.
- Beech Hill Road (2,330 ft.): 2.1 mi., 900 ft. (rev. 500 ft.), 1 hr. 30 min.

Touch-Me-Not Trail

Named for the flower that is so prolific along its course, the quiet Touch-Me-Not Trail forms the easternmost link in Delaware Ridge Trail. Find the trailhead 0.2 mi. south of Middle Mtn. trailhead on Beech Hill Road, and 3.0 mi. north of Beaver Kill Road, northeast of Lew Beach (this is near the corners of Delaware, Sullivan, and Ulster counties). A large trail sign and Finger Lakes Trail signage appear at the parking area.

The trail heads northeast into the woods following the northern edge of a pine plantation in an open field of goldenrod, reentering the woods to the east. Norway spruce appears on the south side as the trail descends slightly along a disused dirt road, soon ascending among a few rotting blowdowns colonized by brassy-orange golden trumpets. The climbing continues to the 2,800-ft. level, where the trail turns southeast, becomes level, descends slightly, and again climbs easily to nearly summit elevation, where it turns northeast again. At the flat summit of Cabot Mtn. at 1.2 mi. (2,970 ft.), the anchor rod of a benchmark may be seen in a stone midtrail, but the benchmark itself is gone. At 1.2 mi., the trail arrives at a lookout point. *This is a vertical ledge, where vegetation projects slightly over the edge of the rock itself. Use caution.* Balsam Lake Mtn. (3,723 ft.) is seen to the left, but the fire tower is nearly impossible to spot without binoculars. South of Balsam Lake Mtn. and farther back on the horizon is Doubletop (3,860 ft.), with the Beaver Kill Range in the foreground. Little Pond (the location of the public campground) is visible directly below, with its sandy beach along the north shore.

The trail leaves across the top of the ledge heading north and descends steeply into the east, leveling at 2,500 ft. in the saddle above Little Pond at 2.0 mi. Little Pond Trail descends to the south at this point. No destination signage exists at this time, but directional marking is adequate. Pointing back into the west, a trail arrow here is hand-painted with the words Beech Hill. From this point the trail continues east, following red markers. Watch carefully as the trail swings north, rising through a low ledge. (A herd path continues a short distance to the right [southeast] before the ledge, indicating that this turn is frequently missed.) Large oak and cherry trees characterize Touch-Me-Not Mtn. at 2.8 mi. (2,760 ft.), the treed-in summit approximated by the junction with the Campground Trail, which descends to the right (south) to Little Pond Public Campground. Signage here is good.

The trail descends to the east, easing as elevation is lost through the thick northern hardwood forest. Soon the trail joins an old woods road as it approaches Big Pond. This area has received high impact from indiscreet campers—there is broken glass and trash scattered along the trail here. Pass the trail register and drop down to Barkaboom Road at 3.9 mi. A Finger Lakes Trail signboard and red markers appear here at the trailhead. Destination signage is absent, but distances to points east can be found at the parking area to the right at 4.0 mi., a short way to the right (south) on the east side of Barkaboom Road. There is also a small parking area here at the trailhead. A signboard at the open, grassy south end of the pond contains a map and information pertaining to both Big Pond and the wild forest area. Big Pond has several designated campsites along its eastern shore, which can be reached by boat (no motors are permitted) or on foot via an unidentified trail that leaves from the trailhead parking area. This area is intensively used. The lake has a substantial population of large trout.

At the trailhead, signage indicates Alder Lake. Regain Touch-Me-Not Trail from the south edge of the parking area where it goes east, passing a stand of conifers and the location of an early homestead on the left, of which only a foundation remains. Walking through an open field, the trail descends slightly into a maple woods. The trail soon ascends, switching back through open forest, climbing through Norway spruce stands and thickets before relaxing through a hardwood forest, following the easterly edge of a ridge at 2,500 ft. Now heading northeast, the trail enters an old farmstead area, where reclaimed pastures are now maturing forests of sugar maple, and passes stone walls and a pair of foundations on the right (east), as well as other evidence of settlement. There is no running or standing water until a seasonal creek, above a beaver meadow on a tributary of Alder Creek, is crossed at 2,300 ft. Having crossed the rocky creek bed, turn left at an intersection where an old road goes off to the right. Climb easily, leveling on a rise where the trail turns right (east) and again ascends gently through an abandoned apple orchard and clearing. Large boulders appear to the left of the trail as it crosses several seasonal rills. The trail descends now, swinging left (north) to join the main confluence of Alder Creek, finally crossing it and rising to meet Alder Creek Road at 6.8 mi. Ahead (east) on the dirt road is Alder Lake at 0.3 mi. To the right 2.5 mi. is Beaver Kill Road (Turnwood).

Touch-Me-Not Trail (map 2: C3–C4)

Distances from Beech Hill Road (2,290 ft.) to
- Cabot Mtn. summit (2,970 ft.): 1.2 mi., 700 ft., 55 min.
- Little Pond Trail (2,430 ft.): 2.0 mi., 700 ft. (rev. 550 ft.), 1 hr. 20 min.
- Touch-Me-Not Mtn. and Campground Trail (2,750 ft.): 2.8 mi., 1,000 ft., 1 hr. 55 min.
- Barkaboom Road and Big Pond (1,970 ft.): 3.9 mi., 1,000 ft. (rev. 800 ft.), 2 hr. 25 min.
- Alder Lake Road (2,090 ft.): 6.8 mi., 1,700 ft. (rev. 550 ft.), 4 hr. 15 min.

Campground Trail–Little Pond Loop Trail

In concert with Little Pond Trail (and a section of Touch-Me-Not Trail), Campground Trail makes possible a fairly short and moderately strenuous loop of 3.1 mi., one that is popular with campers at the Little Pond Public Campground and Day Use Area (New York State Department of Environmental Conservation). Little Pond Campground is located 14 mi. northwest of Livingston Manor on Barkaboom Road, off Beaver Kill Road (CR 54). Enter the campground, pay the day-use fee, and locate the trail directly behind the shower house in the campground's day-use and swimming area parking lot.

The trail and trail register are found to the right of the trail signs. Campground Trail enters the woods heading north and soon turns northwest and flattens out—for the time being. The trail rises steeply beyond 2,300 ft., climbing north through clumps of large sedimentary rock covered in scales of lichen. This ascent continues until Touch-Me-Not Trail junction is reached, on the western summit area of Touch-Me-Not Mtn. at 1.1 mi. (2,750 ft.). Campground Trail ends at this point. Arrive at the wooded junction with Touch-Me-Not Trail and Little Pond Trail at 1.6 mi.

To continue on the loop, hikers must turn left (north-northwest) on Touch-Me-Not-Trail, which provides only broken winter views to the southwest (Middle Mtn. area). Follow the trail, descending through an ash, oak, and cherry woods with some huge specimens of cherry (the small, purple, berrylike drupes that appear along the trail in late summer are black cherries—a preferred food of the black bear). Dropping down through a narrow cleft in the bedrock, walk level along the ridge. Marking is good; signage is poor. A trail arrow pointing west is hand painted with the words Beech Hill (not, as you might expect, Cabot Mtn.), where red markers continue along Touch-Me-Not Trail. To the left (south), at 1.6 mi., yellow trail markers identify Little Pond Trail, which is road width and well traveled. Go left (south). Within a few minutes' walk of the junction a large, open field (Beaver Kill Vista) is entered from the north. Along the northwest side is a dense stand of Norway spruce, and in a depression to the right of the trail is a shallow pond. Pastoral, lowland views open up to the east over Turnwood and into the rolling hills of Mongaup-Beaver Kill Ridge—this is the western foothill region of Big Indian-Beaver Kill Range Wilderness Area and the upper realms of Beaver Kill Valley. Near the south edge of the clearing, a small stone foundation sits to the left of the trail. After reentering the woods the trail forks to the left at a trail arrow and descends into Norway spruce forest, with red pine joining in on the right. This descent continues gradually into hardwoods. The wide, rocky trail passes a beaver meadow to the left, the seasonal outlet forming a deeply etched hollow in the soft soil, where hemlock grows. At 2.7 mi., at campsite 70, Little Pond Trail meets Little Pond itself. Hikers coming around the pond loop from the west may walk past this junction without seeing the east-facing trail signs.

Little Pond Trail continues to the right (west), circling the pond and arriving at the trailhead and remote campsite boat launch/parking area at the site of a solitary stone chimney. The home that stood at this site belonged to the Garrison family, who gave these lands to the state. Photos of the old estate can be seen at the campsite office.

Those seeking to complete the loop by returning to Campground Trail should turn left (east) here, walking through the woods to the rear of the remote walk- or boat-in sites numbered 70 to 75. This will bring hikers in a full circle, back to the day-use and swimming area at 3.1 mi.

Campground Trail-Little Pond Loop Trail (map 2: C4)

Distances from Little Pond Campground (1,990 ft.) to
- Touch-Me-Not Trail (2,750 ft.) via Campground Trail: 1.1 mi., 750 ft., 55 min.
- Little Pond Trail (2,430 ft.) via Touch-Me-Not Trail: 1.6 mi., 750 ft. (rev. 300 ft.), 1 hr. 10 min.
- Beaver Kill Vista (2,370 ft.): 1.8 mi., 750 ft. (rev. 50 ft.), 1 hr. 15 min.
- north end of Little Pond (1,990 ft.): 2.7 mi., 750 ft. (rev. 400 ft.), 1 hr. 45 min.
- return to Little Pond Campground (1,990 ft.): 3.1 mi., 750 ft., 1 hr. 55 min.

Huggins Lake Trail

This trail has gained in popularity in recent years, going from relative obscurity to a destination with its own trailhead parking area. Mountain bikers, skiers, and hikers enjoy the trail, which has posed a management problem because of its use by all-terrain vehicles. The addition of an access barrier has reduced these activities, and hikers can anticipate quiet, peaceful surroundings.

From Holliday and Berry Brook Road, 2.5 mi. north of the Beaver Kill Public Campground, the trail departs from the trailhead parking area, passes around a barrier gate, and leads east and uphill into hardwoods. Signage is posted on the road, but marking along the trail, which is a wide dirt road, is poor or absent. The trail bears left at the first fork after only a few minutes of hiking. (This junction lacks a trail arrow.) Climbing to 2,285 ft., the trail levels, passing to the north of a hill (2,310 ft.) and descending southward.

The lake comes into view to the east, and again as the trail switches back to the left (north) and the final approach is made. Huggins Lake lies cached in a shallow bowl that forms the head of Huggins Hollow. A dam at the lake's south end controls its flow of water into the Beaver Kill. Many wildflowers will be found blooming here throughout the summer—among them aster, sunflower, coneflower, and fleabane. Arrowwood grows next to the lake and produces blue, berrylike drupe bunches by late summer. (Native people used the shrub for arrow shafts.) A campsite is designated to the north of the outlet, 100 yd. from the dam. The short (but hilly) round trip makes for an easy day hike.

Huggins Lake Trail (map 2: C3)
Distance from trailhead on Holliday and Berry Brook Road (1,790 ft.) to
• Huggins Lake (2,230 ft.): 1.9 mi., 700 ft. (rev. 250 ft.), 1 hr. 20 min.

SUGGESTED HIKES

Easy Hike

Trout Pond Trail [rt: 2.4 mi., 1:40]. A level hike to a pair of lean-tos on a small, attractive lake with trout fishing.

Moderate Hikes

Campground Trail-Little Pond Loop Trail [loop: 3.1 mi., 1:55]. A convenient and pretty route, with some climbing, following along Little Pond and across the southerly shoulder of Touch-Me-Not Mtn. Views to the south.

Huggins Lake Trail [rt: 3.8 mi., 2:40]. A short but hilly trail to a quiet lake with a designated campsite.

Strenuous Hike

Cabot Mountain Lookout via Touch-Me-Not Trail [rt: 3.0 mi., 1:50]. A steep hike to one of the few expansive lookouts in the Delaware Wild Forest (continue 0.3 mi., beyond summit benchmark to lookout). Gain access from Beech Hill Road.

Appendix A

CATSKILL 3500-FOOTERS

Mountain	Elevation (ft.)
Slide	4,190
Hunter	4,050
Black Dome	3,990
Blackhead	3,950
Thomas Cole	3,950
West Kill	3,890
Cornell	3,870
Doubletop	3,870
Graham	3,868
Plateau	3,850
Table	3,847
Peekamoose	3,843
Sugarloaf	3,810
Wittenberg	3,790
Southwest Hunter	3,750
Balsam Lake	3,730
Panther	3,730
Lone	3,721

Mountain	Elevation (ft.)
Big Indian	3,710
Friday	3,694
Rusk	3,690
Kaaterskill High Peak	3,655
Twin	3,650
Fir	3,630
Balsam Cap	3,623
Balsam	3,610
Eagle	3,610
North Dome	3,610
Bearpen	3,610
Indian Head	3,573
Sherrill	3,550
Halcott	3,537
Vly	3,529
Windham High Peak	3,524
Rocky	3,508

BIBLIOGRAPHY

Bierhorst, John, *The Ashokan Catskills: A Natural History*, Fleischmanns, NY: Purple Mountain Press, 1995.

Chong, Herb, *The Long Path Guide*, 5th ed. New York: New York-New Jersey Trail Conference.

De Lisser, Richard Lionel, *Picturesque Green County*, Saugerties, NY: Hope Farm Press, 1998.

De Lisser, Richard Lionel, *Picturesque Ulster County*, Saugerties, NY: Hope Farm Press, 1996.

Evers, Alf, *The Catskills: From Wilderness to Woodstock*, Woodstock, NY: The Overlook Press, 1982.

Haring, H.A., *Our Catskill Mountains*, New York: G.P. Putnam's Sons, 1931.

Kick, Peter, *AMC's Best Day Hikes in the Catskills & the Hudson Valley*, Boston: Appalachian Mountain Club Books, 2006.

Kudish, Michael, *The Catskill Forest: A History*, Fleischmanns, NY: Purple Mountain Press, 2000.

Long Path Guide, New York: New York-New Jersey Trail Conference, 1996.

Longstreth, T. Morris, *The Catskills*, New York: The Century Co., 1918.

Van Zandt, Roland, *The Catskill Mountain House*, New Brunswick, NJ: Rutgers University Press, 1966.

Appendix C

HELPFUL INFORMATION AND CONTACTS

The New York State Department of Environmental Conservation

(DEC) Division of Lands and Forests

625 Broadway

Albany, NY 12233-0001

Forest Preserve Management Office: 518-473-9518

Division of Lands and Forests director's office: 518-402-9405

www.dec.ny.gov

> The DEC, through its Division of Lands and Forests, manages the New York State Forest Preserve lands of the Catskills and detached parcels of state land outside the Catskills. The DEC is responsible for search and rescue, planning for management, supervision of campsites, and issuing of camping permits. The DEC also publishes regional trail maps. However, because each state region is run independently, it is easiest to obtain local information from one of the regional offices listed below.

DEC Region 3 Headquarters

21 South Putt Corners Road

New Paltz, NY 12561

Emergency Dispatch: 1-877-457-5680

Forest Rangers: 845-256-3026

DEC Region 4 Headquarters

Stamford Suboffice

65561 State Highway 10

Suite 1

Stamford, NY 12167

607-652-7365

Emergency Dispatch: 1-877-457-5680

State Campsites in the Catskills:
Beaverkill: 845-439-4281
Mongaup Pond: 845-439-4233
Kenneth L. Wilson: 845-679-7020
Bear Spring Mountain: 607-865-6989
Little Pond: 845-439-5480
North/South Lake: 518-589-5058
Woodland Valley: 845-688-7647
Camping reservations: (Reserve America) 800-456-CAMP,
www.reserveamerica.com. Call two days ahead of planned arrival time.
Questions concerning camping reservation service: 800-777-9644
For information about camping discounts go to the DEC website:
www.dec.ny.gov
Travel Information:
Ulster County: 800-342-5826
Sullivan County: 800-882-CATS
Greene County: 800-355-CATS
Delaware County: 866-775-4425

Appalachian Mountain Club (AMC)
New York–North Jersey Chapter
New York City Program Office
5 West 63rd Street, Suite 220
New York, NY 10023
212-986-1430
E-mail: Office@amc-ny.org
www.amc-ny.org

The Appalachian Mountain Club is America's oldest conservation and recreation organization. Since 1876, AMC has promoted the protection, enjoyment, and understanding of the mountains, forests, waters, and trails of the Northeast outdoors. The organization has twelve chapters from Maine to Washington, D.C., and boasts a membership of 90,000. The New York–North Jersey Chapter is active in the Catskills region. AMC encourages people to enjoy the outdoors by offering them a place to stay at its lodges, campgrounds, huts, cabins, full-service camps, and shelters. AMC Books, the publisher of this guide, publishes a variety of books for readers seeking outdoor recreation.

New York-New Jersey Trail Conference (NY-NJTC)

156 Ramapo Valley Road (Route 202)
Mahwah, NJ 07430
201-512-9348
E-mail: office@nynjtc.org
www.nynjtc.org

The NY-NJTC coordinates the construction and maintenance of some 1,850 mi. of hiking trails, including the Appalachian Trail in New York and New Jersey and the Long Path, which connects the metropolitan area with the Catskills and beyond. It also publishes regional maps of the Catskills, Northern New Jersey, West and East Hudson, Harriman State Park, the South Taconics, and the Shawangunks. Some 100 hiking clubs and conservation organizations belong to the conference, along with 10,000 individual members. Applications for individual membership are invited, and the annual fee includes, among other things, a subscription to the *Trail Walker*. This quarterly publication describes the activities of the member clubs and features timely articles, book reviews, and trail updates. It is a reliable source of information on trail closings, relocations, and other potential problems associated with the hikes described in this book.

The Adirondack Mountain Club (ADK Headquarters)

814 Goggins Road
Lake George, NY 12845
518-668-4447
E-mail: adkinfo@adk.org
www.adk.org

The Adirondack Mountain Club (ADK), and its chapters support an active program of hiking, backpacking, and trail maintenance in the Catskills. ADK is an effective advocate for protecting the Catskills. It publishes authoritative articles, books, and maps on the Catskills region.

The Sierra Club

Northeast Field Office
85 Washington Street
Saratoga Springs, NY 12866-4105
518-587-9166
E-mail: informationsierraclub.org
www.sierraclub.org/ny

> The Sierra Club's grassroots advocacy has made it one of America's most influential environmental organizations. Founded in 1892, the club has more than 700,000 members. The Catskills are included in the Mid-Hudson Chapter area. The group conducts outings and speaker socials.

The Catskill 3500 Club

E-mail: membership@catskill-3500-club.org
www.catskill-3500-club.org

> The Catskill 3500 Club is primarily a hiking organization. Candidate members receive notices of trips and outings. A membership patch is given for completing climbs of 35 summits higher than 3,500 ft., four of which must be climbed a second time in winter. A winter patch is available.

The Catskill Mountain Club

P.O. Box 404
Margaretville, NY 12455-0404

> The Catskill Mountain Club is an outdoor recreation association that promotes hiking, camping, kayaking, canoeing, snowshoeing, skiing, and cycling in the Catskills. Founded in 2004, the club also advocates for stewardship of natural resources and maintains trails and facilities in the region, both inside and outside the park boundary.

The Catskill Center for Conservation and Development, Inc.

P.O. Box 504
Arkville, NY 12406-0504
845-586-2611
E-mail: cccd@catskill.net
www.catskillcenter.org

> The Catskill Center for Conservation and Development is a regional advocate for land-use planning and environmental management, and it is active in natural-area and historical preservation, community revitalization, and public review of regionally significant projects. It publishes general interest books and technical studies as well as a newsletter on conservation issues affecting the Catskills. Offices are in the Erpf House on Route 28 in Arkville, and applications for membership are welcome.

The Open Space Institute

1350 Broadway, Suite 201
New York, NY 10018
212-290-8200
www.osiny.org

> The Open Space Institute (OSI) protects scenic, natural, and historic landscapes to ensure public enjoyment, conserve habitats, and sustain community character. OSI has protected more than 100,000 acres through the New York Land Program and through direct acquisition and conservation easements in the State of New York. The Catskills is one of five focus regions for OSI's conservation work in New York.

INDEX

Trail names written in **bold type** indicate that a detailed description can be found in the text.

Where multiple page references appear, **bold numbering** indicates the main entry or entries for the trail or feature.

[Bracketed information] indicates which of the two maps displays the trail and where, by section letter and number.

Appalachian Mountain Club

Founded in 1876, AMC is the nation's oldest outdoor recreation and conservation organization. AMC promotes the protection, enjoyment, and understanding of the mountains, forests, waters, and trails of the Northeast outdoors.

People

We are more than 100,000 members, advocates, and supporters, including 12 local chapters, more than 16,000 volunteers, and over 450 full-time and seasonal staff. Our chapters reach from Maine to Washington, D.C.

Outdoor Adventure and Fun

We offer more than 8,000 trips each year, from local chapter activities to adventure travel worldwide, for every ability level and outdoor interest—from hiking and climbing to paddling, snowshoeing, and skiing.

Great Places to Stay

We host more than 150,000 guests each year at our AMC lodges, huts, camps, shelters, and campgrounds. Each AMC destination is a model for environmental education and stewardship.

Opportunities for Learning

We teach people skills to safely enjoy the outdoors and to care for the natural world around us through programs for children, teens, and adults, as well as outdoor leadership training.

Caring for Trails

We maintain more than 1,700 miles of trails throughout the Northeast, including nearly 350 miles of the Appalachian Trail in five states.

Protecting Wild Places

We advocate for land and riverway conservation, monitor air quality, research climate change, and work to protect alpine and forest ecosystems throughout the Northern Forest and Mid-Atlantic Highlands regions.

Engaging the Public

We seek to educate and inform our own members and an additional 2 million people annually through the media, AMC Books, our website, our White Mountain visitor centers, and AMC destinations.

Join Us!

Members meet other like-minded people and support our mission while enjoying great AMC programs, our award-winning *AMC Outdoors* magazine, and special discounts. Visit outdoors.org or call 800-372-1758 for more information.

APPALACHIAN MOUNTAIN CLUB
Recreation • Education • Conservation
outdoors.org

ABOUT THE AMC IN NEW YORK

The Appalachian Mountain Club (AMC) has two active chapters in New York. The New York–North Jersey Chapter offers more than 2,000 trips per year, ranging from canoeing and kayaking to sailing, hiking, backpacking, and social events. The chapter is also active in trail work and conservation projects, and maintains a cabin at Fire Island. The Mohawk Hudson Chapter serves residents of Albany, Columbia, Fulton, Greene, Montgomery, Rensselaer, Saratoga, Schenectady, Schoharie, Warren, and Washington counties. The chapter offers a variety of outdoor activities for all levels of ability. You can learn more about these chapters by visiting outdoors.org/chapters. To view a list of AMC activities in New York and other parts of the Northeast, visit activities.outdoors.org.

ABOUT THE AUTHOR

Peter Kick, a native of the Catskill Mountains, is a New York State licensed guide and AMC trip leader. The author of several hiking and cycling guides, including AMC's *Discover the Adirondacks* and *AMC's Best Day Hikes in the Catskills & Hudson Valley*, his work has appeared in *Backpacker*, *Sailing*, *Cruising World*, and *Adirondack Life*. Mr. Kick is a life member of the AMC. He lives in Saugerties, New York.

AMC BOOK UPDATES

AMC Books strives to keep our guidebooks as up-to-date as possible to help you plan safe and enjoyable adventures. If we learn, after publishing a book, that trails are relocated or route or contact information has changed, we will post the updated information online. Before you hit the trail, check for updates at outdoors.org/publications/books/updates.

While hiking or paddling, if you notice discrepancies with the trail description or map, or if you find any other errors in the book, please let us know by submitting them to amcbookupdates@outdoors.org or in writing to Books Editor, c/o AMC, 5 Joy Street, Boston, MA 02108. We will verify all submissions and post key updates each month.

AMC Books is dedicated to being a recognized leader in outdoor publishing. Thank you for your participation.

AMC BOOKS & MAPS

EXPLORE THE POSSIBILITIES

AMC Books

AMC's Best Day Hikes in the Catskills and Hudson Valley, 2nd edition

Peter W. Kick

This guide leads beginner and experienced hikers alike along 60 of the region's most spectacular trails, from Westchester County to Albany.

$18.95 • 978-1-934028-45-2

Best Backpacking in the Mid-Atlantic

Michael R. Martin

These 30 overnight trips range in difficulty from intermediate to expert and travel through forests of wild rhododendron at Dolly Sods, across the beaches of Assateague, and over the peaks of New York's Catskill Mountains.

$19.95 • 978-1-934028-86-5

Quiet Water New York, 2nd edition

By: John Hayes & Alex Wilson

This edition reveals more than 100 spectacular ponds, lakes, and rivers ideally suited for canoeing and kayaking. From the Adirondacks to the western plateau to Long Island, use this updated guide to find unique water adventures for beginners and experienced paddlers, birdwatchers and anglers, families with children, and active seniors.

$19.95 • 978-1-929173-73-0

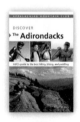

Discover the Adirondacks

Peter W. Kick

With so many wilderness opportunities to choose from in the vast Adirondacks, travelers need this concise travel guide. This guidebook invites first-time visitors or seasoned explorers to experience the 50 best multi-sport trips the Adirondacks have to offer.

$18.95 • 978-1-934028-31-5

Find these and other AMC titles, as well as ebooks, through ebook stores, booksellers, and outdoor retailers. Or order directly from AMC at outdoors.org/amcstore or call 800-262-4455.